FAMA·SEMPER·VIVIT

UNUS·ET·IDEM

Maria m. 1812 1st Marquess of Normandy *ob. s. p.*	Anne Elizabeth m. 1826 Sir Hedworth Williamson d. 1878 Issue	Susan m. 1833 4th Earl of Hardwick	Jane Elizabeth m. 1823 Viscount Barrington *ob. 1883 s. p.*	Georgina, Maid of Honour to Queen Victoria m. 1845 2nd Baron Bloomfield *ob. 1905 s. p.*

Rev William Wren	Charlotte d. unm.	Harriet d. unm.	Amelia d. unm. 1898

Albert Edward Arthur b. 1863 d. aged 8 weeks	Rhoda Caroline Anne (1859–1949) d. unm.	Violet Constance (1864–1927) d. unm.	Frederick Francis (1865–1950) m. 1901 Mabel Alice Magniac d. 1959 Issue	Lionel Charles (1868–1942) m. 1902 Florence Ella Magniac d. 1942 Issue

Palo Alto City Library

The individual borrower is responsible for all library material borrowed on their card.

Charges as determined by the CITY OF PALO ALTO will be assessed for each overdue item.

Damaged or non-returned property will be billed to the individual borrower by the CITY OF PALO ALTO.

The
Real Alice

Also by Anne Clark

Beasts and Bawdy
Lewis Carroll: A Biography

The Real Alice

Anne Clark

LEWIS CARROLL'S
DREAM CHILD

sɒ

STEIN AND DAY/*Publishers*/New York

First published in the United States of America in 1982
Copyright © 1981 by Anne Clark
All rights reserved
Printed in the United States of America

STEIN AND DAY/*Publishers*
Scarborough House
Briarcliff Manor, N.Y. 10510

Library of Congress Cataloging in Publication Data
Clark, Anne, 1933–
   The real Alice.

   Bibliography: p.
   Includes index.
   1. Carroll, Lewis, 1832–1898—Friends and associates.
2. Hargreaves, Alice Pleasance Liddell, 1852–1934.
3. Liddell family. 4. Great Britain—Biography.
I. Title.
PR4612.C57   1981   828′.809 [B]   82-664
ISBN 0-8128-2870-4   AACR2

CONTENTS

LIST OF ILLUSTRATIONS

An asterisk denotes that the picture has not previously been published.

ACKNOWLEDGEMENTS

The author would like to thank the following for their contribution to the preparation of the text: Gerald L. Alexanderson; HRH the late Princess Alice, Countess of Athlone; Capt. Baker (Rifle Brigade); Mrs Mavis Batey; The Marquess of Bath; The Hon Mrs Bull; Capt. M. A. Bullouch (Scots Guards); Dr Sandor Burstein; The Hon Mrs Susan Chaplin; N. V. Clark, Cornhill; *Professor Morton N. Cohen; Denis Crutch; The Late John N. S. Davis; John Field; Mrs Celia Gale; M. N. Gannaway; Dr Selwyn H. Goodacre; The Hon Mrs John Hanbury-Tracy; Jack Hargreaves; Lt.-Col. John Carne Hargreaves; Arthur J. Houghton Jnr; R. Jackman; Charles Johnson; Cmdr. and Mrs Adrian Liddell; Major and Mrs Charles Liddell; Mrs Geoffrey Liddell; James Liddell; Miss Mary Liddell; Sandy McAdams; Miss D. McNair; Stanley Marx; Dr J. F. A. Mason; Graham Ovenden; Brigadier Lewellen Palmer; Emil S. Polk; The Hon Mrs Pretyman; The Lord Ravensworth; Capt. S. J. L. Roberts (Irish Guards); Robert W. Rushmore; G. W. Russ; David H. Schaefer; Justin G. Schiller; Brian Sibley; Major R. J. W. Skene; Miss Mary K. Smith; Dr Jeffrey Stern; The Lord Sudeley; Alan Tompkins; A. Gordon Thomas; The Hon Mrs John Hanbury-Tracy; Mrs Margaret Tye; Mrs Mary Whitehorn. She is also very grateful to the following for the pictures they have lent for reproduction: Gerald L. Alexanderson; The late John N. S. Davis; Dr Selwyn H. Goodacre; The Hampshire County Museum Service; Lt.-Col. John Carne Hargreaves; The Imperial War Museum; Major Charles Liddell; Mrs Geoffrey Liddell; James Liddell; Sandy McAdams; Graham Ovenden; Emil S. Polk; The Hon Mrs Pretyman; Robert W. Rushmore; Major R. J. W. Skene; Dr Jeffrey Stern; A. Gordon Thomas; Mrs Mary Whitehorn.*

The author and publishers would like to thank Mrs Florence Becker Lennon for permission to reproduce an extract from her book, *The Life of Lewis Carroll.*

A QUESTION OF IDENTITY

'Who are *you*,' said the Caterpillar.
Alice's Adventures in Wonderland

SHE WAS Wednesday's child, born at 19 Dean's Yard, Westminster, in the afternoon of 4 May 1852. Her name was Alice Pleasance Liddell and, as such, few people have ever heard of her. Yet simply call her 'Alice', and all the world knows and loves her: for she was one man's dream-child, and that man made her immortal.

Her literary creator's name is almost as unfamiliar as her own. The Reverend Charles Lutwidge Dodgson was a shy, mildly eccentric, though essentially likeable young academic when he first met his child muse. He preferred to publish his flights of literary fancy under a nom de plume. Together Lewis Carroll and his Alice have been eulogised, criticised, psychoanalysed. Their phantasmagoric dream-world has fired the imaginations, fed the minds of poets, philosophers, musicians and artists the world over. They have proved inspirational to creators as diverse as James Joyce and Lennon and McCartney, W. H. Auden and Walter De la Mare, Arthur Rackham and Salvador Dali. Yet the enigma of their own special relationship and the nature of Carroll's genius remain elusive.

At the time of her birth, Alice's father was headmaster of Westminster School and domestic chaplain to HRH Prince Albert. He liked to baptise his own children himself, and he kept to that tradition with this, his fourth child. Alice's baptism took place in Westminster Abbey itself. On 28 July 1852 her father wrote belatedly to the Abbey registrar:

Dear Sir,
    I ought long ago to have informed you that I christened another little girl of mine in the Abbey—Alice Pleasance, daughter

of the Reverend Henry George Liddell and Lorina Hannah
Liddell: born May 4: christened June 17.
Very truly yours,
Henry G. Liddell

Records of birth and baptisms are not readily accessible to the population
at large, but Charles Lutwidge Dodgson publicised his heroine's birthday
for all to read:

'I've seen hatters before,' she said to herself: 'the March Hare
will be much the most interesting, and perhaps as this is May, it
won't be raving mad—at least not so mad as it was in March.'
The Hatter was the first to break the silence. 'What day of the
month is it?' he said.
Alice considered a little, and then said, 'the fourth.'

Dean's Yard,
Westminster, 1846—
Alice was born in the
headmaster's house

When the Caterpillar so rudely asked his famous question, 'Who are *you*?',
he was merely formulating the vital question that every Victorian asked
about everyone with whom he came into contact. Exactly who you were
mattered intensely, probably more so than at any other time in English
history either before or since. The class system in Victorian England was

remarkably complex and had to be adhered to, for God had so ordained it. In the words of the well known hymn:

The rich man in his castle,
The poor man at the gate,
God made them high or lowly
And ordered their estate.

Matters were less difficult for men than for women. A man might perhaps by diligence and good fortune rise to distinction through his career, but for a woman only one career was possible—that of wife. Spinsterhood was infinitely preferable to marriage into the wrong social class, and financial constraints were almost as inhibiting as social ones.

Alice's pedigree was thus of vital importance. It was immaculate. Her paternal grandfather, Henry George Liddell senior, was the younger brother of Sir Thomas Liddell of Ravensworth, who was created Baron Ravensworth in 1821 at the coronation of King George IV. He was not the first Baron Ravensworth: the barony had originally been created in 1745 in recognition of his ancestor Sir Thomas Liddell's defence of Newcastle against the Scots, but it had died out in 1784 for lack of a direct male heir.

Most great families have their occasional eccentrics, and Alice's paternal great-grandfather, Sir Henry St George Liddell, must surely have qualified for that classification. In 1786, for a wager, he set off on an extraordinary tour to Lapland. His companion was Matthew Consett, who wrote the history of their adventures illustrated with engravings by Bewick after their return. Sir Henry brought back with him reindeer which he successfully bred in the grounds of Ravensworth Castle. Even more remarkably, he brought back two young Lap-maidens for the amusement of his friends. Not surprisingly, this caused something of a scandal at the time, though Consett maintained that the young women's virtue remained unsullied. After some eighteen months or so, when they had been exhibited to polite society and the novelty had worn off, they were returned to their native country with a number of gifts as consolation. These trinkets, Sir Henry maintained, would act as a considerable dowry and thus amply repay them for their trouble.

But few of the Liddells proved so outlandish. The family had originally gained its wealth and prestige as merchants in the seventeenth century, and later generations had the foresight to appreciate the value of coalmining and of the steam engine. Alice's great-uncle, the sixth Baronet,

Ravensworth Castle,
the ancestral home of
the Liddell family

was a leading partner in the eighteenth-century colliery company which traded as the 'Grand Allies'. A patron of George Stephenson, he refashioned Ravensworth Castle after a design by Nash. But ironically, the extraction of coal on the estate undermined the foundations of the castle and it ultimately fell into such a state of disrepair that it had to be demolished.

Alice's paternal grandfather graduated at Christ Church, Oxford, and like many a younger brother in noble families, he went into the Church, where his career was in no way distinguished. But he married well. His wife was Charlotte Lyon, fourth daughter of the Honourable Thomas Lyon, brother of the eighth Earl of Strathmore.

On 6 February 1811 their first child, Alice's father, was born at Binchester, Auckland. He was a studious child and an avid reader. 'On my sixth birthday I was promised a great honour and reward,' he wrote in his journal. 'My father took me up into his study and inducted me into the mysteries of the Eton Latin Grammar. I remember the day, the place and the fact as clearly as if it were yesterday. I continued to make pretty good progress under his kind teaching; but I fear that as I went on from day to day I did not regard the honour so great as I did on the first day.'[1]

1 Henry L. Thompson, *Memoir of Henry George Liddell, DD*, 1899, p. 2.

Henry George Liddell, Alice's father, drawn by George Richmond,
1858

With his second brother, Thomas, he went to Bishopton Grove
School, transferring at the age of twelve to 'Beastly Charterhouse'[2], as he
called it in an early letter home. Mr Watkinson, his housemaster, took
exception to his crimson silk watchguard and chain, and Russell, the
headmaster, had a sarcastic tongue. 'Once' Liddell wrote, 'I remember (I
know not on what occasion), he told me "I was as lazy as I was long, and
should bring my father's grey hairs with sorrow to the grave". I was no
doubt somewhat listless, having outgrown my strength, but I hardly
deserved this reproach. It certainly did me no good.'[3]

2 ibid, p. 5
3 ibid, p. 7

Some of Alice's
father's blotting-paper
doodles

Nevertheless, Liddell did have the good fortune to sit next to William Makepeace Thackeray in class. '*He* never attempted to learn the lesson, never exerted himself to grapple with Horace. We spent our time mostly in drawing, with such skill as we could command,' Liddell wrote. 'His handiwork was very superior to mine, and his taste for comic scenes at that time exhibited itself in burlesque representations of incidents in Shakespeare.'[4]

At Easter 1830, a year after he matriculated, Liddell became an undergraduate at Christ Church, Oxford. Three years later he gained the distinction of a double first, and a tutorship was assured in due course. Dean Gaisford, the 'Old Bear' of Christ Church, advised him how to equip himself for the future. 'He recommends me to recover all my French and proceed with German, accompanying this advice with a recommendation to pursue my classical studies, to verse myself in Divinity, and not neglect my scientific pursuits,' Liddell wrote. 'He added that what leisure time I had would be fully occupied by keeping pace with the reading of the day, without which no gentleman can go into society.'[5]

4 ibid, p. 8
5 ibid, p. 24

18

Gaisford appointed him sub-librarian jointly with Robert Scott, who was to play an important part in the establishment of Liddell's academic reputation. It was with Scott that in 1834 Liddell ventured on the greatest scholastic work of his life, the *Greek Lexicon*. Though it was first published in 1843, he continued to revise it for the rest of his life, the eighth version appearing in 1897, a few months before his death. It was a formidable task, for it is estimated that the work contained more than twenty million letters, stops and accents.

Until a few years before the *Lexicon* was published, there was no direct means of translating Greek into English, and Greek could only be interpreted via Latin. Attempts to fill the gap had been made by three scholars, Donnegan, Dunbar and Giles, but the work in each case proved to be inadequate, being unmethodical, unscientific and incomplete.

Dr Johnson, tongue in cheek, defined 'lexicographer' in his *Dictionary* as 'A writer of dictionaries; a harmless drudge', and Liddell's *magnum opus* certainly demanded a great deal of drudgery. Initially, he and Scott met nightly from seven till eleven to work on the project; but from 1840, when Scott married and accepted a College living at Dunloe in Cornwall, the major burden fell on Liddell's shoulders. From that time on, he worked from five o'clock every morning until two, with only a brief meal break, frequently resuming his task in the evening. In July 1842 he wrote to Scott, 'You will be glad to hear that I have all but finished ⊓ , that two-legged monster, who must in ancient times have worn his legs a-straddle, ⋏ else he could never have strode over so enormous a space as he has occupied and will occupy in Lexicons.'

He then inserted a drawing of the creature in human shape (see below), adding, 'Behold the monster, as he has been mocking my waking and sleeping visions for the last many months.'[6]

6 ibid, pp. 74–5

The Dean's sister Harriet*

The *Lexicon* was finally published in 1843 and, despite the high price of forty-two shillings a copy, a second edition was required in 1845. By 1869 six editions had been printed, running into 48,000 copies. The seventh edition produced from electrotype plates brought Liddell profits of £1650.

A Westminster schoolboy once wrote:

> *Two men wrote a Lexicon, Liddell and Scott;*
> *Some parts were clever, but some parts were not.*
> *Hear, all ye learned, and read me this riddle,*
> *How the wrong part wrote Scott, and the right part wrote Liddell.*

Liddell's reputation for scholarship was firmly established with the publication of the *Lexicon*. In 1838 he had been ordained and appointed Greek Reader at Christ Church. His work on the *Lexicon* meant that he became recognised as a leading authority on all matters related to art, and in 1839 he was appointed delegate to decide on the respective merits of various architectural designs for the art gallery at Christ Church. Three

*An asterisk denotes that the picture has not previously been published.

years later he became Select Preacher, winning almost universal approval for that polish, tact and uncontroversial approach which in 1845 led to his appointment as Whitehall Preacher.

Liddell was still unmarried. To his sister Charlotte he wrote, 'I am glad to find that, though my hair is falling off and going grey, I yet feel much youthful ardour and freshness return.'[7] That ardour soon found an object. To Stephen Denison, a friend of his undergraduate years who had been betrothed to Liddell's dead sister Harriet, he confided his matrimonial aspirations. Eager for his friend's success, Denison wrote the following in May 1845 to Thomas Lyon Fellowes, the brother-in-law of Liddell's intended:

Alice's paternal grandmother, Charlotte Liddell née Lyon*

> As I know that Henry Liddell has confided to you a secret (which I need not further particularise) I cannot resist taking the opportunity of half an hour's leisure to say how very great an interest I take in his success and how extremely anxious I am that his hopes should be realised; and as you are so closely connected with the object of his attachment, I believe you will not think me impertinent in saying a few words about one of the dearest friends I have in the world. I have known him so long, and been so very intimate with him, and under such very peculiar circumstances, that I believe no man is better authorised to speak of him than myself. . . . I have now known him about fifteen years as intimately as possible; and I have always noted him down in my mind as the most nearly 'blameless' man I ever knew; the most generous, kind-hearted, amiable fellow, with a delicacy of feeling and taste almost too refined for the rough work of everyday life. I need not speak to you or to anyone of his intellectual powers; they are known to all the literary world. But I may say that I know no one with such abilities and learning who is at the same time so modest and unpretending. If an amiable, excellent, very clever and accomplished man, highly connected, belonging to a delightful family, having innumerable friends, enjoying a reputation both for talent and excellence rarely attained so early in life, and whose prospects of advancement and honours are the fairest that can be, and whose prospects of advancement and honours are the fairest that can be;- if such a man can make a woman happy, Henry Liddell is the man.[8]

7 ibid, pp. 57–8
8 ibid, pp. 57–8

Alice's mother

The woman of Liddell's choice, to whom he became engaged shortly after that letter was sent, was Lorina Hannah Reeve, who was distantly related to Liddell. Born at Lowestoft on 3 March 1826 and baptised there six days later, she was the youngest of the six children of James Reeve and his wife Lorina, daughter of John Farr of Cove. Sadly, James Reeve was not able to see his daughter develop into a poised and talented young woman. He died in July 1827, and thereafter the burden of bringing up the family fell upon Mrs Reeve alone. She was, however, well-connected and provided for, and she ultimately owned the manor at Frostenden.

The Reeves were considerable landowners in Oulton, Suffolk, as early as the sixteenth century, when they were proprietors of the Church of St Michael's, Oulton. They were descended from John Fastoff and his wife Katherine, whose fourteenth-century commemorative brasses are still to be seen in the church. Lorina Liddell's father was the third son of Robert Reeve and his wife Pleasance Clarke. In 1796 Robert's younger sister, Pleasance, had married Sir James Edward Smith, a physician, who became President of the Linnaean Society and of Norwich Museum. His books included *English Botany* and *English Flora* and he was knighted in 1814. He died in 1828 at the age of sixty-nine, but his wife, whom he had married in 1796, lived on until 1877 and achieved the remarkable age of one hundred and three. Dame Pleasance inherited the remarkable topographical collections and cabinets of coins and medals belonging to her brother Robert Reeve, whose knowledge of antiquities was extensive.

Henry Liddell had been in the habit of spending short vacations at the home of his mother's younger sister Susan, who had married the Rev. John Fellowes of Shottesham Rectory, Norfolk. The son of this union, Thomas Lyon Fellowes, married James Reeve's fifth child, Pleasance Elizabeth, and it was through this connection that Liddell became acquainted with his future bride.

There was thus a double link, through Lorina Reeve's brother-in-law and, through Liddell's mother, with the eighth Earl of Strathmore. Moreover the Earl's elder son was John Lyon, who married Mary Eleanor Bowes. The family later took the name Bowes Lyon. A direct descendent of that family, Lady Elizabeth Bowes Lyon, married Albert Frederick Arthur George Windsor and so became Queen of England and mother of Queen Elizabeth II. The family tree is very complex, but it appears that Alice and the present Queen are fifth cousins three times removed.

To the Caterpillar's question it would therefore be appropriate to answer that Alice was a young lady of impeccable pedigree, in every way worthy of becoming Carroll's immortal 'Queen Alice'.

ALICE AND THE QUEEN

Alice Pleasance Liddell

Thomas Lyon (1704–1753) m. (1736) Jean Nicholson

John Lyon m. (1767) Mary Eleanor Bowes
(later Lyon Bowes)

Thomas Lyon m. (1774) Mary Elizabeth Wren

Thomas Lyon-Bowes m. (1800) Mary Elizabeth Rodney Carpenter

Henry George Liddell m. (1809) Charlotte Lyon

Thomas Lyon-Bowes m. (1820) Charlotte Grinstead

Henry George Liddell
m. (1846)
Lorina Reeve

Claude Lyon-Bowes m. (1853) Frances Dora Smith
(later Bowes-Lyon)

Alice Pleasance Liddell
m. (1880)
Reginald Gervis Hargreaves

Claude George Bowes-Lyon m. (1882) Nina Cecilia Cavendish

Elizabeth Bowes Lyon

Elizabeth Angela Marguerite Bowes-Lyon
m. (1923) Albert Frederick Arthur George Windsor (King George VI)

Elizabeth Alexandra Mary Windsor (Queen Elizabeth II)
m. (1947) Prince Philip of Greece (Mountbatten)
Duke of Edinburgh

PURE UNCLOUDED BROW

Child of the pure unclouded brow
And dreaming eyes of wonder![1]

Alice Through the Looking-Glass

WHEN HENRY LIDDELL walked with his bride down the aisle on 23 July 1846 and left for a short honeymoon in North Wales, two important changes had recently taken place in his life.

The first of these was his appointment in January 1846 to the post of Domestic Chaplain to the Prince Consort. To his sister he had written:

It is only an *Honorary* appointment, i.e., there is no pay. Still it is an honour, and the offer is conveyed in very handsome terms, for it speaks of my 'eminent Academical and professional career'; and says the Prince is anxious to attach to his person 'one who has kept the even tenor of his way amid the perils by which his path at Oxford was beset'. So that I suppose I may consider it as a sign that my name is not unknown or unnoticed in high quarters. Also, Mr Anson was pleased to say that the Prince was anxious that the appointment should not be merely nominal, but that he wished sometimes to have personal communication with his Chaplains, yet the duties would not be of such a kind as to infringe upon my time.[2]

This appointment had led directly to his preaching at Windsor: in April 1846 he had been summoned to Windsor to preach for the first time. He also continued to give sermons to packed congregations in the old Palace of Whitehall, where he attracted the notice of many distinguished men, including Canning and Peel.

The second event was his acceptance of the post of headmaster of Westminster School. His marriage plans had made it imperative for him to

1 Dedicatory poem, *Through the Looking-Glass*
2 H. L. Thompson, p. 54

25

seek a position outside Christ Church, where the Dean and Canons were permitted to marry, although the Professors were sworn to celibacy. Dean Gaisford, who had sole responsibility for appointing the new headmaster at Westminster, was breaking with precedent in choosing Liddell. For the preceeding two and a half centuries all Westminster headmasters had been former pupils at the school, whereas Liddell was a Carthusian. But he was known to have found favour, not only with Peel, but also with the Prince Consort.

Liddell's appointment to Westminster School was a calculated attempt to halt a decline unprecedented in the history of the school. Just over a decade earlier, the poet Robert Southey had analysed its failures:

> Some causes of the decline of Westminster are of a permanent nature. Preparatory schools, which were not heard of fifty years ago, have annihilated the under school. King's College and the London University have taken away the day boys who were very numerous in my time. Proprietary schools (another recent invention) are preferred by anxious parents; and too many patrician ones, though the father were at Westminster himself, forsake a falling house and send their boys to Harrow or to Eton.[3]

Financial problems had induced the school to heap domestic drudgery on the boys, instead of employing proper servants. Bullying was rife, discipline was almost non-existent, and conditions were squalid and insanitary. Finally a parent had complained direct to Sir Robert Peel and an inquiry had followed, resulting in the expulsion of the school captain and the resignation of Dr Richard Williamson, the headmaster.

Liddell began by making many radical changes: dismissing weak academic staff and replacing them by men of his own choice; reappraising and reorganising the school's financial affairs; introducing special services in the Abbey for the boys; rationalising the existing accommodation and drawing up plans for improvements. He also reorganised his own accommodation arrangements so that he and his bride could live in a house suitable to their social ambitions, for he realised that parents would be more inclined to send their sons to the school if the headmaster and his wife were socially acceptable.

So acceptable were they, in fact, that in 1847 and 1851 the Prince Consort came to see the school play, and the Queen, as a mark of her

3 John Carlton, *Westminster School*, 1965, p. 54

special approval, contributed eight hundred pounds to the appeal fund for moving the Queen's Scholars into special day rooms.

Before long the new headmaster and his wife started having children of their own. The first was a boy, born at Mrs Reeve's home in Lowestoft on 6 September 1847 and christened Edward Henry, though he was always known to the family as Harry. He was followed on 11 May 1849 by Lorina Charlotte, named after her mother and her paternal grandmother, and baptised in the Abbey by her father at the age of five weeks. Next came another boy, born on 28 December 1850. He was named James Arthur Charles after Mrs Liddell's father, their great friend Arthur Penryn Stanley and Liddell's youngest brother respectively—but to all the family he was known as Arthur.

Alice was born eighteen months later into a London which was still in the process of returning to normal after the Great Exhibition of 1851. Victoria Street, opened for the Exhibition, lay to the west of Dean's Yard. The fashionable world of Whitehall, St James's Park and the famous Nash buildings now extended as far as Regent's Park, visible from the upper windows of the boys' dormitories. The new middle classes were beginning to congregate in the south. The clock tower, housing the

Victoria Street in 1851

27

famous 'Big Ben', was not yet completed, nor had the Queen formally opened the new Palace of Westminster. Dean's Yard was still a peaceful oasis, bounded by a row of eighteenth-century houses incorporating part of the medieval gatehouse where Gilbert Scott's Gothic extravaganza now stands.

The world of elegance to which the Liddells belonged co-existed with the most incredible squalor. While many lived in ease and luxury, thousands more eked out an existence of privation and degradation. It was unsafe to go about alone after dark, and though gas-lighting had helped to offset the gloom and smog of the great metropolis, it had brought attendant problems, for the gas company often neglected to repair the roadways after laying pipes, with the result that poisonous vapours escaped into the streets.

Drainage was another serious problem. *The Lancet* reported that, 'The waters of the Thames are swollen with the feculence of the myriads of living beings that dwell upon the banks and with the waste of every manufacture that is too foul for utilisation', and even as late as 1858 *The Times* told how Members of Parliament had been driven from those parts of the building that overlooked the river by the foul stench from the water. Liddell's cousin Thomas, later Earl of Ravensworth, wrote a poem called 'The Recess', which contrasted the joys of escape to the country with the squalor of London which Members had to endure when Parliament was in session:

28

Blest is the man whom fortune leads
Back to his lawns and bowers and meads;
Who far from London's dingy town,
Can call each passing hour his own;
Who, freed from business, smoke or care,
Inhales again a purer air,
Untainted by the poisonous stream
Of noisome gas, or putrid stream
Mingling beneath the crowded Mall
Compounds of filth unutt'rable.

The Dean of Westminster, William Buckland, who was a notable geologist, saw the danger of inadequate sanitation to the school and had pipe-draining schemes drawn up for the precincts; but despite all the precautions of the sanitary authorities who carried out the scheme, typhoid broke out in 1848, proving fatal to two young scholars and two canons' daughters.

Had it not been for her mother's tenacious will to live, Alice might never have entered this world at all; for Mrs Liddell, always tenderly disposed towards the sick, took the illness herself, and for ten days her life hung in the balance. Liddell's great friend and protégé, Henry Wentworth Acland, was hastily summoned to Westminster. 'Mrs Liddell lives still,' he wrote on the day of his arrival. 'I have been with her since I came, and have fed her every twenty minutes. Liddell's conduct is beautiful.'[4] Acland described her condition as 'desperate', and remained at the headmaster's house until all danger had passed, attending constantly at her bedside.

It was perhaps his sister-in-law's illness that prompted Liddell's younger brother Charles, born in 1813, pupil of George Stephenson and a prominent engineer, to analyse London's water problem. Jointly with Lewis D. B. Gordon he drew up his *Exposition of a Plan for the Metropolitan Water Supply*, a forty-four-page booklet published in 1849. Nothing could have summed up the situation more aptly than the quotation from Coleridge's 'Rhyme of the Ancient Mariner' which prefaced it:

Water! Water every where
Nor any drop to drink.

4 J. B. Atlay, *Sir Henry Wentworth Acland, Bart., KCB, FRS, A Memoir*, 1903, p. 170

The report made the point that, 'A great proportion of the water distributed in London is derived from that part of the Thames which is really the sewer of the Metropolis,' and put forward the theory that the Thames at Maple Durham was the most eligible source for the supply of pure soft water to London.

But Mrs Liddell survived, and Alice duly made her entrance into a world as untainted by the foulness of the surroundings as her parents could make it. Her home was spacious, and there was a bevy of eight resident servants to do the work. The family kept a carriage, as befitted their station, and the headmaster and his wife consolidated their social position and made their mark upon London society to such good effect that, despite the outbreak of typhoid, numbers at the school more than doubled during their tenure of office.

Henry and Lorina Liddell did everything that was expected of them: entertained, promoted music and the arts, and mingled with distinguished and cultured people in a wide range of subjects. They went riding daily in Rotten Row, often in the company of Liddell's old friend William Makepeace Thackeray. Liddell recalled those rides in his personal journal:

> He often used to join Mrs Liddell and myself when riding in Rotten Row. On one occasion he turned to her and said, 'Your husband ruined all my prospects in life; he did all my Latin verses for me, and I lost all opportunities of self-improvement.' It is needless to add that this was a pure fiction—I had trouble enough to do my own verses. At this time *Vanity Fair* was coming out in monthly parts in its well-known yellow paper covers. He used to talk about it, and what he should do with the persons. Mrs Liddell one day said, 'Oh, Mr Thackeray, you must let Dobbin marry Amelia.' 'Well,' he replied, 'he shall; and when he has got her, he will not find her worth having.'

Alice's mother was very much a working partner in her husband's career. While he busied himself with educational and architectural matters, as well as with his preaching, she organised their social life. She also kept a motherly eye on the scholars, particularly those who were ill. She was popular among the boys, who named a school boat after her, and it was she who coached the boys taking female roles in the school plays, showing them how they should walk and talk, and generally teaching them feminine mannerisms. Costumes, too, came under her personal supervision, and so anxious was she to achieve an air of authenticity that she consulted Sir Charles Newton, a distinguished classical scholar, on all matters relating to dress.

The pains which Mrs Liddell took certainly paid off. The annual Latin play was an important event in the social calendar of the day, and influential and prestigious people flocked to see it. The headmaster himself wrote the Prologue, which always referred to topical events. The opening of the Great Exhibition of 1851 and Mrs Bloomer's famous innovation were among the news items that claimed Liddell's attention over the years, and his allusions to the latter caused a considerable social stir. The captain of the school was by tradition responsible for all administrative matters relating to the play, including the maintenance of a detailed account book, and it was he who had the doubtful privilege of reciting the Prologue.

An account of the performance of *Eunuchus* in 1854 was included in a book written with great charm and gentle humour by an old boy of the school, Germain Lavie, who became a Queen's Scholar in 1850 and was elected to Christ Church, Oxford, in 1854. He described the arrival at the play of Mr and Mrs Liddell:

> And now, at about five minutes to seven, the Gods go off into a succession of claps, the young Westminsters stand up, and everybody in the house imitates their example to welcome Mrs Headmaster, who appears leaning on the arm of the Captain, who for this minute or two looks as happy as anyone in knee breeches and buckles can be expected to look. This is a most artfully devised plan to raise the ambition of small town boys who always on play nights wish from the very bottom of their hearts that they might some day, as Captains, enjoy the privilege of escorting Mrs Headmaster. . . .
>
> Five minutes more, and the house again rise, and again the Gods clap, and the band strikes up 'See the Conquering Hero Comes', and presently the hero appears in the shape of the Head Master and his party, though what connection of ideas associates those gentlemen, mostly in grey heads and expensive waistcoats, with conquering heroes or Judas Maccabaeus, no one, as far as my knowledge goes, has yet discovered.[5]

But Liddell's policies were undoubtedly successful, and he was genuinely held in high regard by scholars, parents and the authorities alike. He had come to be looked on as the man responsible for the salvation of the school and, had he not been appointed there, it is virtually certain that the

5 Germain Lavie, *The Westminster Play: Its Actors and its Visitors*, by an Old Westminster, 1855

school would have gone under, a fact recognised even to this very day. His name still means something in the school, and in recent years the house in which he lived was named 'Liddell's' in his honour.

Alice was only eighteen months old when scarlet fever broke out in her home. Two of the Liddell children contracted the disease, and with one of them the prognosis was in every way favourable. But little Arthur, then not quite three years old, hovered between life and death for a week. Alice's mother was five months pregnant at the time, and the doctors insisted not only that she should take no part in the nursing of the child, but that she leave the house immediately until all risk of infection had passed. The full burden of responsibility in this crisis thus fell on Alice's father. Though a nurse was brought in at once, he shared the task of nursing Arthur, whom he described to his mother as a 'dear, angelic little child. I can call him by no other name—so good and patient and gentle he is. I am sitting by his bedside now, while the nurse goes out to get a little air, and every quick-drawn breath goes to my heart. One does not know how one loves them, till a time like this comes.'[6]

Arthur died on 27 November 1853. 'It was a miserable week, each day bringing many alternations of hope and fear,'[6] Liddell wrote.

The continual visits of the doctors, the grave faces, the comings and goings of the undertakers, made no conscious impression on Alice. Neither her father's grief nor her mother's absence held special significance for her. She may have heard the tolling of the knell and seen the mourners, but if she witnessed the bearers leaving the house with that pathetic little coffin on their shoulders, her brow remained unclouded.

On the very day of the funeral her father threw himself almost frenziedly into his work, which he had partially shelved while nursing Arthur. 'I was so worn out by watching and anxiety, added to my usual work,' he wrote, 'that I fell ill on Saturday; and, though I am much better today, they have said that I *must* leave town, and remain quiet for a few days at least. My wife is not allowed to return home.'[6]

A friend let Liddell have the use of his house Tanhurst, a house on Leith Hill, where he went to recuperate. To his friend Acland he wrote: 'I cannot even yet believe that we shall never see again on earth his fair face with those gentle bright blue eyes and silken hair. A more healthy strong child never was. A more docile obedient child never was. I can hardly remember when it was necessary to speak to him a second time. His winning pretty ways are stamped in our memories, I believe, for ever. His

6 H. L. Thompson, p. 9

thoughtful happy disposition made him the favourite wherever he went; and I verily believe the grief of my father and mother is hardly inferior to our own. You will pardon these babblings of fondness. But I watched him alone through that dreadful illness, and it relieves me to write so to those who can, and will, I know, feel with me.'[7]

Recovery was slow, and the whole school shared in the mourning of the headmaster and his family. As a special mark of sympathy, the boys voluntarily decided to forgo that highlight of the academic year, the school play.

Alice's development was meanwhile rapid, and soon she was ousted from her position as baby of the family by a new and most welcome arrival, a little girl born into the family home in the spring of 1854. Family life had almost returned to normal, but Alice's parents had still not recovered from the shock of Arthur's death and were at first unable to decide on a name for their new child. The birth was simply registered as that of an unnamed female child, but eventually the names Edith Mary were chosen.

Alice was now big enough to take an active interest in her surroundings, and the scholars who crossed Dean's Yard or called at the house for breakfast were becoming a familiar sight. Under Liddell's regime the standard attire had been modified to tail-coats, black waistcoats, white stick-up collars and dark trousers. The long black gowns were open in front with V-shaped sleeves, the pointed ends of which were tightly bound with waxed silks. Square-topped caps with tassels were always worn. When Alice looked out of the window she could watch the boys playing football in Dean's Yard. Two trees at either end formed the goals, which were some twenty yards wide, and the number of boys who played at any one time was unlimited. Some twelve or fifteen on each side, regarded as 'duffers' or 'funk sticks', acted as goalies, and anyone who exhibited cowardice on the field was automatically relegated to that position. The games were noisy, boisterous and fun to watch.

The school building itself, with which Alice now gradually became familiar, consisted of a single room, dating back to the sixteenth century and measuring 96 feet by 34 feet. Once it had been the monks' dormitory, and its solid squared stone walls, unplastered, bore the names of countless former scholars. There was a separate library building, where Liddell himself taught the more advanced scholars. One old scholar gave a vivid account of Liddell as headmaster:

7 ibid, p. 10

I remember him as a tall handsome man, well set up, and with a rather scornful expression, a thorough gentleman in every way, with a certain grand manner, which made us proud to have him as our Headmaster. . . . He was always just and reasonable in meting out the punishment for my offences. My first acquaintance of him consisted of oft-repeated interviews at arm's length, I being sent up for 'handings', punishment on the back of the hand with a rod in the centre of the school. These I accepted with the usual expression of scornful amusement which was the etiquette on these occasions.[8]

Alice and her brothers and sisters were kept well away from these rather sordid punishment sessions.

Alice's father never fully recovered from Arthur's death, nor from the earlier shock of his wife's attack of typhoid, for he did not regain his former robust health. He had worked wonders with the school, and in addition, from 1850 onwards, he had served on the first Oxford University Commission, attending no less than 86 of its 87 meetings and always making a significant contribution. The Oxford University Act of 1854 was the direct result of the work of the Commission, which was set up by the government to investigate Oxford University affairs.

By 1854 Liddell had become thoroughly disenchanted with Westminster School, which he now felt was unlikely to prosper at that time in the squalor of the metropolis. Yet there appeared no prospect of moving it into the more salubrious atmosphere of the countryside. He accordingly began to cast his eye around for other openings, and in that same year he was offered the Mastership of Sherbourn Hospital, County Durham. After consideration he decided to decline, but soon there came a much more exciting prospect. Dean Gaisford, the 'Old Bear' of Christ Church, died on 2 June 1855. There were many contenders for the vacant post. 'The man we want must be not only a ripe scholar and apt to teach,' wrote Dr Jelf, one of the Canons, 'but a thorough gentleman, a man skilful and experienced in *governing* young men of the upper classes, a man of sound judgment, unflinching firmness, good temper, courteous manners, business habits, incorruptible integrity.'[9] To find a man with such a vast, almost superhuman range of personal qualities seemed almost impossible; and yet Liddell genuinely possessed them all, and more besides.

Despite various rival claims, Liddell quickly emerged as the most

8 Markham, Capt. F., *Recollections of a Town Boy at Westminster*, 1903, p. 57
9 British Library Manuscript 44381 f.31v

probable contender, but nevertheless, he had his enemies. Dr Pusey, a Canon of Christ Church, had formed a very unfavourable opinion of him only eighteen months earlier when Liddell had preached an uncharacteristically controversial sermon in Oxford, which had been badly received in some quarters and resulted in complaints to the Vice-Chancellor. 'We must struggle with rationalism; but it is miserable to hear it coming down on our young men from those who ought to teach them the truth,' Pusey had written. Now Pusey had terrible forebodings, that this same preacher was to succeed Gaisford, whom he had described to Gladstone as 'a representative of the best of the past, which has been passing away'. And he added, 'Now nothing but what is evil is threatened as his successor. They imagine Liddell.'[10]

Four days later Lord Elcho, Liddell's former pupil and later Lord Wemyss, wrote a letter to Liddell giving him the first news of the appointment which was to improve the fortunes and social standing of the whole family, and to set Alice on the path to immortality:

My Dear Dean,

I went to Lord Palmerston this morning, to urge your appointment. He told me that he had heard so much in your favour, that he had taken the Queen's pleasure about it the day before yesterday, but that his time had been so fully occupied yesterday, that he had not had time to write to you. Upon my asking if I might announce this to you, he begged me to do so, as it would save his writing to ask you to call on him to-morrow morning at 11.30, at which hour he wishes to see you. He added, in his jocose manner, 'you may tell him likewise, that I hope he will excuse my having named him to the Queen, without having previously obtained his consent.' I can assure you that nothing could have given me greater pleasure than to be thus the means of communicating intelligence so pleasing to my old tutor and friend. I rejoice most sincerely at your appointment, as I feel confident that in your hands Christ Church will hold out every possible inducement to us to send our sons there, in the full confidence that you will turn them out *gentlemen* and useful members of society.

Yours ever,

Elcho   6 June 1855[11]

10 British Library Manuscript 44281 f. 181
11 H. L. Thompson, pp. 131-2

Amid cheers, Palmerston personally announced to the House of Commons on the following day the news of Liddell's appointment, which he had had no hesitation in accepting. On 7 June *The Times* made the same announcement, briefly but with pleasure.

A few weeks of the summer term at Westminster still remained, and during this time all the arrangements for the removal of Mr and Mrs Liddell and their four children had to be made. Most of the boys had grown attached to the family, and especially to Liddell himself, whom they were genuinely sorry to lose. Before they left, the whole school assembled and the school captain and the head town boy read out addresses which Liddell kept to his dying day. They then presented the family with a splendid silver vase, which they cherished all their lives; it later passed under the terms of Mrs Liddell's will to their son Harry.

In some ways it was a sad parting. The couple had come to the school nine years previously in robust health and with high hopes and ambitions. They had seen much effort wasted through external factors over which they had had no control. Their lives had been enriched by the birth of five fine children, but in the disease-ridden atmosphere of Westminster they had lost the child who had borne the stamp of Liddell's own features most clearly, and damage which was to some extent irreversible had been done to their own health. Small wonder that, despite their attachment to the boys, they were glad to shake the dust of Westminster from their feet and transfer to new and more prosperous surroundings.

TIME WAS YOUNG

Oh, Time was young, and Life was warm
When first I saw that fairy-form,
Her dark hair tossing in the storm.

'Faces in the Fire'

ALTHOUGH Liddell's appointment as Dean had met with approval in Parliamentary and Court circles, the news was on the whole received in Oxford with a decided lack of enthusiasm. His zealous work for the Oxford University Commission had caused many to look upon him with distrust. He had earned the reputation of 'relentless reformer', a term later applied to him by Charles Dodgson in a clever parody.[1] But, truth to tell, many Oxford men were violently opposed to change, and for such, old Dean Gaisford's passing seemed to signal the destruction of all that was venerable and beautiful in the established order of things. Gaisford had treated the Commission with supreme contempt, and had consistently ignored its communications, an attitude which had been widely applauded in the Chapter.

In the event, such fears proved groundless. Liddell had had enough of controversy at Westminster, and was now determined to avoid it wherever possible. He had a difficult task ahead of him. Academic standards at Christ Church had fallen into a state of decline, and it was now his task to diagnose the reason and put it right. It needed a man of wisdom and mature judgment to do so. At the age of only forty-four, Liddell found himself presiding over a powerful and influential Chapter, whose members were much older than himself. They included Dr Edward Bouverie Pusey, a leading member of the Oxford Movement who had been a Canon since 1828, and Dr Frederick Barnes, who had been a Canon since the turn of the century.

As at Westminster, Liddell began by revolutionising the Deanery. Gaisford had been entirely lacking in social ambition and his life style had been modest. But Alice's parents had other ideas and set to work immediately to build a home and develop a way of living which was to

1 Lewis Carroll, *Examination Statue*, 1864

37

left, A nineteenth-century view of Christ Church, Oxford; *right*, The Deanery, from the garden

transform the Deanery into a glittering social centre, the focal point of Oxford Society for the next thirty-six years.

Alice and her family had not been able to stay on in the headmaster's house at Westminster while the work at the Deanery was carried out, because they had to make way for Charles Broderick Scott, Liddell's successor. Liddell himself was able to take up residence temporarily in the house of Dr Clerke, the Sub-Dean, for he wished to be on hand to supervise the alterations in person; but Alice and the other children did not join him until their new home was ready for occupation.

The alterations on which Alice's parents decided were extensive and included wood panelling in the hall and drawing-room, and the opening out of the long gallery on the first floor to form an extra reception room. Of this the Dean wrote, 'The gallery will be a good place for sound, opening by a wide archway upon the stairs.'[2] The staircase was new and magnificent, and the decorative carving embodied representations of the Liddell family crest. The family always referred to it as the 'Lexicon' staircase, because the Dean paid for it out of the profits of that book. Alice had many recollections of it: 'When my father went up to Christ Church,' she wrote, 'he had some carved lions [wooden representations of the Liddell crest] placed on top of each of the corner posts in the banisters going upstairs and along the gallery. When we went to bed we had to go along this gallery, and we always ran as hard as we could along it, because

2 H. L. Thompson, p. 148

38

we *knew* that the lions got down from their pedestals and ran after us.'[3]

All the woodwork was prepared at a factory in Lambeth, and there was a serious delay to completion because it was destroyed in a fire in the factory before it had been transported to Oxford. But by mid-February 1856, the Deanery was nearly finished. To his mother Liddell wrote:

> As I sit in this now very beautiful house, and admire all that has been done, I feel sensible how worthless it all would be, if we had not kind parents and kinsfolk and friends to join us in admiration. . . . Painters and paperers still linger, but we are now very nearly done, and hope to throw open our doors for an evening musical party next week. They are intending to get up the 'Macbeth' music, with choruses, some glees, and other music, by the help of some of the young men and some ladies, if they are not too prudish to join. . . . I wish you, like my father, had seen the house before it was done, in order that you might appreciate all that has been done. We have spent all my father's magnificent present upon the sideboard, which I hope he will soon come to admire. It is really, or rather will be (for it is not finished), *most* beautiful. I have not yet got anything with your present for my library, for that room at present remains untouched.[4]

About two weeks later he wrote to his mother with another progress report:

> The house is all but finished, and now nothing remains but the pleasant task of showing it to our friends and—paying the bills. We begin with two musical evenings on Thursday and Saturday next, without any dinner parties. All the College will be asked on the two nights, and all whom we know among Heads of Houses, etc., are asked. We very much wish you could all be here. *You* could sit and hear it all quietly in your own bedroom, if you did not feel equal to venturing into such a crowd; for what will, I hope, be your bedroom opens into the gallery where the music will be performed. So, on Thursday evening, think of Madam making her first curtsey at the head of her own stairs in Oxford. This is a strange place for rumours. It has been reported that Mrs Liddell is getting up private theatricals, and that Dr Clerke

---

3 Alice and Caryl Hargreaves, 'Alice's Recollections of Carrollian Days', *Cornhill*, LXXIII 1932
4 H. L. Thompson, p. 148

permits his daughter to personate one of the witches, while the Dean is expected to represent Macbeth![4]

By 25 February the children were installed in the Deanery, in good time for the two musical evenings which took place on 6 and 8 March. As a special privilege Harry and Lorina were allowed to join the fine company; but Alice and Edith were packed off to bed, somewhat to their disappointment. In the long gallery the songs from *Macbeth* were the chief item on the programme, and a well-known Biblical scholar, Ernest de Bunsen, rendered Blücher's 'War Song' with great distinction. Quintin Twiss, who had been Liddell's pupil at Westminster, and other undergraduates joined in, rendering choruses with great spirit. But the strains of the music that filled the lovely new house did not disturb the sleeping children.

Years later in an article which she wrote for *Cornhill* with her son, Alice described the old grey stone home of her childhood:

> The Deanery is a fair-sized house, one side of which looks out into Tom Quad, while the other looks on to a garden which is also overlooked by Christ Church Library. It was very modern for those days in that it had a big bath, but with the un-modern limitation that only cold water was laid on! So the young ladies had a cold both every morning! It was in this house, built by Cardinal Wolsey, but adapted to the comforts of the day, that we spent the happy years of childhood.[5]

When the family moved into the Deanery, Liddell and his wife engaged a young, local woman to act as governess to the children. Her name was Mary Prickett, and she was twenty-three years old. In later years she described her father, James Prickett, as a 'gentleman', but at the time when Mary Prickett was working for the Liddells, he was the butler at Trinity College. He was not, however, to be confused with the run-of-the-mill college servants of his day, but would have been a decidedly superior sort of person, an authoritative man and an able administrator, a man of sufficient education and breeding to deal direct with undergraduates and dons alike. His home was in Floyd's Row, near Folly Bridge, and readily accessible from Christ Church.

Alice's son later wrote of Mary Prickett: 'She was far from being the

5 Alice and Caryl Hargreaves

Alice, Lorina, Harry and Edith Liddell, *c.* 1859

highly educated governess of today, and Alice was not her favourite among the three sisters.'[6] Yet despite her intellectual limitations, Miss Prickett was fully capable of bringing the children up successfully according to the standards of that era, and they spent most of their time in her company. From her they received a general elementary education, and later, when the girls were old enough to require it, masters were brought in to teach them such subjects as French, Italian and German, and mistresses taught them to master music. Unlike Harry, who went to boarding school as soon as he was old enough, Alice and her sisters were always taught at home, for such was the custom of the day. Miss Prickett bore a heavy responsibility, but she was genuinely devoted to the children, to whom she was generally known as 'Pricks'. Charles Dodgson's comments on his portrayal of three Queens in the *Alice* books are interesting:

6 Caryl Hargreaves, 'The Lewis Carroll that Alice Recalls', *New York Times Magazine*, 1 May 1932

It was certainly hard on my Muse, to expect her to sing of *three* Queens, within such brief compass, and yet to give to each her own individuality. Each, of course, had to preserve, through all her eccentricities, a certain queenly *dignity*. *That* was essential. And for distinguishing traits, I pictured to myself the Queen of Hearts as a sort of embodiment of ungovernable passion—a blind and aimless Fury. The Red Queen I pictured as a Fury, but of another type; her passion must be cold and calm; she must be formal and strict, yet not unkindly; pedantic to the tenth degree, the concentrated essence of all governesses! Lastly, the White Queen seemed to my dreaming fancy, gentle, stupid, fat and pale; helpless as an infant; and her just *suggesting* imbecility, but never quite passing into it; that would be, I think, fatal to any comic effect she might otherwise produce.[7]

It is difficult not to see in this description of the White Queen Dodgson's concept of Miss Prickett, formal, strict, pedantic, yet kind. Whether the other Queens bore any resemblance to the Deanery coterie is a matter for speculation. But for better or worse, 'Pricks' was now an established part of the children's daily lives, and was to remain so for as long as they needed her, even accompanying the family on holiday.

Early rising was usual in Christ Church Deanery and, as was the custom in many households in those days, breakfast was taken late when the work of the day was already well advanced. Undergraduates and academic staff were often invited. Mrs Liddell, a warm and sympathetic woman despite her strong sense of propriety, was in her element on these occasions, and from her seat at the head of her own table she was able to draw even the shyest of guests into conversation. But the Dean, seated at the foot of the table, was less at his ease; for though he excelled in academic repartee and intellectual discussion, he was totally lacking in small talk, which he disliked intensely. Always an awe-inspiring figure, he tended to freeze normal conversation on the lips of the undergraduates, who were often uncomfortable in his presence.

Several years were to elapse before Alice and the other children were permitted to join their parents on a regular basis at the dining table. Instead, they took their meals in the nursery under the supervision of Miss Prickett, who was responsible for teaching them table manners, etiquette and general obedience as well as 'reeling and writhing and fainting in coils'. The Liddells were devoted to all their children; but as became their social station they maintained a certain distance between themselves and

7 Lewis Carroll, 'Alice on the Stage', *The Theatre*, 1887

their offspring until the latter were sufficiently housebroken to be socially and intellectually acceptable.

These two people who sat every day at opposite ends of the Deanery dining table were towering personalities, but they were genuinely devoted to each other and rarely clashed. One of the secrets of their successful marriage was that each was dominant in a separate sphere in which the other did not seek to intervene. Between these spheres lay an area off common interest, which included love of family, material and social ambition, and the pursuit of cultural objectives. Added to this was the genuine love and respect which each had for the other, and which resulted in a union giving maximum satisfaction to both parties.

Mrs Liddell's admiration for her husband's academic genius was unbounded. She could not match his brilliance, but she could recognise it for what it was. Nor did she lack intellectual qualities of her own. The Reeve family into which she had been born had introduced her from her formative years to a wide range of academic interests, which included antiquarian and scientific subjects as well as modern languages, art and music, all of which were considered desirable accomplishments for well-born ladies.

Not least of the qualities which the Dean admired in his wife were her graceful bearing and physical beauty. Mrs Liddell had that kind of face which might be described as striking and handsome rather than merely pretty. She could at times be as imperious as she was handsome, nevertheless, there was about her face a certain timelessness which owed much to the tranquillity and, at times, extraordinary gentleness of her expression. Sir William Richmond, the artist, who got to know her when she was about twenty-eight years old, said of her: 'Mrs Liddell was remarkably beautiful, of a Spanish type, although I am not aware if she had any Spanish blood in her veins.'[8] An analysis of the Reeve family tree shows that Spanish connections were unlikely, though a look at a picture of Mrs Liddell, with her dark hair and strong features, shows how Richmond formed that impression of her.

Richmond also said that Liddell himself was 'as handsome a specimen of aristocratic manhood as could be seen in a lifetime'. In this assessment he was almost certainly biased, partly through awe of the Dean's intellectual stature, partly by his grand manner, but also by the genuine appreciation of the human warmth which lay behind the somewhat brusque and dignified exterior.

8 A. M. W. Stirling, *The Richmond Papers*, 1926, pp. 190–91

Sir William Richmond's father, George Richmond, produced a very fine portrait of Dean Liddell in 1858. As a work of art is was beautiful and satisfying, and prints of it were successfully marketed. Yet it cannot be denied that this was a very idealised and youthful representation. In real life, Liddell did not carry his years well. The face and the nose were a little too long, and even at the age of twenty-eight, his hair had receded and grown thin. Within ten more years the light brown colour had turned to grey. He influenced people by his style and elegance, by the splendid hauteur of his manner. It was an image which impressed in the formal and class-conscious society of Victorian England. The children were all exceptionally beautiful, but the only one who resembled his father was Arthur, who lived for less than three years. The others owed their good looks to their mother.

Many believed that Mrs Liddell dominated her husband completely. This was not altogether fair. At an elementary level her word was law in the Deanery, for Liddell disliked trivia and was constantly preoccupied with more weighty matters. But Mrs Liddell deferred to his ultimate authority whenever he chose to exercise it. Nevertheless there were many who noted how she took the leading role in the drawing-room, and often drew the wrong conclusions. An Oxford rhyme of the 1880s ran:

> *I am the Dean and this is Mrs Liddell*
> *She plays the first and I the second fiddle.*

Equally popular were the lines that Arthur Cecil Spring Rice added to the Masque of Balliol:

> *I am the Dean of Christ Church, sir,*
> *This is my wife—look well at her.*
> *She is the Broad and I'm the High:*
> *We are the University.*

And in a sense they were indeed the University for some thirty-six years, unchanging and unchanged and always at the centre of things.

One of the great delights of living in the Deanery was its garden, as Alice and her sisters quickly found. At Westminster School the headmaster's house had had no private garden, and the children had to play in corners of the yard, or by the plane tree which their father himself planted, and which still stands as a living monument to him. But now they had direct and undisturbed access to a private garden of considerable

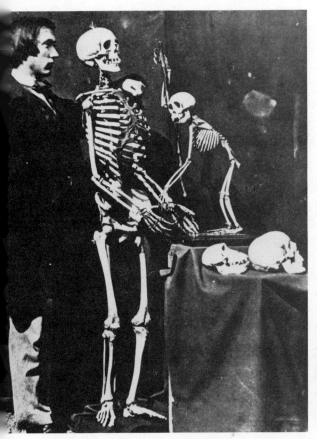

right, Lewis Carroll;
left, His picture of
Reginald Southey,
both *c.* 1856

beauty. It was large and sheltered, with a beautiful rectangular lawn just right for croquet, and surrounded by fine herbaceous borders. Creepers clung to the walls of the house and the Library building which overlooked the garden, and nasturtiums provided a splash of colour all summer long. Side by side with the formal area was a small glade which provided welcome shade from the heat on summer afternoons, and a leafy haunt for adventurous children. The most impressive tree in the garden was a magnificent and ancient chestnut which formed a major set-piece in the imaginative games which the children played.

On the afternoon of 25 April 1856, Alice and her two sisters were playing in the garden when two young men appeared, carrying a quantity of cumbersome paraphernalia which immediately aroused the curiosity of the little girls. As they set up the apparatus, they explained that this was a camera, and that they had come to take pictures of the Cathedral.

45

Reginald Southey, the owner of the camera, had straight, mousey hair, a pleasant countenance, and bright, alert round eyes. The other was twenty-four years old, with thick brown curly hair, rather long by the standards of the day. His eyes were slightly asymmetrical, but they were blue and kindly and full of candour. Alice thought that he must have swallowed a poker, for he stood so stiffly. Though he was only 5 ft 10 ins tall, his slim build and upright stance made him seem taller than he really was. Harry had already made friends with him down at the boats, and Lorina knew who he was at once, for they had made friends at the musical party at the Deanery; but this was Alice's first recorded meeting with Charles Lutwidge Dodgson, a meeting as important in literary terms as that of Dante with his Beatrice.

In his parody, 'Hiawatha's Photographing', Dodgson described what it was like to set up the camera in those days:

> *From his shoulder Hiawatha*
> *Took the camera of rosewood,*
> *Made of sliding, folding rosewood;*
> *Neatly put it all together.*
> *In its case it lay compactly,*
> *Folded into nearly nothing;*
> *But he opened out the hinges,*
> *Pushed and pulled the joints and hinges,*
> *Till it looked all squares and oblongs,*
> *Like a complicated figure*
> *In the Second Book of Euclid.*
>
> *This he perched upon a tripod -*
> *Crouched beneath its dusky cover -*
> *Stretched his hand, enforcing silence -*
> *Said, 'Be motionless, I beg you!'*
> *Mystic, awful was the process.*

Southey's photographic interest was mainly architectural; but Dodgson, whose first camera had been ordered shortly beforehand and was still awaited, always preferred people to places. It was he who suggested the experiment of grouping the little trio in the foreground. Their mother had given the young men permission to use a downstairs cubby-hole in the Deanery as a photographic darkroom for the day, and before each plate was exposed they rushed into the darkroom to pour collodion evenly over its carefully polished surface. The plate was next dipped in silver nitrate solution, and Southey and Dodgson then emerged to expose the plate as quickly as possible, before the solution began to dry out. An exposure time of at least forty-five seconds and usually more was then required, which to the waiting children seemed an age. Despite all his efforts, Dodgson did not succeed in persuading them to sit still; this was hardly surprising, for Alice was not yet four years old and, although Lorina was a mature young lady of six, Edith had only just celebrated her second birthday. Small wonder that they grew impatient and fidgety.

After each exposure the two young men rushed back into the darkroom, where they heated the plate evenly over the fire, before varnishing, draining and drying it. Only when it was completely dry could a print be made from the plate. On this occasion not one of the photographs succeeded, but despite his lack of success in the photographic field, Dodgson was exhilarated by his meeting with the children, and wrote in his diary: 'I mark this day with a white stone.'[9] This was a favourite Latin phrase, its modern equivalent being a 'red letter day'.

Three days later the two young men returned. This time Southey

Three Liddell sisters—Lorina, Alice and Edith—in front of the Deanery, photograph by Lewis Carroll

9 Roger Lancelyn Green (Ed.), *The Diaries of Lewis Carroll*, p. 83

wanted to take a picture of Merton College from the walk in front of Alice's home, 'a much more promising view as far as light goes',[9] according to Dodgson, although the pictures proved to be another failure. Harry was with them almost all the time they were there. Dodgson had already described him in his diary as 'certainly the handsomest boy I ever saw'.[10] Not long before Dodgson and Southey left the garden Lorina went to talk to them, but neither Alice nor Edith emerged.

Next day Dodgson and Southey went back to the Deanery to take away their photographic equipment. They had not been satisfied with the quality of the chemicals and had decided not to attempt any more pictures until better chemicals were available. This time none of the family put in an appearance, somewhat to Dodgson's disappointment.

On 1 May Dodgson's own new camera, which he had had on order from London, arrived in Oxford. It had cost him fifteen pounds, a handsome sum in those days. He was keen to try his hand right away and took some photographs with Southey's spoiled collodion, mainly to get the feel of the camera. But he did not venture back to the Deanery until he had acquired a degree of expertise in carrying out the complicated technical processes.

10 ibid, p. 79

CABBAGES AND KINGS

'The time has come,' the Walrus said,
'To talk of many things:
Of shoes—and ships—and sealing-wax—
And cabbages—and kings—'

Through the Looking-Glass

ALICE and her sisters had stepped into Dodgson's life at a time when there was a void which they were uniquely able to fill. The celibate atmosphere of Christ Church in those days was not a healthy one. For the Students, who were the equivalent of Fellows in other colleges, matrimony meant immediate forfeiture of Studentship, an effective form of banishment from the precincts, and loss of livelihood. The Canons were allowed to marry, but their average age was rather too high for them to populate the houses around Tom Quad with children. But fortune had favoured Alice's father, and he had climbed to high office when he not only already had a fine young family, but when his wife still had many more years of fertility ahead of her. Liddell was always one to seize his opportunities.

Dodgson was very happy at Christ Church. When he had entered its walls for the first time he had discovered his natural habitat, the environment in which he was destined to live out the rest of his life, never quitting it except for holidays. But there was no denying that he missed the companionship of children in general, and little girls in particular. He had come from a large family, having three younger brothers and seven sisters, only two of whom were older than himself.

His childhood had been ideally happy. He had been born on 27 January 1832 in the tiny Cheshire hamlet of Daresbury, where his father had been perpetual curate. His father was only eleven years older than Liddell, and like Liddell he had achieved the distinction of a double first at Christ Church. But he had married younger, thereby forfeiting his Studentship, and had been hustled into the first Christ Church living that had arisen. When the headmastership of Harrow School had fallen

49

vacant he had applied for it, but the fact that he had been away from academic life for some eight years had weighed heavily against him, and he had been rejected. By the time Dodgson reached Christ Church, his father had become Archdeacon of Ripon, but the years of straightened circumstances had taken their toll.

As the eldest son, Charles had been the obvious leader in family games: entertaining the young ones had been expected of him and had come naturally. Always he was at the centre of things, organising the others, writing, conjuring, inventing, and all for their amusement. Even when he went to boarding school, first Richmond and then Rugby, he did not abdicate from the leadership, but kept it up through correspondence with his siblings. His homecoming was always eagerly anticipated, both by Charles himself, and by his fond waiting family.

Dodgson's career at Christ Church began with matriculation in May 1850. He moved into residence in Christ Church in January 1851, gaining a Second Class in Classical Moderations and a First in Mathematics in December 1852. 'I am getting quite tired of being congratulated on various subjects,' he wrote in a letter home. 'If I had shot the Dean I could hardly have had more said about it.'[1] Dr Pusey promptly nominated him for a Studentship. Two years later he gained a First Class Honours in the Final Mathematical School. Professor Bartholomew Prince, that 'little Bat' who twinkled so merrily for Alice and her sisters, said that he had never had such a good set of men, and Dodgson headed the list, finishing eighteen marks ahead of his nearest rival. On 23 January 1855, just four days before his twenty-third birthday, Dodgson took on his first pupil.

By the time that Alice first met him, Dodgson was feeling very satisfied with the way his career was progressing. Although he could not become a Master of Arts in the University until 1857, by which time he would have completed the requisite number of terms, he had been made a Master of the House in honour of Liddell's appointment as Dean. As he saw the old year out quietly in December 1855 he wrote in his diary: 'I am sitting alone in my bedroom this last night of the old year, waiting for midnight. It has been the most eventful year of my life. I began it a poor bachelor student, with no definite plans or expectations: I end it a Master and tutor in Christ Church, with an income of more than £300 a year, and the course of mathematical tuition marked out by God's providence for at least some years to come.'[2] There were even more eventful years ahead, and they all, either directly or indirectly, involved Alice.

1 Stuart Dodgson Collingwood, *The Life and Letters of Lewis Carroll*, 1898, p. 57
2 ibid, p. 65

50

Dodgson had always had literary ambitions, even as a boy, when he had amused himself by writing and editing family magazines. He had had two poems printed in the *Oxonian Advertiser*, but these were poor in quality. Before long he turned his attention to the *Comic Times*, a magazine begun by Edmund Yates in August 1855. Yates liked Dodgson's work, and accepted a few items from him, but unfortunately the magazine collapsed after only sixteen issues. However, although their publisher had deserted them, the regular staff formed a company to launch the *Train*, whose earliest contributors included Yates, Sala, Brough and Smedley. Soon Dodgson found himself writing in their company.

Initially Dodgson had submitted his offerings under the puzzling pseudonymous initials 'B.B', but Yates now wanted him to use a regular pen-name. Accordingly Dodgson submitted a list of four possibles, and left the final decision to Yates. It was a fateful choice. Yates rejected 'Edgar Cuthwellis', 'Edgar U. C. Westhill' and 'Louis Carroll', but opted in favour of the remaining nom de plume. On 1 March 1856 Dodgson noted in his diary, 'Lewis Carroll was chosen',[3] and that same month his poem 'Solitude' appeared in the *Train* under that name.

Alice therefore met Dodgson after his nom de plume had been invented. She entered his natural sphere at a time when his desire to carve out a literary career for himself was already strong. 'I do not think I have written anything worthy of real publication . . . but I do not despair of doing so one day,'[4] he had commented in his diary only a few months earlier. But he had no notion of entering into the field of children's literature, and his writing instincts temporarily took second place to his photography. 'It is my one recreation, and I think it should be done well,'[4] he wrote.

Photographic 'victims' were now essential to Dodgson. This strange 'black art', so called because the chemicals stained the hands, was something entirely new. At first adults, curious to see their own likeness, were not unwilling sitters; but as soon as the novelty wore off their enthusiasm waned and they found themselves too busy to spare the time. Often the photographs failed, so complicated and accident prone were the processes, and there was then the added embrarrassment of having nothing to show for wasted hours.

But with children it was different, at least where Dodgson was concerned, for his charismatic approach overcame all difficulties; and if the children had to sit still for what seemed like an eternity, there were

3 R. L. Green, p. 77
4 ibid, p. 55

always the anecdotes and puzzles to compensate for it all. In those early days of photographic experiment the Liddell children were at hand and eager for his company. Their parents were also co-operative, at least initially. It appears that at that time Southey was regarded with greater favour, though perhaps deservedly, since he had had the greater experience. But the Dean had a genuine interest in photography, which Ruskin, in *Praeterita*, says dated back as far as 1840: 'It must have been during my last days at Oxford that Mr Liddell, the present Dean of Christ Church, told me of the original experiments of Daguerre. My Parisian friends obtained for me the best examples of his results; and the plates sent to me in Oxford were certainly the finest examples of the sun's drawings that were ever seen in Oxford, and, I believe, in England.'[5]

Dodgson spent a lot of time experimenting with his camera when it arrived, but still the major initiatives were left to Southey. On 10 May 1856, after spending a long time watching Southey at work, he went over to the Library which overlooked the Deanery garden. Harry was playing there, and Dodgson called to him from the window, persuading him to come over to Southey's room. 'We had great difficulty in getting him to sit still long enough: he [Southey] succeeded at last by placing him in a bright light, in getting a fair profile.'[6]

Three days later Dodgson took Harry's photograph to show the Dean and was invited to stay for lunch. Mrs Reeve, the children's grandmother, was staying at the Deanery, and she and Mrs Liddell took Harry over for a second photographic session at Southey's. This resulted in another tolerable likeness and several failures.

On the following Saturday Dodgson was invited to dine at the Deanery, where they were holding another musical evening with lots of guests. He reported that the evening was fair as far as the music was concerned, though the rooms were too crowded for real enjoyment, and he excused himself at about eleven o'clock. He might have enjoyed it more if he had had a chance to see Alice and her sisters, but as usual, they had taken their meal in the nursery before being packed off to bed.

Dodgson first photographed Alice and the other children with his own camera on 3 June 1856. It was the first of many such sessions. Their physical attraction and their intelligence made them all ideal subjects for the camera. Dodgson did not like photographing working-class girls, for he thought their ankles too thick. He had already remarked on Harry's handsome appearance, and he described a distant cousin of the children,

5 John Ruskin, *Praeterita*, Vol. II, p. 251
6 R. L. Green, p. 85

Two portraits of Alice
by Lewis Carroll

Frederika Liddell, whom he had met by chance when on holiday the previous summer, as 'one of the most lovely children I ever saw, gentle and innocent looking, not an inanimate doll-beauty.'[7] About the physical beauty of the Dean's daughters he made no comment, though as his photography progressed it spoke more eloquently than words. Alice was already wearing her hair cut in the fringe which she carried with her into adult life. She was the darkest of the children, straight-haired, blue-eyed, and with sturdy limbs. Fatness was regarded as being synonymous with good health where Victorian babies were concerned, and Alice at four years of age had not yet shaken off a certain plumpness of face and form. Her face was gentle and innocent, but she had not yet developed that look of wistful piquancy which later distinguished her from all Dodgson's other child friends.

Lorina's hair was only a little lighter than Alice's, and even at seven

7 ibid, p. 62

she wore it long and curled in ringlets. Edith's was Titian-coloured, also long and, like Lorina's, parted in the middle. As she grew in stature, it grew more abundant and luxuriant, hanging in tight waves and curls about her shoulders in the manner so beloved by the Pre-Raphaelite artists. Mrs Liddell understood the structure of her daughters' faces well, and had chosen for each a distinctive and seemingly timeless style which enhanced her own particular beauty.

When it came to dress, she clothed them all alike, sometimes in cotton, sometimes in muslin, whatever the current mode dictated. Dodgson's photographs of them over the years can be regarded as a kind of fashion parade, showing what the best-dressed Victorian children were wearing year by year. Their accessories were always chosen with care: sometimes they wore little tippet hats, at others larger-brimmed styles. When muffs were in vogue, they carried them, and whether buttoned boots or little black pumps were fashionable, Alice and her sisters were sure to be wearing them.

Every year there was a particular photographic season, at least where an amateur like Dodgson was concerned, for he had to restrict his camera work to those parts of the year when the light was strongest. This meant that the little trio of Liddell sisters was always captured in summer clothing. Presumably those cottons and voiles were replaced in colder weather with warmer fabrics, like wool and velvet, and top coats and mufflers were added according to the season. But their clothes were always charming, the dresses prettily tucked, flounced, spotted or embroidered. Frequently they wore pretty pastel colours, but more often than not they wore white, an indication of their social class. The poorer classes had to stick to serviceable dark colours because only the well-to-do could afford the laundering and upkeep of the delicate white fabrics. There were lots of new dresses in the Deanery, and clothes were never handed down from one child to another, as the wearing of identical dresses made readily apparent.

Among Dodgson's earliest photographs of the little trio is an adorable group in which they are all playing stringed instruments. The dresses are elaborately flounced and trimmed with white broderie anglaise, and peeping down beneath the little frilled skirts are tiny matching pantaloons. It was a charming style, and the picture itself has an appealing quality of innocence. The children's appearance was always a tribute to their mother's good taste.

Dodgson's visits to the Deanery and his photographic sessions were frequent at that time. Harry followed him about constantly like a little

Two portraits by
Lewis Carroll of Alice,
Lorina and Edith

55

dog, going boating with him on the river, and even turning up in his rooms for breakfast. On 5 June 1856 Dodgson and his cousin Frank arranged to go boating with Harry, and to Dodgson's surprise and delight the Dean allowed Ina (as Lorina was often called) to go with them. On the island they had a picnic of ginger beer and biscuits, and the two children were in wild spirits, attracting a great deal of notice from passers-by wherever they went. It was, Dodgson remarked, altogether a '*Dies mirabilis*'.

Shortly afterwards Dodgson left for the long vacation, most of which he spent in the Lake District, while the Liddells went off to Bamborough Castle of which the Dean's father was a trustee. Here the Aclands joined them for a few days. 'The Christ Church undergraduates would have stared had they seen the Dean and the Lee's Reader [i.e., Acland] tramping over moor and fell and, when the exigencies of the route required it, divesting themselves of their nether garments and fording the streams like a brace of Highlanders,' wrote Acland's biographer, J. B. Atlay.[8] Acland was keen to inspect the lighthouse on Fern Island, the famous scene of Grace Darling's heroic sea rescue.

Lewis Carroll's drawing-room

Though Grace herself had died of consumption attributed to her exposure to the elements on that fateful occasion, her father still lived there. Acland described him as 'a tall man, most intelligent and much read', who made birds' nests in safe places to prevent the birds laying eggs on perilous ledges from which the young would be swept to destruction by the gales.

While Mrs Liddell and the children were still enjoying their holiday, the Dean had to return to attend to Christ Church affairs. In September he caught a severe cold, which deteriorated when he was visiting estates in Market Harborough. The family was due back in Oxford for the resumption of term in October, but their father was too ill to get up and greet them. It was the first sign of a further breakdown in the Dean's health.

After the long vacation the intercourse between Dodgson and the family began again, but on 3 November he committed a serious *faux pas*. While out walking he met Lorina with Miss Prickett, and arranged with the governess to come over to photograph the children again in the Deanery, and also to invite the Aclands. It did not seem to occur to Dodgson that Mrs Liddell might take exception to his arranging with the governess not only to use her house and garden again, but to invite other people as well. Perhaps it is not surprising that Mrs Liddell leapt on to her high horse, or rather into her carriage, scooping up her children and the Dean with her, so that on the appointed morning Dodgson arrived just in time to see the whole family driving off. He was dismayed, but failed to understand the significance of what he had done and persisted with his invitations to Acland to be photographed in the Deanery. A few days later he went over to photograph Harry and Lorina again, but found that Mrs Liddell did not wish them to be photographed again until they could all sit for him in a group. Finally Dodgson realised that he had been intruding on the premises for too long and, since the mid-November weather was hardly suitable for photography, he resolved to pack up his paraphernalia and remove it from the Deanery, not returning unless specifically invited to do so.

He did not have to wait long for an invitation. The children's paternal grandfather arrived from his parish in Easington to stay at the Deanery, and he wanted his photograph taken. Dodgson readily agreed and also gave Mrs Liddell two portraits which had been taken earlier, and which he had had coloured for her by a professional artist. He was clearly restored to favour and was invited to another musical evening at the

8 J. B. Atlay, p. 176

Henry Acland

Deanery, where he heard from Mrs Liddell of her plans to send Harry as a boarder to Twyford School in Hampshire, where Dodgson's brothers Skeffington and Wilfred had been educated. She took him into the schoolroom and showed him specimens of Harry's sums and his Latin. When Dodgson offered to teach Harry some arithmetic, however, she said that she thought it would take up too much of his time. Her moods were always uncertain, despite her obvious charm.

Soon afterwards the threatened breakdown in the health of Alice's father took place and he became seriously ill. Acland diagnosed bronchopneumonia and told him that only a visit to Madeira would save his life. To this Liddell replied, 'I expected you to say so, but I am not going to be knocked about in the Bay of Biscay in that little brig *The Brilliant*. I shall not go unless I can go in a man-o-war.'[9]

As it happened, a friend of Acland's, Captain Prevost, had just been given command of one of the Navy's finest corvettes and was about to set sail for the Pacific. Acland accordingly telegraphed to him, and the captain

9 ibid, p. 234

obtained permission from the Admiralty to take the Dean and Mrs Liddell as far as Madeira. The children were to remain in Oxford in the care of Miss Prickett, and on 22 December they said goodbye to their father and mother, who travelled by train to Plymouth.

It was only when they were aboard the train that their escort, Acland, announced that he was to accompany them all the way to Madeira. Liddell was not in the least surprised. 'So I had supposed,' was his only comment.[10] Acland duly landed with them at Funchal, ostensibly to satisfy himself that the climate was suitable for his patient. He stayed there for a week and enjoyed with them 'the sight and taste of turtle, bananas, and green peas.' With the aid of the British Consul, Acland obtained on behalf of the university a magnificent tunny fish, which he had packed in bay salt and crated up in a box eight feet long. At the end of his week's stay, complete with the precious box, and having taken leave of his friends, Acland boarded the West India Mail Company's steamer, *Tyne*, homeward bound from Rio de Janeiro.

The presence on board ship of this great box, addressed to 'Dr Acland, Oxford', convinced the sailors that they had the corpse of a patient in the hold. When they ran into a heavy gale the crew blamed the 'corpse', and finally the Captain told Acland that he intended to throw it overboard. At this, Acland had the crate opened before the assembled crew to convince them of their foolishness. Nevertheless, misfortune did indeed dog the *Tyne*, and on 13 January 1857 she ran aground off the Dorset coast. Fortunately no lives were lost. Ruskin described how the anxious officers, confused crew and hysterical passengers were 'scandalised by the appearance of Dr Acland from the saloon in punctilious morning dress with the announcement that breakfast was ready'.[11] The tunny fish was unscathed, and when it was placed in the university museum, a sham 'epitaph' was devised, mainly by Dodgson, and circulated.

The Liddell children, in the absence of their parents, saw a lot of Dodgson, who was continually calling at the Deanery on one pretext or another. But it was the two eldest, rather than Alice, who chiefly engaged Dodgson's attention at that time. Lorina was at that exact age which Dodgson in those days considered ideal in his child friends, old enough to be a little independent, to go out to riding lessons with Harry, and generally to engage in pursuits for which neither Alice nor Edith was yet ready. When it came to Christmas, Dodgson gave presents only to Harry,

10 ibid, p. 234
11 John Ruskin, *Praeterita*, Vol. 1, p. 380

who got a mechanical tortoise, and Lorina, who received Elizabeth Wetherall's book, *Mrs Rutherford's Children*.

At the end of January 1857 Dodgson arranged with Miss Prickett for Harry to go to him three mornings a week for arithmetic; but a few days later he met Lorina and Miss Prickett out walking, and the governess told him that she had had a letter from Mrs Liddell's mother, expressing fears that Dodgson's lessons might overtax Harry's brain. The lessons were not expressly forbidden, but soon Harry's enthusiasm waned and they died a natural death.

In February 1857 scarlet fever broke out in the house next door to the Deanery. The very name of the disease struck terror into the hearts of the Liddell family, who still remembered the tragic death of little Arthur. Dr Acland immediately ordered them off to Lowestoft, where they stayed with Mrs Reeve until the end of March. It was a heavy responsibility for Mrs Reeve, for the children's parents were still in Funchal, but she had had over thirty years of widowhood and lived for her children and grandchildren.

When the children returned to Christ Church, Harry and Lorina, accompanied by Miss Prickett, lost no time in resuming their friendship with Dodgson. But on 5 May Alice made her first independent entry into Dodgson's diary. It was the day after her fifth birthday. 'I went to the Deanery in the afternoon, partly to give little Alice a birthday present, and stayed for tea,' he wrote.

A few days later a rumour came to Dodgson's ears which temporarily threatened to interfere with the even tenor of his friendship with the children. The Dean and his wife were still in Madeira—'that island of the Atlantic which by its equitable climate and gentle air seems to realise the description given by the great lyric poet of Greece to the islands of the blest,' as Liddell described it.[12] Dodgson's continual hanging about the Deanery in their absence was being misconstrued by some as a passion for Miss Prickett. 'Though for my own part I should give little importance to the existence of so groundless a rumour, it would be inconsiderate to the governess to give any further occasion for remarks of the sort,'[13] he wrote. He therefore resolved to pay no public attention to the children, except in such circumstances as would make misinterpretation impossible.

Nevertheless, the outings with Harry and visits to the Deanery continued fairly regularly. In early June Mrs Reeve came to stay, and shortly afterwards the children were overjoyed by the return of their

12 H. L. Thompson, pp. 261–2
13 R. L. Green, pp. 110–11

left, A portrait of Lorina by Lewis Carroll; *right*, The Dean*

parents. Dodgson was now constantly in the children's company, and Alice was beginning to form a regular part of the little group. Besides the incessant photography, there were games of swinging and backgammon, and many more delights.

The visit to Madeira had been so beautiful and beneficial to the Dean's health that he and his wife resolved to winter there again. But their long absence from the children had been a cause of distress to them all, so that this time they decided to take the entire family. On 18 November Alice and the others said their goodbyes to Dodgson. 'It took a long time to get to the end of the adieus of the dear, loving little children,'[14] Dodgson wrote. Two days later they left for Madeira. Alice was too young to retain any recollections of that winter in the sun, and the experiment of wintering abroad was not repeated, for criticism was levelled at the Dean for his long absences from the Deanery, which not only threw heavy burdens of responsibility on the Sub-Dean and

14 ibid, p. 111

members of the Chapter, but led to major decisions being taken without the benefit of his advice.

During the summer of 1858, there were whispers in the Deanery of an unexpected honour which was about to be bestowed on the College and on the Dean himself. Queen Victoria and Prince Albert had resolved to send the Prince of Wales to the university, and Christ Church had been chosen for him. In making their decision the royal couple had been mindful of the favourable impression Liddell had always made as Domestic Chaplain to the Prince Consort. Arrangements were put in hand for the Prince to go up in 1859. Meanwhile, the Liddells and the Aclands decided to take their summer holiday in North Wales.

Just as the two families were preparing to leave, Liddell and Acland received a Royal Command to dine and stay the night at Osborne. When they rejoined their families, there was much to tell: of the Solent, which was looking its loveliest; of the birthday celebrations of the Prince Consort, and the sports held in his honour by the tenants on the estate and the crews of the yachts. All the Queen's children had been present except the Prince of Wales, and the Queen herself and the Prince Consort had been particularly kind, the latter walking with Acland about the terraces in the moonlight, discussing botany. The Prince of Wales' proposed course of studies and need of a medical adviser was the reason for the summons, and it was agreed that Acland should accept medical care of the Prince while he was in Oxford.

Alice was seven years old when the Heir Apparent matriculated at Christ Church. In a letter to his father, Liddell described the events of that great occasion:

I had not time to write last night, after our grand doings with the Prince of Wales. He came down in a royal carriage (not by special train) at about four o'clock. I received him on the platform, and followed him to his house. The Vice-Chancellor and Proctors then called to pay their respects; then the Mayor and two Aldermen with an address; I standing by and introducing them. Then I went down to Christ Church, where we had the gates shut, and all the men drawn up in the Quadrangle. At five he came, and the bells struck up as he entered. He walked to my house between two lines of men, who capped him. I went out to meet him, and as we entered the house there was a spontaneous cheer. All through the streets, which were very full, the people cheered him well. Then I took him up to the drawing-room, and entered his name on the buttery book. He then retired with his Tutor, Mr Fisher, and put on a nobleman's cap and gown in the gallery, and returned to receive greetings as the first Prince of Wales who had matriculated since Henry V. He was also introduced to the Sub-Dean and Censors. I then *walked* him across the Quadrangle, and across the streets to Pembroke College, where we found the Vice-Chancellor waiting at the door. He took him upstairs, and there matriculated him in due form. This morning at eight he came down on foot from his house to chapel. His Governor is Colonel Bruce, brother of Lord Elgin, a very nice person indeed; and his Equerry Major Teesdale, one of the heroes of Kars, a very pleasing young man. Now you will ask me how it all went off. Very well, *very* well. Colonel Bruce came down to see me this morning, and said everything was done *à merveille*, and that the whole ceremony was a kind of model of how to do this sort of thing, and that the Queen and Prince Consort whould be highly gratified by the account which he would send. The Prince himself is the nicest little fellow possible, so simple, naif, ingenuous and modest, and moreover with extremely good wits; possessing the royal faculty of never forgetting a face.'[15]

Rhoda Liddell

Alice now had direct opportunity of meeting royalty face to face. That autumn was also notable for another important event in the life of Alice and her family: namely, the birth of another little sister, whom they baptised Rhoda Caroline Anne. As time passed it became clear that she would turn out to be as intelligent and artistic as the rest of the family; she was dark-haired, sweet-faced, and from an early age possessed of abundant charm.

During the two years he was in residence, the Prince of Wales lived at Frewin Hall, though for a brief space of time he lived in Acland's house in Broad Street while arrangments were finalised. He attended chapel and lectures wearing the nobleman's gown and cap with its distinctive gold tassel. His Tutor, Herbert Fisher, an equerry, and sometimes Colonel Bruce, always accompanied him to lectures. Occasionally he dined in Hall, though he had his own resident cook at Frewin Hall, for his parents expected him to entertain frequently. He complied with their wishes, but he put on weight, which provoked complaints from the Queen, who was afraid that he would lose his good looks. Prince Albert had warned Liddell

15 H. L. Thompson, pp. 177–8

that it would be necessary for his son 'to remain entirely master (or for his governor to remain so for him)of the choice of society which he might encounter.'[16] In his opinion, 'The only use of Oxford is that it is a place for *study*, a refuge from the world and its claims.'

The Prince of Wales bitterly resented the arrangements which were imposed on him by his parents. What he would have liked above all else would have been to live the life of an ordinary undergraduate. Only ten days after he moved into residence the Prince Consort wrote to Colonel Bruce, 'His position and life *must* be different from that of other undergraduates.'[17] Always noted for his severity towards the Heir Apparent, the Prince Consort made it plain that he expected his son to do well. *Punch* had already noticed the situation and published a poem called 'A Prince at High Pressure', which began:

> *Thou dear little Wales, sure the saddest of tales*
> *Is the tale of the studies with which they are cramming thee.*

The young Prince, who celebrated his eighteenth birthday only a few days after coming into residence, and those in charge of his studies, were besieged with letters from the royal parents; but Liddell continued to be satisfied with his academic progress, and the Prince Consort had to concede that he was doing well.

Though his parents' restrictions irked him, the Prince of Wales enjoyed his time at Oxford. He liked the family at the Deanery, including the children, who were both beautiful and intelligent. The Dean's particular friends Acland and Stanley pleased him so greatly that each of them had the opportunity to accompany him on a tour overseas. Though everyone stood up whenever he entered a room, out of respect, he formed a number of friendships with undergraduates.

On 12 December 1860 Alice's home was the scene of a glittering social event when the Queen paid a surprise visit to Oxford. Alice and the other children were encouraged by their parents to be present, for, Rhoda excepted, they were old enough to start mingling in the right society; and in any event, the Queen was fond of children. Dodgson was also present, and gave an eye-witness account of what happened:

Visit of the Queen to Oxford, to the great surprise of everybody, as it had been kept a secret up to the time. She arrived in Christ Church at about twelve, and came into Hall with the Dean, where Collections

16 Philip Magnus, *King Edward the Seventh*, 1964, p. 30
17 ibid, p. 31

were still going on, about a dozen men being in Hall. The party consisted of the Queen, Prince Albert, Princess Alice and her intended husband, the Prince of Hesse-Darmstadt, the Prince of Wales, Prince Alfred, and suite. They remained a minute or two, looking round at the pictures, and the Sub-Dean was presented: they then visited the Cathedral and Library. Evening entertainment at the Deanery, *tableaux vivants*. I went a little after half-past eight, and found a great party assembled—the Prince had not yet come. He arrived before nine, and I found an opportunity of reminding General Bruce of his promise to introduce me to the Prince, which he did at the next break in the conversation HRH was holding with Mrs Fellowes. He shook hands very graciously, and I began with a sort of apology for having been so importunate about the photograph. He said something of the weather being against it, and I asked if the Americans had victimised him much as a sitter; he said they had, but he did not think they had succeeded well, and I told him of the new American process of taking twelve thousand photographs in an hour. Edith Liddell coming by at that moment, I remarked on the beautiful tableau that the children might make: he assented, and also said, in answer to my question, that he had seen and admired my photographs of them. I then said I hoped, as I had missed the photograph, he would at least give me his autograph in my album, which he promised to do. Thinking I had better bring the talk to an

Edith, by Lewis Carroll

end, I concluded by saying that, if he would like copies of any of my photographs, I should feel honoured by his accepting them, he thanked me for this, and I then drew back, as he did not seem inclined to pursue the conversation.[18]

Dodgson duly got his autograph, and the Prince chose a dozen or so photographs which Dodgson had taken.

During the following Easter vacation the Liddells returned to North Wales and rented a house at 72 North Parade, Llandudno. It was a substantial house, as indeed it had to be to accommodate their establishment. Some of their regular domestic staff naturally remained at the Deanery to take care of it in their absence, but nevertheless they took a surprising number on holiday with them. Besides the Dean and his wife, Alice and the four other children, Harry, Lorina, Edith and Rhoda, Miss Prickett was there, plus Francis, the footman, Maria Warnes, the ladies' maid, Phoebe Hall, the nurse, and Marie Chappins, a twenty-year-old nursery maid from Geneva.[19]

With an establishment of this size, and a built-in love of North Wales, it was hardly surprising that the Dean and his family should think in terms of acquiring a permanent holiday home there. Liddell found a suitable plot of land, completed the purchase and put in hand the construction of a house to his own design. He was a man with a cultivated critical appraisal, an acknowledged arbiter in matters relating to the fine arts, and one whose interest in architectural design had already been given freedom of expression both at Westminster and at Oxford. He might have been expected to produce something of taste and distinction, but in fact the new house, which was not fully completed until the summer of 1862, was an ugly, typically Victorian, folly. Some of its worst features have since been disguised by the restructuring carried out to convert the building to a twentieth-century hotel. Internally it conformed to the social requirements of the day, and it commanded fine views; yet it remained a blot on the landscape. Nevertheless the family enjoyed holidays there for several years, until the popularity of the resort gave rise to an influx of tourists which the Liddells felt spoiled its isolated charm.

Appropriately enough, Dodgson's Christmas present to Alice, Lorina and Edith in 1861 was a book called *Holiday House*, by Catherine Sinclair. In the front of the book he wrote a poem for them, which he had

18 S. D. Collingwood, *The Life and Letters of Lewis Carroll*, p. 85
19 1861 Census, RG/9/4359, Folio 42, p. 14

composed himself. It was an acrostic, embodying in the initial letters of the first lines the names of all three children, and containing the name of the book, forwards and backwards. It was carefully printed in his own hand.

Little maidens, when you look

On this little story-book,

Reading with attentive eye

Its enticing history,

Never think that hours of play

Are your only HOLIDAY,

And that in a HOUSE of joy

Lessons serve but to annoy:

If in any HOUSE you find

Children of a gentle mind,

Each the others pleasing ever—

Each the others vexing never—

Daily work and pastime daily

In their order taking gaily—

Then be very sure that they

Have a *life* of HOLIDAY.

THE GOLDEN AFTERNOON

All in the golden afternoon
Full leisurely we glide;
For both our oars, with little skill,
By little hands are plied,
While little hands make vain pretence
Our wandering way to guide.

Alice's Adventures in Wonderland

By 1862 the excitement of rubbing shoulders with the heir to the throne had virtually died away. Yet this was a year which was to prove singularly eventful for Alice, Lorina and Edith, and in a way which none of them could have expected; for they were about to be made immortal.

These were ideally happy days for the three little girls. The ordeal of learning French and Latin was counteracted by the pleasure of their favourite games, Pope John, Beggar my Neighbour, and even whist. Croquet had also come to the Deanery lawn. As the children tried their luck with the croquet mallets, Dinah the cat often looked on. She was a tabby, whose twin belonged to Harry. The little pair had been named after a popular song of the day called Villikens and his Dinah. Every day the little cats had been subjected to a cold bath, just like their child owners. Sadly, Villikens had died of poison. Though Dinah had been given to Lorina, Alice adored her, and the little cat had become her special pet. So eventually she found the road to fame through *Alice's Adventures*.

All the little girls idolised their father. Their greatest joy at that time was to go out riding with him. Harry had been given a pony called Tommy, but the boy was not much interested in horses and was anyway mostly away at boarding school. The little girls took it in turns to exercise Tommy with their father, who naturally kept a stable of good horses for riding—a necessary social accomplishment—and for the carriage horses. 'I began to ride soon after we went to Oxford,' Alice wrote. 'We were taught up and down a path running at an angle to the Broad Walk [the

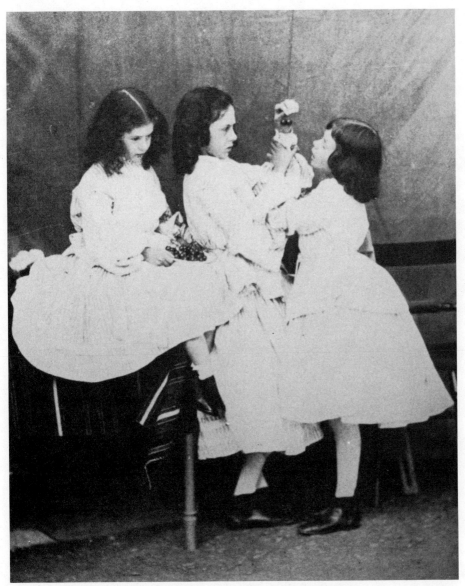

One of the Prince of Wales' favourite pictures of Alice, Lorina and Edith

triangular piece of grass between the two paths being called the Dean's Ham].'[1] Her instructor was Bultitude, the Dean's coachman.

In the colder seasons, or when the weather was inclement, the children went to Dodgson's rooms in the Old Library. They left the Deanery by the back door, escorted by their nurse. 'When we got there,' Alice wrote, 'we used to sit on the big sofa on each side of him, while he told us stories, illustrating them by pen and ink drawings as he went along. When we were thoroughly happy and amused at his stories, he used to pose us, and expose the plates before the right mood had passed.'[1] His stock of stories was seemingly endless. Sometimes they were new; sometimes they were adaptations of old tales. But the interjections of the three little girls led to expansion and adaptation, until the original had been altered beyond all recognition. The stories were 'slowly enunciated in his quiet voice with its curious stutter',[2] which so troubled him in the presence of adults but was unobtrusive in the company of children.

Sometimes, to the dismay of his small guests, Dodgson pretended to fall asleep; but he was always ready to continue after a brief pause. On occasion he told his tales to a purpose: 'Even in mathematics his whimsical fancy was sometimes suffered to peep out,' wrote one child friend, 'and little girls who learnt the rudiments of calculation at his knee found the path they had so imagined so thorny set about with roses by reason of the delightful form with which he would turn a task into a joy. But when the task was over the little girl would find she had learnt the lesson (all unknowingly) just the same.'[3]

Dodgson kept a box of costumes in his rooms for his child models to dress up in. After the photograph had been taken came the privilege of going with him into the dark room to watch while he developed the plates. 'What could be more thrilling than to see the negative gradually take shape, as he rocked it to and fro in the acid bath?'[4] wrote Alice. The dark room was to her a mysterious place and an exciting one, where almost anything might happen. She was not the only child friend who in later years found the smell of the photographic chemicals strangely nostalgic. Alice and her sisters enjoyed the feeling that they were 'assisting at some secret rite usually reserved for grown-ups'.[5]

When the summer was at its hottest, the river was always especially alluring, and Dodgson had fallen into the habit of taking Alice and her

1 Alice and Caryl Hargreaves
2 ibid
3 Isa Bowman, *Lewis Carroll as I Knew Him*, 1972, p. 5
4 Alice and Caryl Hargreaves
5 ibid

Lewis Carroll's photograph of his brother Wilfred and his dog, Dido

sisters out boating several times each summer. It was from him that Alice learned how to handle a boat, and how to feather her oars properly. Occasionally Dodgson let her take the tiller ropes, looking indulgently upon her if the course she steered was somewhat erratic.

These expeditions were always planned with meticulous care. A large basket of cakes was provided by Dodgson, and sometimes a picnic hamper of cold chicken and salad which they ate at Nuneham. There William Harcourt allowed picnickers to land every Tuesday and Thursday and eat their lunch in the special picnic huts which he had built, while they enjoyed the superlative scenery around. Sometimes Dodgson and the children found a haycock, and in its shade they boiled up a kettle to make tea.

Harry was away at school now, and was therefore only rarely able to join the party; indeed these days, if he ever did so, he generally turned out to be something of a nuisance. Usually Dodgson took along one other man to help with the rowing: perhaps one of his brothers, Skeffington or Wilfred, both of whom were up at Christ Church now, sometimes Southey, the photographer, or Augustus Vernon Harcourt, whose uncle owned the house and land at Nuneham. But most popular with Alice and her sisters was Robinson Duckworth, who always sang so well.

On 17 June 1862 the little party went to Nuneham, partly for the benefit of two of Dodgson's sisters, Fanny and Elizabeth, who had come to Oxford to visit him. Duckworth accompanied them. As usual they landed at Nuneham, where the children's first job was always to choose a picnic hut and then to go and borrow crockery, cutlery and glasses from the cottagers who lived down by the river. 'To us the hut might have been a Fairy King's palace, and the picnic a banquet in our honour,' Alice wrote.[6] The woods at Nuneham were a splendid place to wander in, and Dodgson's stories were a constant delight.

The Dodgson sisters were in their early thirties, but they seemed fat and old to the children, who were much inhibited by their presence. But they dined and played games as usual, and then started back. After the party had gone about a mile, they were caught in a torrential downpour which made them abandon the boat and continue on foot. After three miles they were soaked to the skin. Suddenly Dodgson spotted the house where his friend Ranken lodged in the village of Sandford. Thankfully he and Duckworth handed the ladies and children over to Ranken's landlady to get their clothes dried, while the men walked on to Iffley and hired a fly to fetch the party back to Oxford.

To make up for the spoiled afternoon, Dodgson arranged another river expedition for 3 July; but it rained again. Instead, Dodgson stayed at the Deanery and listened to music and singing. The treat of the afternoon was the children's spirited rendering of a negro minstrel song called 'Sally Come Up':

> *Last Monday night I gave a ball*
> *And I invite de Niggers all,*
> *The thick, the thin, the short, the tall,*
> *But none come up to Sally.*
> *Sally come up! Sally go down!*
> *Sally come twist your heel around!*
> *De old man he's gone to town*
> *Oh Sally come down de middle!*

All night the rain fell steadily, but by lunchtime next day the clouds had disappeared. After lunch Dodgson and Duckworth changed their clerical black for white flannels and straw boaters; but they kept their black boots on, for white tennis shoes had not been thought of in those days. When

6 ibid

Alice and her sisters appeared, they were all dressed identically in white, and made a charming picture as they clustered about the two young men.

At Folly Bridge Dodgson chose a boat with his usual meticulousness. This time they could not go to Nuneham, for picnickers were not allowed to land there on a Friday. Instead, they rowed up the river in the opposite direction to Godstowe, a journey which took them all of two and a half hours.

As usual the three children were stowed away in the stern. 'I rowed *stroke* and he rowed *bow* . . . and the story was actually composed *over my shoulder* for the benefit of Alice Liddell, who was acting as "cox" of our gig,' wrote Robinson Duckworth, many years later. 'I remember turning round and saying, "Dodgson, is this an extempore romance of yours?" And he replied, "Yes, I'm inventing as we go along."'[7]

Alice, too, retained clear recollections of that historic outing:

> The beginning of *Alice* was told to me one summer afternoon when the sun was so hot we landed in meadows down the river, deserting the boat to take refuge in the only bit of shade to be found, which was under a newly made hayrick. Here from all three of us, my sisters and myself, came the old petition, 'Tell us a story,' and Mr Dodgson (that is Lewis Carroll) began it.
>
> Sometimes to tease us, Mr Dodgson would stop and say suddenly, 'That's all till next time.' 'Oh,' we would cry, 'It's not bedtime already' and he would go on.
>
> Another time the story would begin in the boat and Mr Dodgson would pretend to fall asleep in the middle, to our great dismay.[8]

A quarter of a century later Dodgson himself also recalled the occasion:

> Many a day we rowed together on that quiet stream—the three little maidens and I—and many a fairy tale had been extemporised for their benefit—whether it were at times when the narrator was 'i' the vein', and fancies unsought came crowding thick upon him, or at times when the jaded Muse was goaded into action, and plodded meekly on, more because she had to say something than because she had something to say—yet none of these many tales got written down: they lived and died, like summer midges, each in its own golden

7 S. D. Collingwood, *The Lewis Carroll Picture Book*, 1899, p. 359
8 *The New York Times*, 4 April 1928

afternoon until there came a day when, as it chanced, one of my little listeners petitioned that the tale might be written out for her.[9]

Not a line, not even a word suggests that Alice was Dodgson's favourite before that fateful July afternoon; but from that time forward she was his heroine, his dream-child, his muse. Later he tried to explain that special quality which Alice possessed, and which inspired him to write as he had never written before:

What wert thou, dream-Alice, in thy foster-father's eyes? How shall he picture thee? Loving, first, loving and gentle; loving as a dog (forgive the prosaic simile, but I know no earthly love so pure and perfect), and gentle as a fawn: then courteous—courteous to all, high or low, grand or grotesque, King or caterpillar, even as though she herself were a King's daughter, and her clothing of wrought gold: then trustful, ready to accept the wildest impossibilities with all the utter trust that only dreamers know; and lastly, curious—wildly curious, and with the eager enjoyment of Life that comes only in the happy hours of childhood, when all is new and fair, and when Sin and Sorrow are but names—empty words signifying nothing.[10]

Even to the little girls, it was obvious that that day's story-telling was something special, better than ever before. When it was all over, and Dodgson escorted the children back to the Deanery, Alice implored him to write out the story for her, and albeit somewhat reluctantly, for it was by no means an insignificant task, he agreed.

Next day the children took the 9.02 train to London with their parents. The object of the visit was to spend a few days there, viewing the Exhibition in South Kensington, and visiting the picture galleries as well. Dodgson was aboard the same train, and bent on a similar mission. Even if he had been inclined to forget his promise of the night before, the children would not have let him; and so he made use of the journey to jot down the chapter headings.

The Liddells lingered on in Oxford longer than usual during the summer vacation, and Dodgson too, though term had ended. On 1 August Dodgson and Harcourt called at the Deanery to ask permission to take the children to Nuneham. The little girls entertained their visitors with a song, 'Beautiful Star' by J. M. Sayles:

9 Lewis Carroll, 'Alice on the Stage'
10 ibid

Lewis Carroll, photograph by Rejlander

Beautiful star in heav'n so bright,
Softly falls thy silv'ry light,
As thou movest from earth so far,
Star of the evening, beautiful star,
Beau-ti-ful star
Beau-ti-ful star
Star of the even-ing
Beautiful, beautiful star.

75

Penmorfa,

Llandudno.

My dearest Papa!

Many many happy returns of your birthday, the 6th of Feby. That makes you (as you were born in "William the Conqueror's" time) 797 years old. Yesterday we had another gale it left off at 12 Edith and I had our beds moved down into Harry's room, we lay on two mattresses on the floor and were very comfortable indeed little Rho-da had her little cot down into Mama's room where Rhoda and Ina slept and Mama was in the Blue Room, altogether we were very jolly. We shall be very glad to see you again. We are reading "Fairy Barns," we like it very much have you read it? Mama has. We went to the town

Next day they all went to Nuneham as planned, and with them Margaret and Ida Brodie, daughters of Sir Benjamin Brodie, the Professor of Chemistry. When they returned from their excursion, they played croquet on the Deanery lawn. Alice was in contact with Dodgson every day. Soon there was another boating expedition, and the trio made Dodgson go on with what he described as his 'interminable fairy-tale of Alice's Adventures'. 'A very enjoyable expedition—the last, I should think, to which Ina is likely to be allowed to come—her fourteenth time,'[11] Dodgson commented in his diary. For Ina was growing up fast, and at fourteen she was physically very mature for her age. Two days later the family left for Llandudno, and as they were driving away, they caught a last glimpse of Dodgson crossing the quadrangle.

By mid-October Alice was back in Christ Church. Dodgson had been arranging for the artist at Shrimpton's, a local fine art dealer's, to colour some of his photographs of the children. His attention to detail was always meticulous, and he wanted to arrange for the artist to call and have a

11 R. L. Green, p. 185

today with Mademoiselle Duê Mr
Bagots governess. she ran after us to try
and catch us but she could and we had
a great bit of fun. The sun made its first
attempt to make a sunset, there has not
been any appearance of one before today
since you left. I have been trying to illu-
minate I have not anything more to tell
you. as I shall be able to tell you better

by mouth which is better than letters

Tremain ever

your affec^{ate} and loving daughter
Alice Pleasance Liddell.

Thursday evening
5th of Feb 1863.

---

sitting in order to get the likeness as close as possible to the children's
colouring. He therefore took an early opportunity to call on Mrs Liddell
to arrange it, but she simply avoided the issue. 'I have been out of her
good graces ever since Lord Newry's business,'[12] Dodgson commented.

Lord Newry was a protégé of Mrs Liddell's, and his family seat was
very near to Penmorfa, the Liddells' new holiday home in Llandudno.
Lord Newry had wanted to hold a ball at Oxford, but this would have
contravened the general rules for the undergraduates of the college, even
allowing for the special privileges accorded to the aristocracy. A great deal
of ill feeling had arisen from the matter. It is possible that Mrs Liddell was
already looking around for suitable husbands for her daughters,
particularly Lorina, and Lord Newry would certainly have been highly
eligible. But whatever her motives, she certainly favoured the young man.

Alice next met Dodgson in the quadrangle in mid-November, a
rather rare occurrence since the Lord Newry dispute. But that chance
meeting was enough to stiffen Dodgson's resolve to write down *Alice's*

12 ibid, p. 188

Adventures for her, and he began it that very afternoon. A few days later Alice and Edith asked him over to the Deanery. Their new hobby was collecting the crests on notepaper and calling cards of noblemen, and at their request Dodgson helped them to mount them in their albums. Ina did not come down as she had a cold, and Mrs Liddell, who was pregnant and still inclined to be tetchy, did not appear either.

Alice's Adventures were nowhere near ready for presentation at Christmas, but by 10 February the tale had become sufficiently important to Dodgson for him to turn back the pages of his diary and mark up the day on which he had first told the story. By now Alice had resumed her former intimacy with him, for her mother had relented. Dodgson had completed the text and had made that fair copy which was in future always referred to as the manuscript, lettering it in his own special printed characters. As he went along, he had left spaces on the page for the insertion of the pictures, just as the medieval limners used to work. But the pictures, which were to be an integral part of the page, were nowhere near complete. Dodgson had never had a drawing lesson in his life, but he wanted to make the illustrations as good as possible, to please Alice. The creatures were even more difficult than the rest to portray adequately, but Alice's father obligingly lent Dodgson a natural history book from his own library to help him with the drawings of animals and birds. Meanwhile his efforts to immortalise his heroine continued in another direction, and he began to write a poem embodying a description of Alice. He decided to call it 'Life's Pleasance', a word play on Alice's second name, and publish it in the magazine called *College Rhymes* which he edited for a short while. But in the event the poem had to wait until 1871 for publication, when it was used as the dedicatory poem in *Through the Looking-Glass* (see pages 128–9).

Alice was now considered sufficiently grown-up to stay up all evening when guests were invited to the Deanery. On 10 March 1863 she carried out her first public engagement. It was the wedding day of the Prince of Wales and Princess Alexandra of Denmark, and in honour of the occasion three new trees were planted in the Broad Walk by Alice, Lorina and Edith. A large crowd gathered to watch as the three girls carried out the formal planting and gave names to their trees. Alice's was called 'Albert', Edith's 'Victoria', and Ina's 'Alexandra'. Alice made a little speech, 'Long life to this tree, and may it prosper from this auspicious day',[13] as she completed the ceremony. Afterwards they went to the

13 ibid, p. 193

78

Torpid race. There they met Dodgson, who escorted the children and their grandmother, Mrs Reeve, who had come to stay with the family for a while, to watch an ox roasted whole near Worcester College. It was a spectacle that none of them enjoyed, according to Dodgson's diary. Perhaps it offended their humanitarian feelings.

That evening Dodgson and his brother Edwin, then nineteen years old, toured the principal streets with Alice to show her the illuminations. There were enormous crowds of people, but all were well conducted. Every college was lit up. The illuminations were a wonderful spectacle and there were abundant fireworks. 'It was delightful to see the thorough abandonment with which Alice enjoyed the whole thing,'[14] wrote Dodgson.

'I clung tightly to the hand of the strong man on either side of me,'[15] recalled Alice, many years later. One of the illuminations particularly caught her fancy: it embodied the words 'May they be happy' in giant letters of fire. Next morning Dodgson drew a caricature of it for Alice. Underneath were two hands holding birches with the words 'Certainly not'.

By the beginning of April 1863 Alice's mother was approaching her confinement, and Alice, Lorina and Edith, together with Miss Prickett, were sent to stay with the Dean's parents at Hetton Lawn, Charlton Kings. They were deeply attached to their grandparents, but truth to tell they were a little bored, with only the old couple and their maiden aunts, Charlotte and Amelia Liddell, to entertain them. They missed their parents, the hustle and bustle of College life—and they missed Mr Dodgson. Finally they sought, and obtained, permission to invite him over to lunch. It was Ina, as the eldest, who penned the invitation. The letter brought him immediately, as they had known it would.

Alice and Miss Prickett waited for him on Cheltenham Station, and together they walked the mile and a half to the house. After lunch the whole party went in a carriage to Birdlip, where Alice, Ina and Miss Prickett got out and walked with Dodgson over Leckhampton. 'The children were in the wildest spirits,'[16] wrote Dodgson, who dined with them that evening before returning to the Belle Vue Hotel for the night.

Next day it rained, and Dodgson spent all day with the girls indoors, mostly in the schoolroom. It was a fine old building and had been known as Bolton House before old Mr Liddell acquired it. Its new name derived

14 ibid, pp. 193–4
15 Alice and Caryl Hargreaves
16 R. L. Green, p. 195

from Hetton Hall, the seat of his wife's family. It possessed one particularly fine feature of some significance which captured the imagination of the little girls: a gigantic mirror above the fireplace in the drawing-room. Whether the seeds of *Through the Looking-Glass* were already beginning to germinate at this stage would be difficult to say, but certainly that mirror, which still exists, bears a remarkable resemblance to the one drawn by Tenniel in that book.

Life was very quiet in Cheltenham at that time, for it was Easter week. But there was one outstanding event, the performance of a celebrated Viennese conjuror called Herr Döbler. The *Cheltenham Looker-On* advertised his 'wonderful tricks of sleight of hand', and added, 'As there are no other public entertainments provided for the good people of Cheltenham in the Easter week, they will, doubtless, be glad enough to avail themselves of the opportunity afforded them of visiting Herr Döbler's "Enchanted Palace of Illusions"; and avail themselves Alice and her sisters certainly did, escorted by Dodgson and no doubt chaperoned by Miss Prickett.

The day after this entertainment Alice, Edith and Miss Prickett walked into Cheltenham with Dodgson, who was leaving to stay in Tenby, and went on to the local riding school. They stayed on at Hetton Lawn until

Edith, photograph by Lewis Carroll

mid-April, and when they finally returned to Oxford, they met Dodgson on the train. On their very first day back they all went down the river together, Harry, the three girls and 'Pricks', plus Dodgson of course. Miss Prickett was there at Mrs Liddell's specific request, but Dodgson did not seem to think the stipulation unreasonable. Ina had matured early, and had become so tall as to look 'odd without an escort'.

Four days later, Alice was laid up with a sprained leg. Dodgson went to see her and stayed with her and Rhoda for about an hour. Less than a fortnight later Alice was fit enough to go on the river with the others, and Dodgson, the stammerer, was by this time so much at ease in their company that he sang them a song of his own composition, set to a cento of popular melodies. He called it 'Miss Jones'.

On Alice's eleventh birthday Dodgson gave her a book, Charlotte M. Yonge's *Scenes and Characters; or, Eighteen Months at Beechcroft*. On the fly-leaf he had written, 'Alice P. Liddell, from C. L. Dodgson. May 4th /63'. It was a book that she treasured, and it stayed in her personal library for the next sixty-five years.

The new baby to which Alice's mother had just given birth was a little boy. The Prince of Wales had done them the honour of consenting to be godfather, and it was he who chose the names, Albert Edward Arthur. The other godfather was Arthur Penryn Stanley. But the child was not strong, and so great was the alarm that the Dean was fetched out of morning chapel one day to baptise it. Alice, Lorina and Edith wandered forlornly around the meadow with Dodgson, despondent and silent. The baby died on 28 May, only eight weeks old. Dr Pusey, the controversial figure who had clashed so often with the Dean in the meetings of the Chapter, wrote immediately to Mrs Liddell: 'Human sympathy avails but little. Yet you will let me express mine at your quick bereavement of the little one whom God lent you for so short a time. It is a sore trial; only our good Father knows how to make all work together for good.'[17]

In June the newly wed Prince and Princess of Wales favoured Oxford with a visit. Already Alice's second cousin, A. G. C. Liddell, a grandson of the second Lord Ravensworth, had caught an intriguing glimpse of the young woman who was one day to become Queen of England. Young Adolphus' home was at Park Cottage, East Sheen, but during term time he was away at Eton. Just before the royal wedding, he had seen her leaving Windsor in her carriage. With half a dozen or so of his school friends he had run alongside her carriage for about a mile. 'I had

17 H. L. Thompson, p. 187

Lewis Carroll's song,
'Miss Jones', written
in his own hand

The Prince and
Princess of Wales

a stunning view of her,' he wrote home. 'She grinned away like beans, and
so did her mother. . . . She is very pretty indeed, with a jolly colour, has a
beautiful complexion, and looks quite merry, but a little shy.'[18]

Alice and the rest of the children were wildly excited at the
impending visit, for the royal couple were actually coming to stay in the
Deanery. The entire household was flung into a flurry of preparation. The
royal bedchamber was splendidly furnished. Among the many gorgeous
trappings was a photograph album with the plume of the Prince of Wales
emblazoned on a magnificent onyx, and when Dodgson was treated to a
preview of the bedchamber, he volunteered to fill it up with *cartes de visite*
from his own albums. The job of filling it took him about a couple of
hours, and when he had finished he got a note from Lorina begging him to
come over and help them with a stall which they were setting up in St
John's Gardens for a bazaar on the following day. Alice spent most of the
day on the work and Dodgson was with her for about four hours, putting
up cards and arranging items. After dinner, he joined the Liddells at the
Music Hall, where they heard a performance of 'Little Toddlekins'.

Next day the Prince and Princess of Wales arrived in Tom Quad at
about one o'clock. While Alice and her sisters looked on, and the whole of

18 A. G. C. Liddell, *Notes from the Life of an Ordinary Mortal*, 1911, p. 46

Christ Church with them, the royal couple stood under a special awning where the Princess presented prizes to the Volunteers. After lunch the children went back to their stall, where they were shortly joined by Dodgson. When the royal party arrived the children were selling some white kittens, rather like Persians. As Alice was too shy to offer hers to the Princess, Dodgson did it for her. But Alice was disappointed, for the Princess had already bought Ina's kitten.

After the Prince and Princess of Wales had moved on, the bazaar was opened to the general public, and in no time at all the place was filled with a dense mob. When the proceedings were over, the children went back to the Deanery in a fly which Dodgson hailed for them. That night there was a splendid banquet in Hall, and many grandees and ladies in fine clothes were present. There was music—much too loud during dinner—and after the healths had been drunk came the melodic voices of the Orpheus Club singing for the royal couple.

Next day was Commemoration, at which the Prince was given the honorary degree of DCL. After an excellent cold collation at All Soul's College, the Liddell children, including Alice, returned for another stint at the bazaar. At four o'clock they went back to the Deanery where they had a game of croquet on the lawn with the Prince and Princess of Wales, who left Oxford on the following day.

A week later Dodgson was allowed the privilege of photographing the royal bedroom, with its magnificent bedstead, and Alice posed with Ina for him in the window of the princely bedchamber for an external shot

The Prince and Princess of Wales in the Deanery garden

of the Deanery. That evening Alice went with Dodgson, Miss Prickett, Ina and Edith to Sanger's Circus. All things considered, the royal visit to Oxford had been a memorable occasion for the little girl.

During the last few months, Alice's meetings with Dodgson had been almost continuous, and instinctively, Dodgson felt that it was too good to last. Relationships between the Liddells and Dodgson could not, however, have been more cordial when, on 25 June 1863, Alice went with Edith to his rooms to ask him to organise a boating trip to Nuneham. There were ten in the party: Alice and her three sisters, her mother, father and grandfather, Harcourt, Viscount Newry, and Dodgson. They took a four-oar boat, and the three younger men rowed all the way, while the others managed the stroke oar in succession. 'We had tea under the trees at Nuneham,' wrote Dodgson, 'after which the rest drove home in the carriage (which met them in the park), while Ina, Alice, Edith and I (*mirabile dictu!*) walked down to Abingdon Road Station, and so home by railway: a pleasant expedition, with a *very* pleasant conclusion.'[19]

Two days later Dodgson sent a note to Mrs Liddell, urging her to send the children over to be photographed. But after Dodgson's death some member of his family cut out a page—no doubt a highly significant one—from Dodgson's diary, and altered the preceding paragraph to conceal the fact that something was missing. The handwriting was clearly different from Dodgson's own. The record recommences on 30 June, when the Liddells left for their usual holiday in Llandudno.

What did that missing page contain, and what prompted someone to clip it from the book? We shall probably never know. But it undoubtedly contained details of a major breach between Alice's family and Dodgson, for the children, with whom he had been associating almost daily, are not mentioned again until 5 December, long after their return to Oxford, when Dodgson describes the Christ Church theatricals: 'Mrs Liddell and the children were there, but I held aloof from them, as I have done all this term.' Held aloof? And from Alice? Shy and quick to take offence Dodgson certainly was; but it was never his habit to ignore his child friends, any of them, much less Alice. Whatever the quarrel was, it is impossible to believe that it was of Dodgson's, or the children's, making.

A fortnight later Dodgson went over to the Deanery at 5 pm, nominally for croquet, though they never got round to it. All the same it was an odd pretext for an invitation in mid-December. He stayed until 8 pm, 'making a sort of dinner of their tea', as he put it, and generally

19 R. L. Green, p. 199

enjoying himself with the children. The whole time was spent in music and conversation. The Dean was away, and Mrs Liddell, then six months pregnant, was with them for only part of the time. It was a 'white stone' day for Dodgson. But if Dodgson imagined that this heralded a return to the old, privileged friendship, he was very much mistaken. In May 1864 he recorded that he had applied in vain for permission to take Alice, Edith and Rhoda on the river; Mrs Liddell had made it clear that she would not let any of the children enjoy these innocent expeditions in future.

Was Dodgson ever 'in love' with Alice in the adult sense of the words, and if so, did she reciprocate? Did he ever broach the subject of matrimony, or even hint at the prospect? And if so, was it *then*, in that summer of 1863? And with Alice only 11 years old, was it possible, would it have been decent?

Such a relationship was not as improbable as it might seem on first consideration. The custom in Victorian England was very different from that of the present day. Social and economic constraints necessitated that men chose younger and waited longer. On the whole substantial age differences between husband and wife tended to be commoner. It was the era when Ruskin fell in love with the twelve-year-old Rose La Touche. Significantly, Dodgson's own younger brother fell in love with the fourteen-year-old Alice Jane Donkin, niece of William Fishburn Donkin, the Savilian Professor of Astronomy at Oxford, but agreement could not be reached on the subject of matrimony. Dodgson recorded the advice he gave: 'Wrote Wilfred a long letter on the subject of Alice Donkin, as things are not on a satisfactory footing at present and urged on him the wisdom of keeping away from Barnby Moor [the Donkin family home] for a couple of years.'[20] Wilfred ignored his advice and married his Alice, but not until nearly six years later. In the autumn of 1865 Dodgson consulted his uncle, Skeffington Lutwidge, on two successive evenings. 'On each occasion we had a good deal of conversation about Wilfred, and about A. L. It is a very anxious subject,'[21] Dodgson wrote. This close link between his anxieties about Wilfred's courtship and his own relationship with Alice Liddell is a strong argument for concluding that he was romantically attached to her and that matrimony was what he wanted.

It is impossible to overlook the length and strength of Dodgson's attachment to Alice, which, considered in the context of his lifespan, cannot altogether be explained away by the fact that their immortality was in a sense shared. Certainly Alice's descendants were under the impression

20 Ms. Diaries of Lewis Carroll
21 ibid

that Dodgson had asked for Alice's hand, even that she had resented her parents' rejection of Dodgson, though if this occurred, it was presumably at a time when she could not have been old enough to know her own mind. Oxford rumour, too, insisted that he was a suitor who had been rejected.

Clearly, however, Alice's parents expected a much better match for her. She was beautiful, intelligent, cultured and well-connected. The cream of the aristocracy passed through Christ Church, and there were ample opportunities for Alice to attract the attention of a prospective husband who was both wealthy and prestigious. Dodgson's family was cultivated and well-bred, but he came from less distinguished social stock than the Liddells, and his means were modest. He was not the sort of man to attempt to court Alice without her parents' consent, and this he did not have. They could not at that stage have foreseen the fame that his literary talent would bring him, but in any event it is doubtful whether that would have made any difference to their decision. Moreover, financial matters came relatively low on Dodgson's list of priorities, a modest sufficiency being all that he required; and though his potential was considerable, his perfectionism and sense of moral obligation stood in the way of personal financial gain, and what he had he usually succeeded in giving away.

In general terms the Liddell family continued to flourish. Frederick, Crown Prince of Denmark, had come into residence at Christ Church, though his studies had to be broken off prematurely when war broke out between Denmark and Prussia over the Schleswig-Holstein question. But his presence had established beyond all reasonable doubt that despite the Dean's somewhat bold and forthright letters to his sovereign suggesting that she was being too rigorous with the Prince of Wales, his standing in the Royal Family was in no way diminished. It had also underlined the position of Christ Church as the most prestigious of all Oxford colleges, and of the Deanery as a social and cultural centre without equal in Oxford.

At the end of the year the Liddells' old friend Arthur Penryn Stanley, who had been their neighbour at Christ Church, became Dean of Westminster, but their disappointment at losing him as a neighbour was tempered by their pleasure at his marriage to Lady Augusta Bruce, Lady-in-Waiting to Queen Victoria. Alice's father had preached the sermon at Stanley's ordination many years previously, and the family went to hear his farewell sermon at Christ Church on 29 November 1863; Liddell wept on his departure. But three days before Christmas came an occasion of unalloyed pleasure: the marriage of Stanley and Lady Augusta in

Westminster Abbey. Liddell himself performed the wedding ceremony. It was evening, and fog filled the ancient Abbey; the congregation was almost lost in the vastness of the nave. Years afterwards Liddell recalled that ceremony, and how 'the dim lights just showed the clustered pillars — their lower parts only, for as you looked up they disappeared and vanished into the gloom above.'[22]

Mrs Liddell's healthy pregnancy and the hope of further progeny tended to ease the pain that the family had felt when the infant Albert had died earlier in the year. Now the new year was filled with promise. Violet Constance was born on 10 March 1864, healthy, vigorous and good-looking. In looks, like all the Liddell daughters, she favoured her mother, and like all the children she was to become intelligent, artistic and cultured.

But despite this special happiness, there was still a cloud on Alice's horizon. The rift between Dodgson and their parents was a calamity to all the little girls, but especially to Alice. She was a most affectionate, tender-hearted child and deeply attached to him. Although he and the family in general avoided each other, Alice often saw him from afar as he crossed Tom Quad or strode about the High Street and St Aldate's with that stiff and curiously jerky gait. It pained her not to be able to go to him as before, to bask in his affection and enjoy his inimitable nonsense. There was now a void in her life which could never be filled in the same way again. Though she was still a child, the instincts of womanhood were stirring within her. She was in no danger of drowning in a pool of her own tears; but her sorrow was none the less real for all that.

22 H. G. Liddell, *Funeral Oration*, 12 March 1876

AN OBSTACLE THAT CAME BETWEEN

My notion was that you had been
(Before she had this fit)
An obstacle that came between
Him, and ourselves, and it.

Alice's Adventures in Wonderland

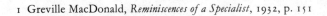

WE DO NOT KNOW for certain when Dodgson began to think of publishing *Alice's Adventures*, though clearly it was at some time between 13 November 1863, when he started to write the story, and 10 February 1864, when he wrote in his diary the date when the tale was first told. Shortly after that he lent the manuscript to the novelist George MacDonald and his wife, who tried it out on their children. Their response was enthusiastic. In later years their son Greville recalled hearing it:

I remember that first reading well, and also my braggart avowal that I wished that there were sixty thousand volumes of it. Yet I distinctly recall a certain indignant grief that its characters were only a pack of cards; and I still look on that *Finis* as a blemish upon the sublime fantasy. Doubtless Charles Dodgson felt that a child must never be deceived even by a fairy tale. And he was right; though there would have been little or no risk of this, had he left his immortal narrative just a fairy tale that needed no justifying.[1]

With the MacDonalds' encouragement to back his own judgment, Dodgson now felt sufficiently confident to make an approach to his friend Thomas Combe, a printer to the university who was associated with the Clarendon Press. Combe arranged for a trial page to be set up so that

---

1 Greville MacDonald, *Reminiscences of a Specialist*, 1932, p. 151

Dodgson could see how it would look in print; but the result did not satisfy him, and on 2 July 1863 he received a further trial page, larger than the first.

Two weeks later Dodgson called on Combe with his first drawing on wood. Combe was an art collector of considerable importance, who specialised in the work of the Pre-Raphaelite artists. Dodgson found him sitting for a bust for Thomas Woolner, one of the original Pre-Raphaelites. Woolner looked at Dodgson's half-length drawing of his heroine and condemned the arms immediately. It was absolutely essential, he pointed out, to work from a live model. Dodgson needed little convincing, and thereafter began to draw from life. Less than three weeks after meeting Woolner, he called on the engraver Orlando Jewitt in Camden Town and handed over to him a block that he had drawn, to be cut on wood. Jewitt not only gave some excellent general advice, but agreed to improve a little on Dodgson's block when he cut it.

The original manuscript fair copy of *Alice's Adventures Underground* contained some eighteen thousand words, but the published story was almost twice as long, possibly because the MacDonalds or Thomas Combe suggested doubling the text for publication. The title *Alice's Adventures Underground* was permanently reserved for the manuscript fair copy which was to be presented to Alice herself. Dodgson had second thoughts, however, about the title of the published version, toying with 'Alice's Hour in Elfland' before the final title, *Alice's Adventures in Wonderland*, occurred to him on 28 June 1864.

Lewis Carroll and the MacDonald children

There can be no doubt that Dodgson took Woolner's advice and thereafter used a live model. Some of the drawings had already been slotted in alongside the text and formed an integral part of the artistic whole. But those which had not been done were drawn from a live model. None of the extant letters and papers reveal the identity of Dodgson's model, although certainly Alice herself did not sit for the pictures. Her hair was short, straight, dark and cut in a full fringe, while Dodgson's heroine had long waving hair, worn in a style much favoured by the Pre-Raphaelites. And Alice was already ten years old when the story of her adventures was told, though the storybook heroine is only seven. But one member of the family was ideally suited to sit for the pictures: Edith, who was eight years old on that fateful day. Her hair was long, waving and luxuriant, and she was used to posing for Dodgson's photographs, so that she was fully at ease with him. Though he saw precious little of the children between July 1863 when he discussed his drawings with Woolner and September 1864 when he completed the last of the pictures, there were no other obvious models.

Lewis Carroll's title page for *Alice's Adventures Underground*

Dodgson was intensely preoccupied with the visual arts, and both in his photography and in his drawing he was heavily influenced by the Pre-Raphaelites. He spent much of his time with important artists, often working side by side with them in their studios. In this, the most creative period of his life, he numbered among his friends Arthur Hughes, Rosetti, Millais, Holman-Hunt, Munro, Ruskin, Watts and others. His creative mood was Pre-Raphaelite, and little Edith Liddell, though still a small child, possessed that elusive, ethereal style of beauty which was so beloved by the Brethren. By exaggerating the melancholy mouth, soulful eyes and abundant waving hair, Dodgson intensified his drawing in a manner which was truly typical of that artistic movement. Since Dodgson first drew his *Alice* pictures, many artists have illustrated his works—but no other illustrator has equalled the poignant intensity of his finest drawings.

Dodgson eventually decided to use a professional illustrator for his book, and his friend Tom Taylor suggested John Tenniel, to whom he gave Dodgson a letter of introduction. When Dodgson paid a visit to Tenniel for the first time in January 1864 he found him sufficiently interested in the idea of illustrating the book to agree to study the manuscript.

As a boy Tenniel had lived in Kensington, where his best friends were the sons of the painter John Martin. Although his friendship had fostered in him a keen interest in drawing, he had been dissatisfied with the few formal lessons he attended at Academy schools and instead he had

6

how she was ever to get out again: suddenly she came upon a little three-legged table, all made of solid glass; there was nothing lying upon it, but a tiny golden key, and Alice's first idea was that it might belong to one of the doors of the hall, but alas! either the locks were too large, or the key too small, but at any rate it would open none of them. However, on the second time round, she came to a low curtain, behind which was a door about eighteen inches high: she tried the little key in the keyhole, and it fitted! Alice opened the door, and looked down a small passage, not larger than a rat-hole, into the loveliest garden you ever saw. How she longed to get out of that dark hall, and wander about among those beds of bright flowers and those cool fountains, but she could not even get her head through the doorway, "and even if my head would go through," thought poor Alice, "it would be very little use without my shoulders. Oh, how I wish I could shut

62.

She was a good deal frightened by this very sudden change, but as she did not shrink any further, and had not dropped the top of the mushroom, she did not give up hope yet. There was hardly room to open her mouth, with her chin pressing against her foot, but she did it at last, and managed to bite off a little bit of the top of the mushroom.

* * * * *

"Come! my head's free at last!" said Alice in a tone of delight, which changed into alarm in another moment, when she found that her shoulders were nowhere to be seen: she looked down upon an immense length of neck, which seemed to rise like a stalk out of a sea of green leaves that lay far below her.

turned to the British Museum, where he studied sculpture and anatomy. When the Government set up a Commission to beautify the Houses of Parliament, Tenniel was sent to Munich to study fresco techniques, but the result of the art work instituted by the Commission was a failure, for though the paintings of the various artists were initially acclaimed as works of major importance, all the frescoes faded rapidly.

In 1850 Tenniel joined the staff of *Punch*, and when Leech died in 1864, Tenniel succeeded him as leading *Punch* cartoonist. As early as 1842 he had begun producing book illustrations for *Hall's Book of British Ballads*. In 1845 he illustrated *Undine*, and his pictures for *Aesop's Fables* (1848) and *The Gordian Knot* (1860) were highly regarded. But his reputation as a book illustrator rested largely on his drawings for *Lallah Rookh*, published in 1861. By the time Dodgson approached him, he was already collaborating with Leech and Cruikshank on *The Ingoldsby Legends*. Their edition of this work appeared in 1864.

Ruskin held Tenniel in high esteem, and said of him, 'Tenniel has much of the largeness and symbolic mystery of imagination which

Sir John Tenniel

belongs to the great leaders of classic art; in the shadowy masses and lines of his great compositions there are tendencies which might have won his adoption into the school of Tintoret.'[2] His work was almost always executed in pencil, and his fine lines were not ideally suited to wood block: they reproduced better in his later works when steel was widely adopted. He did not normally use a model, and his skill in portraying animals was an outstanding feature which would particularly have appealed to Dodgson.

In April 1864 Tenniel accepted Dodgson's commission, and a month later he received the first galley proofs, taken from the beginning of the third chapter; the author did not send the first chapter off to be typeset until a month later. This was not greatly changed from the original version, but Dodgson had had to do a great deal of work on the text besides simply augmenting it with additional material. *Alice's Adventures Underground* had contained a lot of private jokes which were amusing to

2 John Ruskin, *The Art of England*, 1883, Lecture 5, p. 195

93

Alice and her sisters, but which Dodgson felt would be unsuitable for a
wider audience. There were references to the earlier boating expedition
with the Dodgson sisters, when the party had got drenched in a rainstorm
and the children's clothes had been dried off at Sandford. The negro song,
'Sally Come Up', which the children had rendered with such spirit, had
reappeared as 'Salmon Come Up'. Their games of croquet, their school
work and their friends were all referred to in the text. Now, Gertrude and
Florence became Ada and Mabel, to spare the feelings of real children who
might have recognised themselves. 'Salmon Come Up' was left out, the
mouse's tale was refined, and the caucus race replaced the drying of the
clothes. There were two completely new chapters, 'Pig and Pepper' and
'A Mad Tea Party'. The Marchioness was dropped, but the Ugly Duchess
now made her appearance. Three extra poems were included, 'Speak
Roughly to your Little Boy', 'Will You Walk a Little Faster' and ''Tis the
Voice of the Lobster'.

Though Alice was the heroine, Lorina and Edith appeared in *Alice's
Adventures* as the Lory and the Eaglet respectively. All three little girls can
be found at the bottom of the treacle well, as Elsie (L. C., Lorina
Charlotte), Lacie (an anagram of Alice) and Tillie (for Matilda, Edith's

A Tenniel cartoon
from *Punch*, entitled
'Alice in Bumbeland'

nickname). Dodgson and Duckworth are, of course, the Duck and the Dodo. The Mad Hatter was possibly derived from a *Punch* article called 'Mad as a Hatter', which ends: 'We think we can venture to observe that the madness of a hatter must be, from the nature of his calling, peculiarly one of those things that are said to be more easily *felt* than described,'[3] while the caterpillar smoking a hookah on a mushroom may owe its existence to the *Punch* illustration of a frog sitting in a similar position and smoking two huge pipes.[4] The croquet match recalled not only the game which the children had played with the Prince and Princess of Wales, but also *Castle Croquet*, a game of Dodgson's own invention, which he had taught the children to play, and the rules of which he published.

Though Dodgson had been lucky enough to persuade Macmillan to publish his book, he had decided to bear the expense of publication himself, including the payments to the artist, who was paid an outright sum and not on a royalty basis. This gave Dodgson a much greater degree of control over the finished product. Even though he was to pay for it from his own pocket, he was singularly fortunate, as an unknown writer, in getting a firm as prestigious as Macmillan to publish his work under their own imprint.

Alice saw very little of Dodgson these days, for the breach with the family was too great for the old, easy friendship to be resumed. She was puzzled and hurt by her mother's attitude towards Dodgson, as were Lorina and Edith also; for all of them loved him dearly, though none with the same intensity as Alice herself. Her interest in the progress of the book was undiminished by these problems, and Dodgson found ways of keeping her informed at all stages. Though she was not exactly consulted, she was kept in the picture both literally and metaphorically. No detail was too trivial to claim her attention.

The summer vacation of 1864 was an exceptional one for the Liddells. The whole family, now augmented by another little girl, Violet Constance, born on 10 March 1864, migrated to Llandudno. Penmorfa had already become a home from home. It stood in secluded surroundings of quite exceptional beauty at the south-east corner of the Great Orme's Head. It faced due south, and the view extended over the Conway Estuary to the summits beyond. The headland rose up wild and steep behind. Before it the sea was so shallow that when the tide was out and the sun set over the island, dramatic colours lit the rugged hills and reflected in glittering tints on the wet sands. Matthew Arnold considered them the

3 4 January 1862
4 21 December 1861

finest sunsets in the British Isles. For many years the Great Orme's Head was untouched by carriage roads, and few people frequented its wild slopes, which were scored by rough paths and sheep tracks. Here the search for wild flowers rewarded the family with rare finds.

A more romantic spot for the picnics in which the family and their friends delighted could scarcely be imagined. They passed much of their time in drawing and sketching. The Dean loved teaching his daughters how to use the pencil and brush, and suggesting suitable views. All of them enjoyed expressing themselves in paint and pencil, but none was more apt a pupil than Alice. They took long drives and scrambled over the hills in blazing sunshine, for it was a summer of seemingly endless fine weather.

The Aclands had come to stay nearby, as was their custom, and the two families were rarely out of each other's company. Samuel Wilberforce, the Bishop of Oxford, and Mr and Mrs Gladstone also occupied houses in the vicinity, spending a great deal of time with the Liddells. Matthew Arnold, too, was staying in Llandudno for the Eisteddfod. He wrote to his mother, 'There are one or two people here: the Liddells, with whom we dined; the Scudamore Stanhopes, him I knew slightly at Oxford; the Dean of Chichester; a clergyman or two, who have called.'[5] Sir Charles Newton and his wife Mary, daughter of Joseph Severn, passed the summer as house guests of the Liddells. Mary Newton painted a picture of Mrs Liddell at about that time, which was generally considered to be a very fine likeness of her as she was in her prime.

Despite the tranquil setting, the summer holiday was not without its occasional excitements. One day Gladstone was out walking with the family on the Great Orme's Head when he suddenly came to an abrupt stop and clung to Alice's father, for he could not bear to look down from so great a height to the sea below. It was difficult to know what to do, for they had reached a point on the steep, rocky path from which it was as difficult to retreat as to advance. They decided to go down; but the path became worse. The Dean made Gladstone close his eyes and led him slowly down, while the rest of the family walked between him and the seaward side, forming a kind of buttress: for the children themselves knew no fear. It was a hazardous and difficult undertaking, and everyone was relieved when they found themselves safely on lower ground.

The family's normal preoccupation with the visual arts was intensified still further that summer by the visit of the artist William

5 Letters of Matthew Arnold

Richmond (later Sir William), whose father had produced a fine crayon drawing of the Dean in 1858. From 1861 onwards the young Richmond had been establishing a reputation for himself by going to stay in the houses of notable people while he worked on their portraits. He had become very friendly with Acland, who was also an excellent amateur artist, and spent a lot of time with Acland's friend Donkin, who was dying of consumption. During his stay with Donkin, Richmond painted a fine head of the sick man and afterwards gave it to Acland as a present. Acland showed the picture to the Dean, who thought so highly of it that he immediately commissioned Richmond to paint a portrait of Alice, Lorina and Edith.

Richmond was already commissioned to paint a portrait of the three children of Lawrence Pemberton of Sunderland, but as soon as that commitment had been honoured, he travelled to Llandudno where he spent about seven weeks as a house guest of the Liddells. Richmond described the family's lifestyle at Penmorfa as 'very merry and homely', and found their company delightful. He joined their walking and sketching expeditions, but particularly recalled how 'sometimes, when the day had been too hot and the moon was full, a long, enchanting expedition was made by moonlight through a silver, shimmering, mysterious land.'[6]

Richmond remarked on the awe which most people felt in the presence of the Dean; but he himself never felt any restraint in his company. He felt instinctively that the Dean disliked humbug. Although he hated shyness in others, the Dean was himself the shyest of men. Richmond thought that this shyness was at the root of his somewhat aloof manner, which could always be broken down by a straightforward approach. Curiously, the complete contrast between the characters of Liddell and Acland seemed to cement their friendship all the more firmly. Each had a distinction of character which the other recognised and respected. Where Acland was impulsive, Liddell was prudent. Acland was impressionable and incurably optimistic, which sometimes annoyed the Dean, who could not conceal his irritability. But though he was brusque even to the point of rudeness, Acland took it all in good part; for his respect and affection for the Dean was so great that he felt occasional faults of manner counted for nothing.

Richmond felt that either Acland or Liddell could have distinguished himself had he taken up art as a profession. In his view Acland had the greater genius, but the Dean had the greater accuracy of eye and hand.

6 A. M. W. Stirling, p. 190

Richmond's father, George Richmond, had drawn portraits of both men. His picture of Acland, done in 1846, is pleasant, though less aesthetically satisfying than his likeness of Liddell.

The Dean was never rude to Richmond, for the painter took care always to think before he spoke. 'Those who were rash enough not to do so, brought a cartload of bricks down on them without delay,' he wrote. 'His relationship with his family was beautiful. They feared him not one whit, although he would at times reprimand them with asperity if they were inaccurate or made what he considered silly statements.'[7]

Richmond, who regarded himself as 'a kind of tame cat in the family', said that it would be difficult to decide between the beauty of the daughters, whom he painted on several occasions. Their mother, he commented, dressed them 'most picturesquely, leaving me nothing to design in the way of garments. I saw my chance of making a picture and took it.'[8] Alice, Lorina and Edith were enthusiastic and co-operative sitters. 'The girls entered into my scheme with unexpected avidity and kindness,'[9] he recorded. Richmond himself realised that he was a strict taskmaster, who liked to begin work before seven o'clock in the morning; yet in all the long hours of patient sitting, never a word of complaint fell from their lips. He liked to work for eight to ten hours every day and never put brush to canvas without his sitters before him, except when he was working on the background alone. In this case he chose as his setting a wildly romantic spot on the Great Orme's Head. He began by making an elaborate full-sized cartoon, which was then underpainted in tempera and finished with coachpainters' copal, which he bought in Llandudno. This was a deep varnish which had the advantage of drying very quickly and which at the same time proved exceptionally durable. Many years later he visited the Liddells again and saw the picture. There was not a mark or a crack on any part of the picture, he said, which was as fresh as the day when he last touched it; and indeed, so it remains to this very day. While painting the picture, Richmond had very much in mind the beautiful St Jerome in the National Gallery. His aim had been to obtain great clarity and purity of colouring. He regarded that as the greatest merit of the picture, and he was absolutely right.

While Richmond and the three eldest girls were involved in the portrait, Mrs Liddell's friend Mary Newton occupied herself by decorating the doors of the rooms with pictures of flowers, which

7 ibid, p. 192
8 ibid, p. 192
9 ibid, p. 192

98

Richmond called 'pleasant blots of colour'. The Dean, as always, worked on the *Greek Lexicon*. His study was next door to the room used as Richmond's studio. Every day, promptly at twelve o'clock, the Dean sneezed. Alice and the other children often teased him about it, but its cause remained a mystery. Both portrait and *Lexicon* were set aside at one o'clock for lunch, but the sittings were resumed in the afternoons. And in the late afternoon or early evening, artist and sitters together were dragged off by their family and friends to enjoy a long ramble over the grand promontory in that summer of unbroken sunshine.

Instead of dinner the family had a common high tea in which the children participated. Alice and the others vied with each other for the privilege of sitting next to their father, unless some favoured guest usurped the coveted place. After the meal the Dean remained with the family, for he did not smoke and rarely drank. In the evenings he often read aloud, while Richmond sketched and the girls busied themselves with their sewing. During Richmond's visit, 'Enoch Arden' came out, and the Dean read it and other poems in the same volume. Richmond noted that Liddell read it very splendidly, with 'restrained dramatic force and great feeling'. His favourite part was the sermon in Aylmer's Fields. 'When Enoch comes back and looks in at the window, and sees the new husband and his wife of his youth among their children, he fairly broke down,' Richmond recalled. 'The strong, stern man was moved beyond his power of restraint—for so it was with him—a very sensitive, tender, emotional nature was hidden under what many people thought a hard, critical exterior. Possibly he had to harden himself lest his emotional side might impede his judgment, but his near friends knew that a tenderer, more affectionate man did not exist than Henry George Liddell.'[10]

During those weeks Richmond and the Dean became very close, somewhat to the surprise of the young painter, who modestly felt that he knew too little to interest the great man. But Liddell's judgment in matters of art was excellent, and he appreciated Richmond's talent. Richmond profited intellectually from his contact with the whole family. 'Long walks and serious talks led me into a region of thought and desire I had not known before,' he wrote. 'He liked to talk about current Art as well as ancient Art with me, and was an admirable listener. He drew all the best of one out, as Mr Gladstone did. One could not help trying to be at one's very best in such company, which stimulated to the acquirement of knowledge, the perfection of taste, and the increase of effort.'[11]

10 ibid, pp. 191–2
11 ibid, p. 192

And if Richmond, a mere outsider, felt this, Alice and her sisters and brothers must have benefited considerably from daily contact with this remarkable man. She drank in all that her father had to offer. Her eager curiosity was never satisfied. She dreamed, she imagined, and she created. She revelled in beauty, in art, in music, literature and poetry. And that particular holiday, when she was in daily contact with artists, must surely have increased her own interest in painting and drawing. She was now twelve years old, and though all the Liddell children possessed outstanding beauty, Alice was Richmond's favourite. In describing his portrait he wrote, 'Little Alice, to whose pretty face and lovely colouring no reproduction can do justice, is seen on the right in profile, peering at the big volume on her sister's lap.'[12]

Alice and her sisters were naturally eager to see the painting, but Richmond would not allow so much as a glimpse until it was finished. On the day he completed it, he went off on a long walk by himself, filled with a gnawing anxiety about their verdict. His fears were entirely groundless, for the picture was breathtakingly beautiful. The family's response was enthusiastic, and Richmond confessed that he had never felt happier. In later years he said that he regarded that picture, which was called 'The Sisters', as a milestone in his career, representing the end of the first period of his work as an artist.

Rhoda was then only four years old, and during that same holiday Richmond painted her separately, but did not finish the picture. A. M. W. Stirling, Richmond's biographer, regarded it as one of the most attractive portraits he ever achieved:

The little girl, in the dark beauty of whose baby face is a delightful mingling of shyness and pathos, stands holding a basket of fruit over her arm, from which she has extracted a rosy apple. The attitude of the child is very lifelike, the colouring is rich and full of depth; while the wistfulness on the baby face is accounted for by a sad conviction of the futility of earthly hopes. For the painter kept promising her that if she sat still she would eventually reap her reward by being allowed to eat the grapes which she was carrying, and with prophetic wisdom she foresaw the issue—that this promise was never fulfilled![13]

12 ibid, p. 193
13 ibid, p. 195

'The Sisters' (*l to r*, Edith, Lorina, Alice), painted at Llandudno by William Richmond

Some years later Richmond touched the picture up and sent it as a present to the Dean. The artist considered that it was quite as good a painting as 'The Sisters', though in an entirely different manner.

'The Sisters' was very well received by the press. One critic wrote:

Young Mr Richmond has, in his charming picture 'The Sisters', achieved a success and aroused a surprise not soon to be forgotten. These three sisters, who might be daughters of Italian Giorgione or Palma Vecchia, are grouped in a landscape glowing in the subdued light wherein Venetian painters delighted. There is something in this work allied to the style Pre-Raphaelite, a careful touching in of detail, a love for harmony of colour, a pensive question of sentiment—each sufficient to move interest without arousing repulsion. Seldom has a young painter put forth work of better promise.

That most exacting of critics, Ruskin, was full of enthusiasm about the work, but took issue with the artist on one minor point, the inclusion of Lorina's shoes, and wrote to him: 'My dear Willie, you have made one great mistake. The rest of your picture being supremely beautiful, why the devil didn't you paint the damsel's feet instead of her shoes? Perugino would never have made such a mistake!'

When the family returned to Oxford, the portrait attracted a great deal of attention. A black and white print of the picture was marketed, and proved very popular. Dodgson was also privileged to photograph the painting, which he particularly admired. Richmond, when he was an old man, claimed that Dodgson had been present during the painting sessions, and had related many of the episodes from *Alice's Adventures*; but in this his memory seems to have been at fault. Yet Dodgson almost certainly did visit the family on at least one occasion at Penmorfa. One of Alice's own photograph albums, crammed with well-known photographs by Dodgson, contains a photograph of Penmorfa. Seated on the steps in the foreground, Alice, Lorina and Edith act almost as Dodgson's signature. But the picture was probably taken in the Easter vacation of 1862, when Penmorfa appeared complete from the outside, though inside it was still far from finished. Dodgson's diary for this period is missing.

Dodgson, meanwhile, had finished the pictures in the manuscript fair copy of *Alice's Adventures Underground* at Croft on 13 September 1864; he did not immediately give it to Alice, perhaps because he was at that time still heavily involved in discussions with Tenniel and Macmillan about the printed version. It was not until 12 October that Tenniel was able to show

A Christmas Gift
to
a Dear Child
in Memory
of
a Summer Day.

Lewis Carroll's dedication to Alice in *Alice's Adventures Underground*

him a single drawing on wood, the only thing that he had completed, of Alice standing by the pool of tears, and the rabbit hurrying away. Initially they agreed on about thirty-four pictures, but the number was finally increased to forty-two, partly by splitting some preparatory drawings. Little more than a fortnight later Dodgson went to London and called on Dalziel, the engraver, who was able to show him several proofs, including four from 'Father William', and strongly advised printing from wood blocks.

On 26 November 1864 Dodgson finally presented the manuscript of *Alice's Adventures Underground* to Alice Liddell. It was her Christmas present. All along he had hoped to be able to give her the printed version at the same time, but that was not to be. Tenniel was permanently behind schedule, and when his mother died he wrote to Dodgson in great distress. Generously Dodgson begged him to set aside the work for a while, yet he was anxious to press ahead with publication before Alice grew too old to enjoy it. Perhaps he failed to realise that she would never be too grown up to love his literary offering.

Lewis Carroll's last portrait of Alice, Lorina and Edith

A GRAVE AND GENTLE MAID

'Tis now a grave and gentle maid,
At her own beauty half afraid,
Shrinking, and willing to be stayed.

'Faces in the Fire'

TENNIEL FOUND Dodgson a difficult taskmaster. Though the author had every respect for his illustrator's ability, his own visual concept of the scenes in the book was so clearly defined that he wanted to use Tenniel simply as a draughtsman to commit his own ideas to paper. Tenniel was a patient man, and it says much not only for his character but also for his faith in Dodgson's literary creativity that he accepted all his criticism patiently.

It had been decided that the heroine of the printed book should bear no physical resemblance to the real Alice. Dodgson wanted his artist to use a live model and sent him the photograph of a little blond child called Mary Hilton Badcock, the daughter of a canon. She could not have been more different from Alice Liddell. Beyond accepting the notion of the blond hair, Tenniel disregarded Dodgson's request. 'Mr Tenniel is the only artist who has drawn for me', Dodgson wrote, 'who has resolutely refused to use a model, and declared he no more needed one than I should need a multiplication table to work a mathematical problem! I venture to think he was mistaken and that for want of a model, he drew several pictures of "Alice" entirely out of proportion—head decidedly too large and feet decidedly too small.'[1]

As usual in matters relating to art criticism, Dodgson was right. A childless widower, Tenniel had had little experience of drawing children, and his Alice often looks more like a miniaturised adult than a real child. Yet for all that his illustrations are curiously satisfying. Both author and illustrator were concerned primarily with characters, and very little with

1 Martin Gardner (Ed.), *The Annotated Alice*, 1970, p. 25

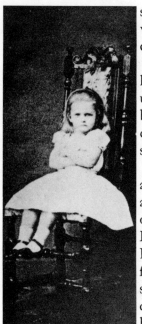

Mary Hilton Badcock, suggested by Lewis Carroll as a model for Alice

setting. Tenniel's background is rarely more than a little cross-hatching, which has the effect of focusing the attention of the reader sharply on the characters themselves, whether animal or human.

Dodgson was no less difficult with his publishers than he was with his illustrator, a fact which he himself fully realised. 'The day when they undertake a book for me is a *dies nefastus* for them. From that day till the book is out . . . there is no pause in "the pelting of the pitiless storm" of directions and questions on every conceivable detail,' Dodgson wrote some two decades later.[2]

On 13 May 1865 the Clarendon Press sent Dodgson the first page, and Macmillan forwarded a specimen volume bound in bright red cloth and blank except for the first page so that he could get an idea of the look of the finished product. The colour of the cover had been chosen by Dodgson himself, because he felt that it appealed strongly to children. Perhaps it is significant that red was the predominant colour in the soft furnishings of his rooms in Oxford. Dodgson was not, however, entirely satisfied with the sample, and wrote to the publisher on 24 May 1865, 'I don't quite like the look of gilt edges at one end. As I want it to be a *table* book, I fancy it would look better with the edges merely cut smoother, and no gilding.'[3]

Tenniel finally handed in the last of the illustrations on 18 June 1865, and by the end of the month two thousand copies of the book had been run off. The very first copy was bound up in white vellum, and Alice received it at the Deanery, specially delivered and just in time for the third anniversary of the famous boating expedition when the tale had first been told. Dodgson said nothing in his diaries about Alice's response to his gifts, either of the manuscript of *Alice's Adventures Underground*, or of *Alice's Adventures in Wonderland* in its printed edition. The breach with the family was now virtually complete, and Mrs Liddell made Alice burn all Dodgson's letters, which must have been numerous. The taboo was not lifted until Alice was a married woman and could decide these things for herself. Even the fame which Dodgson began to attract as an author did not alter Mrs Liddell's attitude on this point. What makes this fact even more surprising is that Alice's mother was an avid autograph hunter, who wrote to notables in the hope of a signature, and had a large collection of letters from the famous. One short and unimportant letter from Thackeray to her husband was prized so highly by her that she not only

2 Pamphlet, *The Profits of Authorship*, 1884, as quoted in S. D. Collingwood, *The Life and Letters of Lewis Carroll*, p. 226, no surviving copy being known
3 D. Crutch, (Ed.), *The Lewis Carroll Handbook*, 1979, p. 31

kept it till her dying day, but specifically mentioned it in her will. Sadly, none of Alice's letters to Dodgson seem to have survived either. It is inconceivable that Dodgson himself would ever have parted with them, unless asked to return them, but presumably they were destroyed with a great many of his personal papers immediately after his death.

In April 1866 Mrs Liddell, a keen collector of such items, wrote to Holman Hunt asking for his autograph. He replied:

Alice's mother*

> My Dear Madam,
>   Having heard of your extraordinary beauty I am exceedingly anxious to obtain your photograph prepaid by return of post.
>   Your Obedt. Servt.
>   W. Holman Hunt

Mrs Liddell wrote him a charming letter in return, and enclosed a photograph, not of herself, but of Alice. He answered from his home at Tor Villa, Campden Hill, on 11 April 1866:

> Dear Madam,
>   I am somewhat ashamed at finding that my note of last week—which I wrote without any idea that it would ever leave the room in which it was dictated—has reached a lady kind enough to deserve a much better one. I can scarcely however profess very sincere repentance for my part in the passing joke seeing that it has procured me a portrait of so interesting and graceful a young lady as your daughter. I make a rule to demand the photograph of each lady that applies to me for my autograph but I am sorry to say that many take no notice whatever of my claim, a fact which leads me to the conclusion that most autograph seekers are very dishonest people—or very indifferent in enthusiasm which prevents me from attending to other collectors as I should do.
>   Believe me
>   Yours obediently
>   W. Holman Hunt[4]

Alice and her family had stayed on in Oxford long after the end of term on account of the Oxford elections, which continued from 13 to 18 July 1865.

4 Autograph letter, private collection of the Marquess of Bath

It was customary in those times for the voting to be spread over several days, but the Dean's interest went far beyond the mere casting of his vote and going away to await the public announcement of the result. He was a staunch supporter of Gladstone, whom he actually nominated, personally leading the way to the poll. Sir William Heathcote and Gathorne Hardy, who later became first Earl of Cranbrook, also stood, and two out of the three had to be elected. The Sub-Dean, Archdeacon Clerke, on the other hand, was Chairman of Gathorne Hardy's campaign committee. Dodgson, a lifelong Conservative, watched the outcome with a critical eye, and wrote a political squib called *The Dynamics of a Parti-cle*, a copy of which was sent to Hardy by Lygon, who became Earl Beauchamp. He described it as 'the only squib worth having'.[5] Sir John Mowbray, one of Hardy's supporters, wrote in his diary on the first day: 'We leave off ten ahead, 385 to Gladstone's 375. This of course reveals nothing. At 3 o'clock we were 50 ahead, but then they began to pour in voting papers. The Dean of Christ Church in particular has polled a large number against us.'[6] The votes were counted daily, and the results made public. When the final results were announced, Heathcote had 3236, Hardy 1904 and Gladstone 1724, giving Hardy a majority of 180 over Gladstone. Hardy wrote later, 'This was the crowning triumph of my life, unsolicited and unexpected, but I always feel that Gladstone misrepresented the constituency, and proved it by declaring himself unmuzzled when defeated—not a very honest outbreak!'[7] 'It is very vexatious,' wrote Liddell. 'To think that Oxford should reject Gladstone!'[8]

After the election was over the family went to Llandudno to await the Dean, who went to Switzerland on a walking tour with Acland and the second son of the latter. They made first for Engelberg, but had scarcely settled in there when the Dean slipped on a mossy stone while descending a steep slope and badly injured his leg. As he was quite unable to walk, help had to be fetched, and he had to stay on the mountain until it was dark, when a *chaise-à-porteurs* reached him. For a whole week he had to stay at the hotel, and then Acland took him in easy stages to Paris where he called in M. Nelaton, the Emperor's own surgeon, who discovered that the small bone of the leg was broken. This had to be properly set at once, and Liddell was fortunate that he sustained no permanent damage.

It was while she was at Penmorfa in the summer of 1865 that Alice

5 A. E. Gathorne Hardy, *Gathorne Hardy, First Earl of Cranbrook: A Memoir*, 1910, p. 179
6 ibid, p. 179
7 ibid, p. 180
8 H. L. Thompson, p. 262

Lorina Liddell*

heard again from Dodgson. Some two weeks previously he had had a letter from Tenniel, who was 'entirely dissatisfied with the printing of the pictures of *Alice's Adventures in Wonderland*', and this prompted Dodgson to call in all copies of the first printing. Not all the recipients of the book complied with Dodgson's request, but naturally Alice did as she was asked. The author's original intention was to have the special binding removed from Alice's copy and transferred to the new version when it was ready, but this proved impractical and Dodgson kept it himself.

Alice received her copy of the new first edition of *Alice's Adventures in Wonderland* on 14 December 1865. The date of the edition was 1866, but it was on sale in time for the Christmas market of 1865, and Macmillan reported that by 30 November five hundred copies had already been sold. Alice's own copy was not in white vellum, as her copy of the 1865 edition had been, but instead, perhaps for practical reasons, it was bound in blue Levant morocco with a roundel of Alice holding the pig on the front and her initials below, in gilt. Dodgson could not have realised it at the time, but he would have done Alice a greater service had he allowed her to keep the original rejected copy, for less than twenty of these are known to have

Alice's personal
presentation volume
of *Alice*

survived and their value is considerable. Although Dodgson's verdict on the new edition was that it was 'very *far* superior to the old, and in fact a perfect piece of artistic printing,'[9] the difference was in no way sufficient to justify scrapping the entire first printing.

On the whole the book was well received by the critics. First to review it was the *Reader*, which on 18 November 1865 pronounced it 'a book to put on one's shelf as an antidote to a fit of the blues'. The *Spectator* reported that 'big folks who take it home to their little folks will find themselves reading more than they had intended, and laughing more than they had any right to expect', and though *The Times* was more preoccupied with Tenniel's fine illustrations than with the text, it pronounced it 'an excellent piece of nonsense'.

In August 1866 Dodgson wrote to Macmillan asking his opinion about getting *Alice* translated into French and German, and adding: 'It will probably be some time before I again indulge in paper and print. I have, however, a floating idea of writing a sort of sequel to *Alice*.'[10] He did not begin work on the latter project until the Christmas vacation of 1867–1868, but, Macmillan's reaction to the concept of foreign translations being favourable, Dodgson set to work to find suitable translators. His Aunt Caroline introduced him to a language teacher called Antoinie Zimmerman, who was undeterred by the difficulty of translating into German a book that relied so heavily on puns, poems and parodies. She began work at once, substituting German nursery rhymes for English ones where necessary to get the desired effect. In April 1867 Dodgson located an unknown French translator called Henri Bué, who worked at incredible speed and translated the entire book in only two months. Meanwhile, Dodgson took French lessons from Bué's father so that he could more readily criticise the finished product. Both books were published in 1869, the German edition preceding the French by about four months. Alice received a copy of *Alice's Abenteuer im Wunderland* bound in green morocco gilt with her initials on the sides, and of *Adventures d'Alice au Pays des Merveilles* similarly bound in red morocco, and initialled. Dodgson had written inside: 'Alice Pleasance Liddell—From the Author.' It was not until 1872 that an Italian translation, *Le Avventure d'Alice nel Paese delle Meraviglie*, translated by T. Pietrocòla-Rossetti was published, but in due course Alice received a copy of that book too, bound in citron morocco.

Though she continued to collect such tribute from Dodgson, Alice

9 R. L. Green, p. 236
10 Morton N. Cohen, *The Letters of Lewis Carroll*, 1979, p. 94

left, The German title page of *Alice*, published 1869; *right*, Antoinie Zimmerman

saw very little of him these days: she was now into her teens and maturing rapidly. She had passed through the somewhat difficult phase of adolescence and emerged as a beautiful young woman. Her complexion was exceptional. That elfin piquancy was in no way lessened with the passage of time. The eyes were still wistful, the hair still cut in the straight fringe across the forehead.

It was probably in the December of 1866 that Alice had a rather serious accident. The Dean was obliged to preach in the Cathedral every Christmas day, so that the family usually spent at least part of the Christmas vacation in Oxford. As Old Tommy, the pony which the children had ridden when they first came to Oxford, had become unfit, the Dean bought a bigger pony. On Boxing Day Alice was out riding with her father when the new pony crossed its legs and fell with her on the Abingdon Road. Alice was in great pain and the matter was plainly serious, so the Dean was obliged to leave Alice by the side of the road while he rode off to summon assistance. In his absence some passing strangers saw the child and came to her aid. They had a wagonette with them, and went to a nearby farm where they borrowed a feather bed on which to send her back to Oxford. 'The bottom of the wagonette was not quite long enough when the door was shut, and this caused me great pain,'

Alice recalled, 'so perhaps I was not as grateful as I should have been, for, when I got home and Bultitude was carrying me indoors, I said to him, "*You* won't let them hurt me any more, will you?" at which, as he told my mother afterwards, he "nearly let Miss Alice drop".' Clearly, Bultitude the coachman was very attached to his young mistress, and indeed to the whole family. 'As it was, I was on my back for six weeks with a broken thigh. During all these weeks Mr Dodgson never came to see me,'[11] Alice added.

Dodgson was not to be blamed for failing to call and see his muse after this accident had occurred, nor should the incident be confused with an earlier minor accident when Alice had suffered a sprain and had been unable to manage a boating expedition; for that was in midsummer, Dodgson had visited and Alice had rapidly recovered. But he was no longer a welcome visitor where Alice's mother was concerned and he may have felt it wiser to stay away. On 11 May 1865 he had written in his diary, 'Met Alice and Miss Prickett in the quadrangle: Alice seems changed a good deal, and hardly for the better—probably going through the usual awkward stage of transition.'

The glittering social life at the Deanery continued unabated. There were some who alleged that the standing receptions at the Liddell home would come to an abrupt halt when the children were all safely married off to wealthy heirs and heiresses; but as the Dean and his wife produced two more children, Frederick Francis, known familiarly as Eric, and Lionel Charles, born on 7 June 1865 and 22 May 1868 respectively, there seemed no imminent danger of that situation arising. The birth of these two sons brought the final total to ten, including the two little boys, Arthur and Albert, who had died in infancy. With Lionel, last of this long line of children, the Dean finally produced a child who inherited not only his intellect, but also his fair curling hair and facial features.

In the summer of 1867 Richmond spent another summer with the family at Penmorfa. The artist, whose memory for fine detail was somewhat imperfect in his old age, recalled that he spent his time painting another portrait of Rhoda, this time with a little pet dog. Yet the portrait was in fact of Violet, who had been too young to be painted in 1864. Of this new portrait he wrote:

> I always think, although one is not a good judge of one's own work, that this portrait which I painted of that singularly picturesque child

11 Alice and Caryl Hargreaves

The Dean, photographed at Llandudno*

is among my best works of that kind. I had been much a attracted by the Velasquez of the Infanta in the Louvre and rather emulated it. The child had a pet dog, a pink and white toy creature that I detested because it was always either barking or dribbling at the mouth, but it was a pretty sight to see the child teaching it tricks, and so I painted them. Only one thing I left unfinished, which I completed afterwards in Oxford; the chair upon which the dog is seated under command of his mistress. The colour of the picture is very good and rich, so much so that my father when he saw it, asked me why I always did my best work for the Dean of Christ Church. I do not know! Perhaps the Dean stimulated me, or perhaps his children were possessed of the kind of beauty that attracted me; but one cause may be that I painted the picture swiftly—it went without a hitch, a rare event, but most successful work is done so; I apprehend when one is swift, one's vision is clear and one's aim decided.[12]

12 A. M. W. Stirling, p. 242

left, Eric and Violet Liddell*; *right*, Richmond's portrait of Violet

Even so the final result was less satisfactory than the portrait of Rhoda. Violet is in a blue velvet gown with a snowy collar and big sleeves slashed with white. 'The child's dark beauty and the old-world richness of her dress enhance the foreign atmosphere of the whole,' commented A. M. W. Stirling. 'Yet there is a stiffness and artificiality about the pose which is entirely absent from the earlier picture of the pathetic, shy child with the fruit; the influence of Velasquez is too apparent; even the pink and white dog—perhaps because the artist hated it—shares the general air of unreality. The portrait, in short, is a fine imitation of old Spanish art, but it exhibits the defects of all imitations in a loss of identity both of the portrayer and portrayed.'[13]

During Richmond's visit to Penmorfa the Liddells exercised all their old fascination. 'This visit brought me still more into touch with that charming family,' Richmond wrote. I had much talk with the Dean, who

13 ibid, pp. 194–5

Alice and Edith, photographed at Llandudno*

liked to hear me describe Rome, which he had never visited.'[14]

It was inevitable that the Dean's lovely daughters should attract a wide circle of admirers. Alice's range of interests was wide and varied. Though she was brought up in a more than ordinarily conventional atmosphere, there were certain areas in which her tastes and habits, like those of her parents, could be considered rather daring. The family's attendance at the professional theatre, at circuses and even music-halls would have been regarded as an impropriety in certain narrow-minded individuals, particularly since the head of the family was a man of the cloth. The Dean's friend Wilberforce, Bishop of Oxford, frowned upon the professional theatre in all forms. Some would have frowned on the Liddells' participation in amateur theatricals, even within their own home; but Alice loved acting and miming and playing games of charades. Small wonder that young men like Lord Newry, who wrote plays for the

14 ibid, p. 243

professional theatre, were drawn to seek her out.

Alice loved music, too, and the Liddells did a great deal to encourage music in Oxford. They not only held frequent musical entertainments in the Deanery, but supported anything which would enhance and extend the quality of musical life in Oxford. The Dean even went to the lengths of arranging a performance of Bach's *St Matthew Passion* in the Cathedral before an audience of twelve hundred people, which gave great offence in some quarters. Oxford was fortunate to have in the University at that time two men of exceptional musical genius, John Stainer (later Sir John), and Charles Hubert Hastings Parry (later Bt). Both found a welcome at the Deanery.

Stainer, the elder of the two men, had been a child prodigy who could play Bach's Fugue in E Major when he was seven years old. He was a chorister at St Paul's Cathedral from the age of nine, having a very fine voice as well as great musical skill. He matriculated at Christ Church on 26 May 1859 and proceeded to Bachelor of Music there. In 1861 he became organist to the university, took his B.A. degree in 1864, and two years later, having attained a Doctorate in Music, was appointed examiner.

Stainer founded the Oxford Philharmonic Society and conducted its first concert on 8 June 1866. His church music had a greater vogue than that of any other English composer: during his lifetime he composed over one hundred and fifty hymn tunes. Stainer received every encouragement from the Liddells in his musical ventures, and served on the committee, set up in 1871 and chaired by the Dean, to produce a new University Hymnal. The insertion of Milton's hymn on the Nativity was at Liddell's direct insistence, and when others objected that there was no suitable tune to fit the metre, Stainer at once undertook to write one. H. L. Thompson, who served on the committee, wrote afterwards: 'One can remember many delightful criticisms which fell from the Dean's lips: they were the ripe judgement of a master of the English tongue; and the many warnings on the score of orthodoxy which were uttered by the otherwise silent mentor of the committee, Mr John Griffiths.'[15]

In December 1865 Stainer eliminated himself from the matrimonial stakes by marring Eliza Cecil Randall, only daughter of Alderman Randall of Oxford. But Parry, eight years younger than Stainer and four years older than Alice, was still available. He was the son of Gambier Parry, a great art lover who had a superb collection of Italian paintings. Indeed, he was an amateur artist of considerable talent, who instilled into

15 H. L. Thompson, p. 237

Alice, *c.* 1867

his son at an early age faculties of artistic appreciation which fitted in very well with the interests of Alice and her family.

Like Stainer, Parry was a child prodigy, and his compositions were preserved from the time he was nine years old. He was encouraged by his father, a high churchman, to take a keen interest in church music, and by the time he reached the age of sixteen, he had composed every form of Anglican church music, including piano and organ pieces, madrigals, songs and fugues. At Eton he took a leading part as both pianist and singer in the Eton Musical Society, and he excelled at cricket. He was still at Eton when he passed his Bachelor of Music examination at Oxford, and having Matriculated at Exeter College he went up to Oxford in 1867.

With Parry's background it was virtually inevitable that he, too, should begin haunting the Deanery. Many were the musical entertainments and social evenings that he shared with Alice's family. It was he who was mainly instrumental in founding the University Musical Club. All the Liddell sisters sang well, but at that stage neither Rhoda nor Violet, the best singer in the whole family, was old enough to attract any real notice. The three eldest girls, with their beauty and sweet harmony, as well as their accomplishment as soloists, were the centre of an admiring circle.

If Parry ever entertained hopes of matrimony with Alice or one of her sisters, he gave them up and married Lady Elizabeth Maude Herbert in 1872; but he continued to associate with the Liddells and in March 1873 he wrote for them three trios for female voices, dedicated to 'Imogen', 'Eda', and 'Rosiepaw'. Alice was Rosiepaw, Imogen and Eda being Ina and Edith. The trios included a setting of Ben Jonson's 'Hymn to Diana', a madrigal, and 'Take O Take Those Lips Away'. For Alice herself he set and dedicated 'A Lament', by Shelley, *Opus* 14. The last verse reads:

> *Out of the day and night*
> *A joy has taken flight;*
> *Fresh spring, and summer, and winter hoar,*
> *Move my faint heart with grief, but with delight*
> *No more—Oh, never more!*

Ruskin, too, was coming more and more into contact with the Liddells at this time. Liddell and Acland had done their best to get him elected to the vacant Professorship of Poetry at Oxford, but without success. Ruskin was very disappointed. It was then suggested in certain quarters that he might be appointed one of the curators of the university art galleries, and Ruskin wrote to Acland, already one of the curators: 'If you are tired of that curatorship and think that I can be of any use, I will do the best I can. But in no phrase of politeness I tell you that you are fitter for the place than I, and, working with your old friend the Dean, and entering into the fruit of your effort for many years, you had much better stay as you are, if you are not weary.'[16]

The Dean and Acland were the only curators, and if Ruskin were to be offered a curatorship, one of them would have to resign. Neither of them actually wished to do so. Together they had built up the gallery from an unsorted, virtually uncared-for mass of art work into an organised and exceptionally fine collection, supplemented by enlightened and judicious acquisition policies. Liddell wrote to Acland, 'Are you sure positively certain that Ruskin would like to be Curator of the Galleries? Have you it in writing? And can his inclination or wish in August be depended upon in November?'[17]

16 J. B. Atlay, p. 369
17 ibid, p. 369

Eric Liddell*

In the end nothing came of it; but in 1869 Ruskin became first Slade Professor of Fine Art at Oxford. He delivered his inaugural lecture in February 1870. The lecture-room at the Taylorian Institute was crowded to suffocation long before the lecture was due to begin, and Acland had to ask the audience to adjourn to the Sheldonian Theatre so that all who wanted to, could listen in comfort. The excitement caused by Ruskin's lectures was almost unbelievable and scarcely seemed to diminish as long as he continued as Slade Professor. He brought a new and special appreciation of art which was unique in his day, and the Liddell family were among those who benefited. His lectures were thronged with ladies as well as men, and this he somewhat resented. He had come to Oxford, he claimed, to spread the light among the members of the university, but its beams were 'caught by the bright toilets and luxuriant head-dresses of his fair auditors'.[18]

18 ibid, p. 371

In 1871 Ruskin made a munificent gift of £5000 to endow a Master of Drawing at Oxford: it was handed over to Acland in a most unorthodox manner when Ruskin was lying ill at Matlock. 'There, Henry, that's to endow the Masters,'[19] he said, and gave him the cheque. As Acland's visit was that of doctor to patient, he demurred, but as the state of Ruskin's health forbade argument, he accepted and handed the cheque over to the trustees.

Soon after Ruskin arrived in Oxford, Alice became his pupil. She amply repaid the trouble he took with her. Ruskin was pleased with her progress, and in 1870 he presented her with Sir Walter Scott's *Minstrelsy of the Scottish Border*, which he inscribed with the words, 'Alice P. Liddell, First Prize for Time Sketch, 1870.'

Richmond knew Ruskin intimately and had every respect for him. All the same, he had reservations about him as a teacher:

> Ruskin . . . would have made me his pupil if I would have decided to copy birds' nests, fruit and primroses for the rest of my life. I copied one picture so well that when Ruskin saw it he did not know it from the original. I also copied, to please him, one or two of Turner's watercolours made to illustrate Rogers' *Italy*, and did these also to his satisfaction; but when it came to spending my whole time in such work, I struck! Ruskin's limitations were always before me, and I remember listening with contempt to his outrageous criticisms of Michelangelo, Raphael and other giants. When Ruskin wrote of twigs, of clouds, of glaciers, mountains and inanimate nature he was always enlightening, but when he touched on Epic Art he was entirely out of his element. Out and out Ruskinism would be fatal to any student. . . . His eloquence conquers judgment and while under the spell of it, a pliable or receptive mind loses for the time being its individuality of judgment.[20]

Before long Ruskin started lending Alice some of his Turners to copy. Early in 1871 he sent her a letter from his family home at Denmark Hill giving her advice about painting: 'I have sent you a little vignette of Turner's—which you must not be frightened by, as if it were too difficult. Turner's *method* is as simple as a child's—and you will need no skill to copy his works.' Alice's influence with the artist was not inconsiderable. He resolutely set himself against formal parties, yet she could inveigle him

19 ibid, p. 371
20 A. M. W. Stirling, p. 195

into attending. 'I am horribly vexed with myself for having been at the Prince's party (it was all your fault. . .) and now I don't think I can come to Christ Church today and what will mama say of me? [You] will know quite well which party I would rather have been at. But please tell me a time when I can come and show you how to do this sky—& other skies.'

Ruskin had some recollections of Alice's influence over him:

I never went to official dinners in Oxford if I could help it. . . . When The Princess of Wales came, one winter, to look over the Art Galleries, I had of course to attend . . . and then came the commands to dinner at the Deanery. . . . The day before, or the day before that, the Planet Saturn had treated me with his usual adversity in the carrying out of a plot with Alice in Wonderland. For, that evening, the Dean and Mrs Liddell dined by command at Blenheim; but the girls were not commanded; and as I had been complaining of never getting a sight of them lately, after knowing them from the nursery, Alice said that she thought, perhaps, if I would come round after papa and mama were safe off to Blenheim, Edith and she might give us a cup of tea and a little singing, and Rhoda would show me how she was getting on with her drawing and geometry, or the like. And so it was arranged. The night was wild with snow, and no one likely to come around to the Deanery after dark. I think Alice must have sent me a little note, when the eastern coast of Tom Quad was clear. I slipped round from Corpus through Peckwater, shook the snow off my gown and found an armchair ready for me, and a bright fireside and tea coming up.

Well, I think Edith had got the tea made, and Alice was just bringing the muffins to perfection—I don't recollect that Rhoda was there; (I never did, that anybody else was there, if Edith was; but it is all so like a dream now, I'm not sure) when there was a sudden sense of some stars having been blown out by the wind, round the corner; and then a crushing of the snow outside the house, and a drifting of it inside; and the children all scampered out to see what was wrong, and I followed slowly;—and there were the Dean and Mrs Liddell standing just in the middle of the hall, and the footmen in consternation, and a silence, and—

'How sorry you must be to see us, Mr Ruskin!' began at last Mrs Liddell.

'I never was more so,' I replied. 'But what's the matter?'

'Well,' said the Dean, 'we couldn't even get past the parks; the snow's a fathom deep in the Woodstock Road. But never mind; we'll be very good and quiet, and keep out of the way. Go back to your tea, and we'll have our dinner downstairs.'

'And so we did, but we couldn't keep papa and mama out of the drawing-room when they had done dinner, and I went back to Corpus, disconsolate.'[21]

Next evening Ruskin dined at the Liddells' with the Princess after all. While the company was assembled, 'The door from the nurseries opened; and enter Rhoda—in full dress! Very beautiful! But just a snip too short in the petticoats, a trip too dainty in the ankles, a dip too deep of sweet-briar-red in the ribands. Not the damsel who came to hearken named Rhoda—by any means; but as exquisite a little spray of Rhododendron ferrugineum as ever sparkled in Alpine dew.

D'Israeli saw his opening in an instant. Drawing himself to his full height, he advanced to meet Rhoda. . . . "*This* is, I understand, the young lady in whose art education Professor Ruskin is so much interested!" I had never given Rhoda a lesson in my life (no such luck!) yet I could not disclaim the interest.'[22]

Rhoda Liddell*

21 John Ruskin, *Praeterita*, Vol. III, pp. 62–9
22 ibid, Vol. III, pp. 62–9

WELCOME QUEEN ALICE

'Then fill up the glasses with treacle and ink,
Or anything else that is pleasant to drink:
Mix sand with the cider, and wool with the wine—
And welcome Queen Alice with ninety times nine!'

Through the Looking-Glass

THOUGH ALICE had virtually lost contact with Dodgson, he still went on with his literary offerings to her. His ideas of a sequel to *Alice's Adventures in Wonderland* were slow in developing. One major obstacle was Tenniel's initial refusal to illustrate the book, coupled with Dodgson's personal reluctance to write it until the question of the illustrator had been settled. Dodgson approached a number of other illustrators, but all refused for one reason or another. Finally Sir Noel Paton, who was too ill to undertake the work, reminded him that Tenniel was the only possible choice. Dodgson approached him again, promising to pay Tenniel's publishers for five months of his time, and finally Tenniel agreed, though he made it plain that the work would have to proceed at his own pace. The commission was accepted in June 1868.

A personal bereavement now claimed Dodgson's attention. Archdeacon Dodgson, his father, died on 21 June 1868, leaving him head of a family of ten unmarried brothers and sisters. As his father had occupied a rectory, Dodgson now had to find a new home for the family, disposing of surplus furniture and effects, and acting as executor. But after a few weeks had elapsed, he took the lease of a house at Guildford and the move was arranged.

It was January 1870 before Tenniel was able to show Dodgson the first batch of rough sketches, but thereafter the momentum increased. If he had seemed critical before, Dodgson was now even more so. He had no intention of permitting a repetition of the recalled first printing of *Alice's Adventures in Wonderland*. By 15 April 1870 he had already criticised a trial title page which Macmillan had had printed for him, and although Dodgson's criticisms were all to do with seemingly unimportant matters,

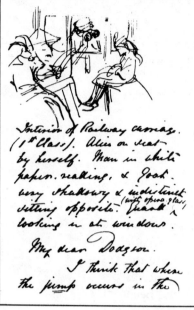

Interior of Railway carriage. (1st Class). Alice on seat by herself. Man in white paper. reading. & Goat. very shadowy & indistinct (with opera glass) sitting opposite. Guard looking in at windows.

My dear Dodgson.

I think that when the jump occurs in the railway scene you might very well make Alice lay hold of the Goat's beard as being the object nearest to her hand - instead of the old lady's hair. The jerk would naturally throw them together.

Don't think me brutal, but I am bound to say that the 'wasp' chapter doesn't interest me in the least; & that I can't see my way to a picture. If you want to shorten the book I can't help thinking - with all submission - that there is your opportunity.

In an agony of haste

Yours sincerely

J Tenniel.

Portsdown Road.
June 1. 1870

A letter from Tenniel to Lewis Carroll about *Through the Looking-Glass*

like misplaced punctuation marks and bad spacing, there is no doubt that the final form was far superior to the first.

Early in 1871 Dodgson decided to consult a number of his friends about Tenniel's drawing of the Jabberwock, an imaginary beast which Tenniel portrayed to such good effect that Dodgson was afraid it would frighten his child readers. He consulted about thirty mothers, asking for advice as to whether he should retain the picture as a frontispiece, as Tenniel had intended, transfer it to its proper place in the book, or omit it altogether. He finally decided to transfer it to its correct context, and to use a picture of the White Knight as frontispiece instead. Perhaps significantly, he did not apparently consult any of the family at the Deanery.

While working on the book, Tenniel got his revenge for Dodgson's continual carping criticism by getting him to drop a chapter. 'Don't think me brutal, but I am bound to say that the "wasp" chapter doesn't interest me in the least, and I can't see my way to a picture. If you want to shorten the book, I can't help thinking—with all submission—that *there* is your opportunity.'[1] Dodgson took Tenniel's advice.

1 S. D. Collingwood, *The Life and Letters of Lewis Carroll*, pp. 148–9

On 11 October 1871 Dodgson received five finished sheets of *Through the Looking-Glass* from Clay, the printer, and he recorded that the book was printing off rapidly. On 21 November he telegraphed to Clay his authority to electrotype all the rest of the book. Meanwhile, he had prepared a little address in pamphlet form called *To All Child-Readers of Alice*, which was to be inserted in copies of the book. Macmillan now told him that advance orders already accounted for 7500 out of a print run of 9000, and they accordingly decided to print off a further 6000. The book was dated 1872, but it was in the bookshops in time for the Christmas market.

Alice's personal copy was originally to have had a looking-glass incorporated in the cover, but the idea did not prove practical. Instead, Dodgson had one specially bound up for her in red morocco, a perfect partner to the blue copy of *Wonderland* which she had already. Dodgson received his order of a hundred cloth bound copies and three in morocco on 8 December, and he took care to dispatch Alice's copy together with cloth-bound ones for Lorina and Edith before any others went out. Their reactions to receiving the book are nowhere recorded.

Through the Looking-Glass was an immediate commerical success. By 27 January 1872, Dodgson's fortieth birthday, 15,000 copies had been sold. Though it lacked something of the spontaneity of *Alice's Adventures in Wonderland*, many critics feel that its structure is tighter and more carefully worked out. Like its forerunner, it is dramatic in presentation and relies for its effect on dialogue, with an abundance of puns, word plays and songs. Both books are crammed with memorable phrases and unforgettable characters, and the books are as perfectly matched as Dodgson could make them, even down to the number of chapters—twelve in each. Just as the children's earlier interest in croquet played an important part in the first book, so their later delight in chess formed a framework for its sequel. As Alexander Taylor aptly noted, Dodgson's intention was not to work out the moves of the game in correct sequence, but to illustrate the implications of the moves, providing 'a carefully worked-out sequence of moves designed to illustrate the queening of a pawn, the relative powers of the pieces—the feeble king, the eccentric knight and the formidable queen whose powers include those of rook and bishop—and finally a checkmate.'[2]

Most important of the poems in the book is 'Jabberwocky'. This takes as its first and last verse the 'Stanza of Anglo-Saxon Poetry' which

2 Alexander L. Taylor, *The White Knight*, 1952

Dodgson had composed as early as 1855 to amuse his family.

> *Twas brillig, and the slithy toves*
> *Did gyre and gimble in the wabe:*
> *All mimsy were the borogoves*
> *And the mome raths outgrabe.*

The poem indicates Dodgson's complete ignorance of the Anglo-Saxon language and poetic tradition: he knew nothing of its basic vocabulary, its inflexions and word order; and he was apparently unfamiliar with the sprung rhythm which Anglo-Saxon poets employed. His poem was rhymed, a convention unknown in Old English. Yet none of this matters. Enlightened scholars and general readers alike found their imaginations captured by the poem. Even Liddell's co-author of the *Greek Lexicon*, Robert Scott, wrote a German translation of the poem in February 1872 which he claimed was the original, Dodgson's being a mere translation. He wrote to Dodgson:

> Are we to suppose, after all, that the Saga of Jabberwocky is one of the universal heirlooms which the Aryan race at its dispersion carried with it from the great cradle of the family? You really must consult Max Müller about this. It begins to be probable that the *origo originalissima* may be discovered in Sanscrit, and that we shall by and by have a *Iabrivokaveda*. The hero will turn out to be the Sun-God in one of the Avatars; and the Tumtum tree the great Ash *ygdrasil* of the Scandinavian mythology.[3]

A month later Augustus Vansittart, Fellow of Trinity College, Cambridge, translated 'Jabberwocky' into Latin elegiacs under the title '*Mors Iabrochii*' for Trinity College Lecture Rooms, where every week an English passage had to be translated into Greek or Latin. After the undergraduates had made their translations, Vansittart's own was circulated as a model. Though *Through the Looking-Glass* tended to be less popular with translators than *Alice's Adventures in Wonderland*, translations of 'Jabberwocky' continued to appear, and the poem has made almost as strong an appeal to illustrators as a separate entity as *Alice's Adventures*.

 The most significant character in *Through the Looking-Glass*, apart from Alice herself, is the White Knight, for it is impossible to overlook

---

3 S. D. Collingwood, *The Life and Letters of Lewis Carroll*, p. 143

certain similarities between the Knight and Dodgson himself. Tenniel
appears to have been aware of this, for his drawings of the White Knight
bear a resemblance to the illustrator in the same way that the pen portrait
resembles the author. There are, moreover, certain poignant moments in
the scenes between the White Knight and Alice, particularly in the excised
'Wasp in a Wig' chapter. This fascinating episode, thought for over a
century to have been irretrievably lost, turned up in Sotheby's salerooms
in July 1974 in the form of six galley proofs amended by Dodgson and
bearing his instruction to the printer to leave it out.

The wasp chapter should have appeared after Alice's affecting
farewell to the White Knight and on the brink of the brook which she
must cross to become a queen. Alice pauses to speak to a rheumaticky old
man with a face like a wasp, whom she will be powerless to help after
crossing the brook. His churlish responses to her efforts to help offend her
but she makes allowances for him: 'Perhaps it's only the pain that makes
him so cross.' Dodgson was right, artistically, to omit the chapter, for it

Alice music by
C. H. R. Marriott,
dedicated to Alice and
the Queen of Hearts
respectively

127

somes as something of an anti-climax after the leave-taking of the White Knight; but clearly both incidents are allegorical references to the inevitable parting of the ways between Alice and her old friend. Dodgson recognises in the queening of his Alice that she has grown up. She is nearly twenty, Dodgson nearly forty. They are 'half a life asunder'.

Underlying the charm and wit of *Through the Looking-Glass* is an intense preoccupation with transience of beauty, with death and decay, and loss of maidenhood. The introductory poem says all that needs to be said about Carroll and his Alice, their past, their present, and their future:

> *Child of the pure unclouded brow*
> *And dreaming eyes of wonder!*
> *Though time be fleet, and I and thou*
> *Are half a life asunder,*
> *Thy loving smile will surely hail*
> *The love-gift of a fairy-tale.*
>
> *I have not seen thy sunny face,*
> *Nor heard thy silver laughter;*
> *No thought of me shall find a place*
> *In thy young life's hereafter—*
> *Enough that now thou wilt not fail*
> *To listen to my fairy-tale.*
>
> *A tale begun in other days,*
> *When summer suns were glowing—*
> *A simple chime, that served to time*
> *The rhythm of our rowing—*
> *Whose echoes live in memory yet,*
> *Though envious years would say 'forget'.*
>
> *Come, hearken, then, ere voice of dread,*
> *With bitter tidings laden,*
> *Shall summon to unwelcome bed*
> *A melancholy maiden!*
> *We are but older children, dear,*
> *Who fret to find our bedtime near.*
>
> *Without, the frost, the blinding snow,*
> *The storm-wind's moody madness—*

Within, the firelight's ruddy glow
And childhood's nest of gladness.
The magic words shall hold thee fast:
Thou shalt not heed the raving blast.

And though the shadow of a sigh
May tremble through the story,
For 'happy summer days' gone by,
And vanish'd summer glory—
It shall not touch with breath of bale
The pleasance of our fairy-tale.

Alice had indeed grown away from Dodgson now. The Liddells' star continued in the ascendant. In the year 1870 they went to Llandudno for their last holiday at Penmorfa. The Dean had weighty matters to consider and used the vacation to come to an important decision. The Vice-Chancellorship of the University had fallen vacant, and Liddell had been invited to accept it. Not since Dean Aldrich in the seventeenth century had a Dean of Christ Church held both offices together. Liddell was now fifty-nine years old, and had many responsibilities over and above those which were strictly required of him. He wrote to his friend and colleague, Bartholomew Price, with whom he had been closely associated for years in the management of the Clarendon Press, inviting him to join the family at Llandudno and ponder the vital problem.

When he returned to Oxford, Liddell accepted the office. He was now Head of the University for all practical purposes, presiding over all public assemblies, chairing all committees, and having a major part in the appointment of all Professors, Preachers and Examiners. Except on those rare occasions when the Chancellor himself visited, he had to preside over all public ceremonies. Liddell was ideally suited to the work, bringing to it the impartiality of judgment for which he was well-known. Professor Max Müller wrote of his performance as Vice-Chancellor: 'There was a restraining influence in his very presence, people seemed ashamed of lowering themselves before him by selfish, ungenerous or unacademic behaviour. No gossip was allowed in his presence, no insinuations were tolerated against anybody not present to defend himself.'[4]

Shortly before Liddell's appointment as Vice-Chancellor, Lord Salisbury had been installed as Chancellor. At that time the Conservative

4 H. L. Thompson, p. 233

Lewis Carroll's last photographs of Alice
(*right*) and Lorina (*below*), 1870

The Dean at his desk

Party was in opposition, but when the Party returned to power in 1874, Disraeli appointed him Secretary of State in India, and four years later Foreign Secretary. In 1885 Lord Salisbury became Prime Minister. Liddell was never a close friend of Lord Salisbury, but the two men enjoyed a smooth and cordial relationship. Peel, Gladstone, Disraeli and now Salisbury: such was the distinguished line of Prime Ministers who dined at the Deanery with Alice and her family. Alice herself did not indulge in politics. That sort of thing was simply not done by well brought up young ladies in her day. All the same, she was politically well-informed, for the Dean expected his family to take a proper interest in all that went on in the world.

Temperamentally Lord Salisbury and the Dean were very different. The Dean was always impeccably dressed. Not so Lord Salisbury. 'Throughout his life my grandfather was eccentrically indifferent to his own appearance,' wrote Lord David Cecil. 'In later years, and when he was Prime Minister of England, he was refused admittance to the Casino in Monte Carlo because his clothes were so disreputable that he was taken to be a tramp.'[5] Lady Salisbury also had little interest in matters of dress but she had a magnetic personality. Lord David Cecil wrote of her: 'Though not pretty—she was short and square, with strong, aquiline features—she was yet made attractive by her fresh skin, shapely hands and piercing blue eyes; and still more by the vitality which radiated from her whole person and was audible even in the quick, firm sound of her footsteps. It showed most of all in her conversation, which was alive with strong opinions and vigorous humour and an appreciative interest in the personality of whomever she was talking to.'[6]

On the very day that Lord Salisbury was installed as Chancellor of the University, Dodgson's friend, Henry Parry Liddon, a great preacher and a firm favourite in the Deanery, sought and obtained Lady Salisbury's permission for Dodgson to photograph her children. 'I fancy *Wonderland* had a great deal to do with my gracious reception,' Dodgson wrote afterwards. Next day Lord Salisbury and the children called at Dodgson's rooms and he photographed them. In the afternoon Lady Salisbury brought the children again, leaving the children with him while she went to make some calls, though not before she had looked at the seven first pictures of *Through the Looking-Glass*, the title of which had originally been suggested by Liddon. Mrs Liddell was not to be outdone. Dodgson

5 Lord David Cecil, *The Cecils of Hatfield House*, 1973, p. 221
6 ibid, p. 226

Lord Salisbury, Chancellor of Oxford
University; a contemporary undergraduate
portrait*

wrote: 'This morning an almost equally wonderful thing occurred, Mrs
Liddell brought Ina and Alice to be photographed, first visiting my
rooms, and then the studio.'[7] It was the last time that Dodgson
photographed them.

By 1871 the Liddells had abandoned Llandudno as a holiday resort
and were looking for vacations of a different kind, yachting and a gay
social life now being of greatest importance to Alice and her sisters. On 24
July 1871, when Alice was about to embark on her new adventure, Ruskin
wrote to her from Matlock: 'You may do some useful work while you are
yachting. . . . Look at the sky at sunrise and sunset, every day (and
therefore don't dance on deck till one in the morning). . . . And I wish you
fair winds—just enough to require some pretty sailing—I wish you pretty
skies—wakeful eyes—at right times—and happy thoughts at all times.'

7 R. L. Green, p. 288

Only a few days earlier he had lent her another Turner to copy, and had written asking her 'to be kind enough always to keep the little Turner away from the light, above all not in sunshine when you are not at work on it. And you know you must not let anybody else try to copy it (except Ina and Edith).'

It was the custom of the day for the upper classes to go on a 'grand tour' of Europe as a kind of culmination to their education. Alice, Lorina and Edith set out on just such a tour on 7 February 1872. Lorina was perhaps rather old for her first adventure away from parental care, being twenty-three by now, but it was natural for the three girls to go everywhere together, and it is possible anyway that political unrest had deterred them from undertaking such a tour previously.

Paris, their first objective, was still severely battle-scarred after the insurrection of 1871, and everywhere there were grim reminders of the consequences of mob violence. Many buildings had been scarred or destroyed by shellfire, while others had been blackened and devastated by deliberate arson. Trees had been felled and the recollection of recent carnage still haunted the memories of those who had lived through that terrible time. It was not a happy time to visit Paris, though once inside its galleries one could forget the battle stains outside. Alice looked at the treasures of the Louvre with an artist's eye, and felt herself enriched by the experience.

Marseilles, Monte Carlo and Nice were obvious resorts to head for, and there the sisters were able to enjoy a more temperate climate. Some three weeks after leaving England they boarded a private yacht, the *Kathleen*, and set sail for Italy. Dean Liddell was particularly interested in his daughters' account of that country. Like them he had visited Venice, but although in 1855 he had published a celebrated *History of Rome*, he had never been there himself. The highlight of their visit to Rome was an audience with the Pope, which they attended veiled and clad in black from head to foot as custom demanded.

While in Rome, Alice received a long, newsy letter from Prince Hassan, son of Ismael Pasha, Khedive of Egypt, who was at Christ Church at that time, having matriculated on 18 October 1869. Mrs Liddell, who never missed an opportunity of encouraging her daughters to mingle with the mighty, had urged him to write on the grounds that Alice would enjoy receiving letters from England. He had a great deal to relate about the royal occasions which he had attended, and notably of a special thanksgiving service in St Paul's Cathedral where everyone had tried to get a glimpse of the Queen and the Prince and Princess of Wales.

Most adventurous of the girls' exploits was the ascent of Mount Vesuvius. Part of the journey was by pony, but the final phase was by *chaises-à-porteurs*. Capri, Pompeii, Sorento all formed part of the programme, and in Milan they went to La Scala to hear Verdi's opera *Aida*. They returned to England just in time for the celebration of Alice's twentieth birthday.

Alice's education was now regarded as finished in the formal sense, though naturally the daughter of the Dean of Christ Church had been trained from birth to absorb knowledge and indulge in cultured pursuits, and that was a continuing process. The faithful Miss Prickett had finally relinquished her charge of Ina, Alice and Edith in the previous year. She now had a new occupation: that of wife and stepmother. On 22 March 1871, in the Parish Church of St Aldates, she had married Charles Foster, a prosperous local wine merchant. Her husband's first wife had died, and he was in need of companionship. For Mary Prickett this was an excellent match. At thirty-eight years of age, a Victorian spinster, particularly one without a substantial fortune, had precious few prospects of matrimony.

An illustration by the Dean from his book, *The History of Rome*

Alice*

Her situation as governess in a family of the Liddells' social standing had stood her in good stead, however. Years of close contact with cultured and distinguished people had given her a considerable social advantage. Her new husband was a prosperous man, with a business at 3, St Aldate's Street and cellars in the Corn Exchange. In addition he owned the fashionable Mitre Hotel in the High Street, one of the three best hotels in Oxford. At the time of his marriage, this was let out to Mrs Sarah Venables, a widow, but in due course the Fosters moved in there themselves, and Mary Foster became the proprietress. Her husband, meanwhile, carried on his wine business and had an excellent reputation in Oxford. He was well acquainted with the social requirements of the day and was called in to most major Oxford functions, not merely as a wine expert, but as overall organiser. Clearly he and his new wife were complementary to each other.

Sadly, Alice and her sisters returned to a household in mourning after the unexpected death on 9 March 1872 of the Dean's father. He was eighty-four years old and had died peacefully at his home, Hetton Lawn, Charlton Kings. His wife, the former Charlotte Lyon, granddaughter of the eighth Earl of Strathmore, had predeceased him by only a few months. But Alice's grandmother had been in very poor health for many years, so that her death could be said to have been a merciful release from a vegetable existence. Her grandfather, on the other hand, had been active

Aunt Amelia, the Dean's spinster sister*

to the last, and had passed painlessly into the next world. He had been much loved locally for his kindly disposition and readiness to participate in acts of human charity. His last gift to the village was a pump, which had only just been completed when he died. He was buried in his wife's grave in the local churchyard on 14 March, and as the burial party returned, a rainbow stood over the old family home.

Alice's grandfather left three sons and daughters. As a second son, he had narrowly missed a title, plus the Ravensworth Castle and estates, but he had been comfortably circumstanced and had been able to make generous provision for his children. The Dean received ten thousand pounds, and his younger brother, William Wren Liddell, the Rector of Cowley in Gloucestershire, received seven thousand pounds. His youngest brother, Charles Liddell, the famous engineer, received two thousand pounds and the entire real estate, including Hetton Lawn and a house which the old man had built himself on the site of an old Wesleyan meeting house. Alice's two spinster aunts, Charlotte and Amelia Liddell, received an annuity of three hundred pounds, and Alice and her brothers and sisters were given three hundred pounds each. The Dean's wife received a thousand pounds, as did Alice's Aunt Marion. The latter had been a rather beautiful woman when she married Charles Liddell, but in later years she became a very unsympathetic character who frankly disliked children and could not be bothered even with her own grandchildren, let alone with those of her various in-laws. Although she observed the outward courtesies, children sensed that there was something lacking, and a slight but unladylike predisposition to alcohol,

Alice's Aunt Marion
and Uncle Charles
Liddell

though never actually discussed in family circles, did not pass unnoticed.

Alice's art studies were still an absorbing interest in her life. During her holiday abroad she had kept a journal which she illustrated. As a writer of prose, Alice was disappointing, particularly bearing in mind the avidity with which she read the world's best literature and discussed it with the world's greatest scholars. She was by no means inarticulate, but though she could pen a graceful social letter, though her written work was always grammatical, the level of prose was frankly uninspired. This was the case when she was twenty; it remained so to the end of her life. Some vital creative urge was lacking, and no amount of learning by rote, no dissection and analysis could alter that fact. Yet place a pencil or paint brush in her hand, and Alice was transformed. She could bring romanticism to her work; she could take something as transient as a handful of flowers, a geranium leaf, perhaps, or a few pansies, and capture that fragile beauty for ever. Often she worked at landscapes. Like Picasso, she had her 'blue' period, but her work was always accurately representational, and she specialised in fine lines. When treating family scenes, she did so with wit and humour.

Two examples of Alice's artistry: *right*, A watercolour painting by Alice*; *opposite*, An original watercolour composition, painted on vellum—a floral design for a decorative fan, contained in the original exhibition mount from the Oxford School of Art*

Ruskin's art school was intended to bring art not only to the rich, but to the artisan classes. Alice, though strictly maintaining the social distinction between herself and certain of the other students, was formally enrolled there and indeed entered into the spirit of the school with a certain sense of social mission. Mostly she did not go to the classes with the rest. Instead, Ruskin went to her at the Deanery. But like the other pupils she produced work and exhibited it under the formal imprint of the school. Though she signed her work, she left blank the space for 'stage', 'age', 'occupation' and 'master'. There was a certain air of patronage about her participation after all.

She continued to copy Turners lent to her by Ruskin. In one undated letter he wrote: 'I thought you had chosen the Goodwins for yourselves— I think them a little too difficult for you at present—at least. Try . . . the quite light Turner sketches. . . .' His letters to her were surprisingly flirtatious, given the nature of Victorian society, and it says something of the character of Alice herself that she should continue to receive letters written in such a teasing vein. 'It is very pretty of you to sign your full sweet name—it is like a little breath of soft air from a garden of herbs. . .' he wrote on one occasion, and on another, 'I meant to have had audience of you for a moment after lecture, but was tired and afraid to stop . . . but if you *would* be a beautiful and audible sibyl both—on Tuesday afternoon— would you? Could you—will you? How the days pass—like Sibylline leaves.'

It has always been assumed that Ruskin was only interested in the child Alice; yet it is clear that he appreciated her as a beautiful and cultured young woman, and that she herself frankly rather enjoyed this relationship with the great man.

BEYOND ALL IMAGING

Ye golden hours of Life's young spring,
Of innocence, of love and truth!
Bright, beyond all imagining,
Thou fairy-dream of youth.

'Solitude'

IN 1872 an event occurred which was to have far-reaching consequences for Alice, and indeed, to some extent for the entire family at the Deanery. Queen Victoria decided to send her youngest son to Christ Church.

Prince Leopold George Duncan Albert was born on 7 April 1853 at Buckingham Palace. A few days later Queen Victoria, who made a rapid recovery after the birth, wrote to her uncle, King Leopold of the Belgians, 'I can report most favourably of myself, for I have never been better or stronger. Stockmar will have told you that Leopold is to be the name of our fourth young gentleman. It is a mark of love and affection which I hope you will not disapprove. It is a name which is dearest to me after Albert's.'[1] The new baby was baptised by the Archbishop of Canterbury in the private chapel at Buckingham Palace on 28 June 1853, and Alice's father was among the clergy who officiated. The list of sponsors was impressive: the King of Hanover, the Princess of Prussia, Princess Mary of Cambridge and the Prince of Hohenlohe Langenberg.

Unfortunately Prince Leopold was not a strong child, and had the misfortune to inherit haemophilia, that curse which struck a number of the royal houses of Europe. This robbed him of many of the ordinary pleasures of childhood, for he was not able to join in the games of his brothers and sisters. Perhaps it was this physical defect which turned Queen Victoria against him initially. 'A very common-looking child, very plain in the face, clever but an oddity—and not an engaging child though

1 *The Illustrated London News*, 5 April 1884

140

amusing'[2] is how she described him. To her daughter Victoria she later wrote of him: 'It is a great pity that he holds himself so ill for he has a fine figure with fine limbs and chest.'[3] She also said that he had an 'unfortunate defect in his throat and speech',[4] though by the time he reached Oxford he had long outgrown these handicaps.

In early childhood Leopold was, according to custom, placed in the care of governesses, and his love of music, history and art very quickly emerged. But his ill-health continually interrupted his formal education, and in 1861 he was sent to Cannes to escape the perils of an English winter. On 14 December 1861, while the boy was still in France, his father died.

Widowhood inclined the Queen to draw her children closer around her, with the sole exception of the unfortunate Prince of Wales, and in 1863 she took Leopold with her to Germany. When in England, several of the masters at Eton used to visit Leopold regularly at Windsor to give him lessons, but later he had a succession of regular tutors. In due course, Robinson Duckworth, who had been in the boat when *Alice's Adventures in Wonderland* was first told, and who had since became a canon, was appointed tutor, followed by the devoted Robert Hawthorn Collins, who remained with him in the all-important years at Oxford. By the time Leopold was ready to embark on his life as an undergraduate, he had long since won over his mother's affection by his kind and gentle manner, his application to those matters of the arts which had been regarded as his late father's particular preserve, and his obvious scholastic abilities.

Leopold matriculated at Christ Church in 1872, and began his career as an undergraduate in November of that year. Acland, who was appointed to supervise his medical care while he was at Oxford, actively joined in the search for suitable accommodation for the young Prince. Wykeham House, near St Giles's, was chosen, but Acland insisted on separate drainage, refusing to allow the Prince to run the risk of contamination from the main drainage of the town, knowing well how susceptible the Royal Family were to typhoid.

Every day, health permitting, Leopold attended lectures with the other undergraduates. His special studies were political economy, languages and history; but he went to Ruskin's lectures on art, too, and never missed an opportunity of broadening his cultural background. Science also fascinated him and Acland saw to it that every facility was made available to him to follow that interest. He loved singing, and he

2 Marina Warner, *Queen Victoria's Sketchbook*, 1979, p. 121
3 HRH Princess Alice, *For My Grandchildren*, 1966, p. 10
4 ibid, p. 10

played the harmonium, accompanying his own hymn singing. He was no mean performer, and was well able to sing in public when the occasion seemed right.

Though his physical disability did not permit him to lead a fully normal life, he liked to entertain at Wykeham House, and undergraduates and men of distinction alike found a warm and friendly welcome there. He counted Ruskin, Max Müller, the great philologist, and the controversial Benjamin Jowett, the Greek scholar, among his friends. Outside the university, Gounod, Sullivan and Tosti were close companions, and through the Oxford Musical Club he met Hubert Parry. Chess was one of his favourite pastimes, and he was a regular attender both at the Chess Club and at the meetings of the Oxford Union Debating Society. Most of his undergraduate friends were drawn from Loder's Club, which was composed entirely of Christ Church men, and to which he belonged. Though unable to participate in any form of sporting activity on account of his haemophilia, he was an enthusiastic member of Bullingdon Cricket Club, taking a keen interest in all its activities.

In describing him as plain, Queen Victoria had done her youngest son an injustice. Though not very tall, he was a rather handsome young

Wykeham House

man with a most engaging manner. An American journalist described him
most aptly:

> He is a young man . . . rather small in stature, not more than five feet
> six inches in height, very slender, and animated in his movements,
> with a slight stoop forward when he walks. He looks eminently like
> an Englishman, and bears the marks of geniality in his face and
> manners. His eye is blue, his moustache diminutive and blonde, and
> his features are like those of the rest of his family, his nose being
> slightly aquiline, and his mouth small. . . . In his right hand he
> carried a slender cane, and on the fingers of his left hand, when he
> stroked his moustache, was observable a large number of gold rings,
> embossed, jewelled, and enamelled, evidently tokens of honour.
> Prince Leopold is as far removed as possible from what is known as
> the English cad or snob. He is not even a swell. He has nothing about
> his dress whatever of the loud style which young England affects.[5]

It was only natural that the Dean and his wife should take a special interest

left, Prince Leopold
(*left*) sits for a portrait
by W. D. Campbell at
Wykeham House;
right, Prince Leopold
with Princess Louise,
his favourite sister

5 Anon, *The Life of the Duke of Albany, The Scholar Prince*, 1884, p. 13

this page and opposite,
Three portraits of
Alice by Julia
Margaret Cameron,
1873

in this gentle and talented young man; only natural that his visits to the Deanery should become more and more frequent; for was not the Dean his mentor; was not the Deanery at Christ Church the hub around which the social life of Oxford revolved? And was not the Dean's wife sympathetic and understanding; and were not her daughters charming, gifted and very beautiful?

Alice's beauty had by now attracted the attention of another distinguished photographer. Having decided that the influx of tourists was now making Llandudno and undesirable resort, the family had cast about for a new centre. The Isle of Wight seemed an obvious choice. The Queen's frequent presence at Osborne made it an important social centre, and it was a haunt of yachtsmen, members of the Royal Yacht Squadron being a wealthy and privileged class. Above all, the presence at Freshwater of the Tennysons and Julia Margaret Cameron lent it a coterie atmosphere unequalled anywhere in the country.

Mrs Cameron was a most remarkable woman. At the age of forty-eight she had taken up the art of photography in a potting shed. M. S. Watts, the second wife of the artist George Frederick Watts, described the secret of Mrs Cameron's success as a photographer:

She used to say that in her photography a hundred negatives were

destroyed before she achieved one good result; her object being to overcome realism by diminishing just in the least degree the precision of the focus. Thus when a real success was attained, she was able to give to her work a poetry and a mystery far removed from the work of the ordinary photographer, far even from that of the very best who have followed her. While other photographs, after long aquaintance, weary the eye, hers remain always an abiding pleasure. She had much correspondence with Signor [Watts] on the subject of principles of composition, and quotations from his words were often written below her pictures.[6]

Watts was closely connected with Mrs Cameron's family circle and undoubtedly had a strong influence on her work. Her sister was married to Thoby Prinsep, and Val Prinsep, the painter, was their son. For many years Watts lived with the Prinseps, and he was a frequent visitor to the Isle of Wight.

Mrs Cameron was an indefatigable lioniser, who photographed many of the great men and women of her day. Her sitters included Trollope, Browning, Holman Hunt, Darwin, Herschel, and of course the Tennysons. It was her presence even more than that of Tennyson that drew people to Freshwater. She entertained at her house, Dimbola Lodge, and she joined the parties at Farringford, home of the Tennysons. She was a difficult woman to refuse, and under her influence the Poet Laureate was known even to join in the dancing and general merriment.

Alice had relatives in the Freshwater coterie. The Dean's cousin, Adolphus Liddell, had been a close neighbour of Mrs Cameron and her great favourite and idol, the poet Sir Henry Taylor, when he lived at Park Cottage, East Sheen. His son, also called Adolphus Liddell, described Henry Taylor: 'He wore a cape and wide-awake, an uncommon get-up in those pre-aesthetic days. . . . He was a very tall man, though he had rather a stoop, with a very fine head and a long grey beard, and a somewhat languid, dreamy expression. . . . He could make himself very agreeable, and was popular with my mother and the other ladies of Sheen, while the men were inclined to scoff at his unlikeness to the ordinary type.'[7] Of Mrs Cameron he wrote: 'She had an intense devotion for great men in general, and Henry Taylor in particular. From what I can remember her devotion must have had its drawbacks, as she not only larded on the butter very thick, but took almost entire possession of her idol. . . . Mrs Cameron had

6 M. S. Watts, *George Frederick Watts: The Annals of an Artist's Life*, Vol. 1, 1912, p. 207
7 A. G. C. Liddell, p. 4

Alice's father by Julia Margaret Cameron*

such indomitable resolution and utter indifference to snubbing, that I fancy the idols, or at any rate their families, often found her worship somewhat excessive.'[8]

The house at East Sheen was very near to the home of another of the Dean's cousins, Augustus Liddell, who was Deputy Ranger at Richmond Park. At one time the Duchess of Gloucester, one of the daughters of King George III, spent a whole summer in his house, so that Augustus was as much accustomed to mingling with royalty as the Dean. Later he became Ranger in Windsor Great Park. He was an excellent shot and in later years was often in the company of the Prince of Wales. When Adolphus Liddell started spending his summers at Cowes, where his friend Captain Legard owned a 45-ton schooner called the *Kohinoor*, Augustus took a house nearby. Soon Adolphus Liddell junior fell victim to Mrs Cameron's camera. Augustus, on the other hand, was a keen amateur photographer himself, and so developed a special rapport with her.

8 ibid, p. 5

Alice's family began renting a house on the Isle of Wight regularly, and immediately found themselves in a congenial environment there. Before long, Mrs Cameron began photographing various members of the family. As a lioniser, she naturally found herself drawn to the Dean, but Alice, too, was an excellent subject for her camera, and perhaps her fame as 'Alice in Wonderland' lent her additional charm in the kindly woman's eyes. One of her photographs of Alice is strongly influenced by G. F. Watts' portrait of his child-bride Ellen Terry, entitled 'Choosing'. Like Ellen, Alice is seen in profile against a romanticised background of flowers. On 24 April 1873 Charles Dodgson called to see the Dean on business, and Mrs Liddell took him into the drawing-room to look at photographs. 'Alice showed me the large ones Mrs Cameron had done of them,' Dodgson recorded. He himself was an old friend of Mrs Cameron, and had photographed her with her two little boys. He did not entirely approve of her style, nor she of his. Dodgson had written to his sister Louisa of Mrs Cameron's pictures, 'Hers are all taken purposely out of focus. Some are very picturesque—some merely hideous—however she talks of them as if they were triumphs of art, *She* wished she could have had some of my subjects to do *out* of focus—and *I* expressed an analogous wish with regard to some of *her* subjects.'[9]

The close of the year 1873 was marked by a significant event in the lives of the family at the Deanery. Lorina became engaged. Her fiancé was William Baillie Skene, younger son of Patrick George Skene of Edinburgh and Pitlour House, Strathmiglo, Fife. He had matriculated at Corpus Christi College, Oxford, on 3 March 1856 at the age of seventeen years, and had been an exhibitioner from 1858 until 1860, when he gained his Bachelor of Arts degree. He took his Master of Arts degree in 1863, and was a Fellow of All Souls College, Oxford from 1864 until the time of his marriage.

William Baillie Skene inherited substantial estates from his father. These included not only large holdings of land in Strathmiglo, Auchtermuchty, Portmoak, Orwell and Abernethy, but also in Sutton, Wareham, Orlestone and New Romsey. Most of his lands and properties were let out, but he went in for sheep farming at Pitlour. However, he was at heart a true academic and deeply entrenched in the way of life at Oxford. Ultimately he became Treasurer at Christ Church, maintaining that office until his death.

9 M. N. Cohen, p. 66

Patrick Skene, Lorina's father-in-law*

The excitement of the girls at this, the first wedding in the Dean's family, was considerable. In view of a recent bereavement on the Skene side of the family it was decided to make the wedding a quiet affair, but for all that it was carefully planned and attended by a great many people. Alice, of course, was to be a bridesmaid, and so were Edith, Rhoda and Violet, and their dresses were planned with infinite care.

The wedding took place in the Cathedral at Christ Church on Saturday 7 February 1874. Lorina, on the arm of her father, looked very beautiful. The Brussels lace which adorned her dress and which her mother had given her was extremely valuable, and the gown was trimmed with natural orange blossom. The bridesmaids' dresses were of Chinese silk and eau de nil. The reporter from the *Oxford Times* was quite carried away by the splendour of it all:

10 14 February 1874

A more beautiful morning than that which favoured the occasion of this auspicious marriage, and added splendour to the bridal procession could not well be imagined or wished for. The dull cheerless fogs of the previous day had, during the night, been transformed into a coating of hoar frost, which covered the venerable pile in which the ceremony was to take place. At an early hour the sun burst forth in splendour, and the beautiful rays of light, as they reflected upon the white and glittering surface of the morning frost, added lustre to the opening day. Then in pleasant and beautiful relief the parti-coloured dresses of the ladies placed the finishing touches upon nature's lovely picture, and the procession, on its way to the Cathedral, formed such a scene of beauty as would have stirred the inspiration of poetic genius and poetic power.[10]

A red carpet had been laid out along the whole route from the Deanery to the Cathedral, and little girls from the Bluecoat school lined the walk with flowers in their hands. Friends of the family thronged to Christ Church to witness the bridal procession, the ladies attired in their most elegant gowns. At 11.45 am Lorina emerged from the Deanery leaning on her father's arm. Alice and her remaining sisters followed closely behind. Next came Harry, Eric and Lionel; and in the group of relatives and

Pitlour House, Lorina's home*

friends who then followed came Prince Leopold, with Alice's great-aunt Mrs Fellowes on his arm.

All along the route ladies and little girls strewed flowers before the bride's feet. The service, which was choral, was conducted by Archdeacon Clerke, the Sub-Dean, the Warden of All Souls, and the Rev. William Wren Liddell, Alice's uncle. Afterwards the family returned to the Deanery for the wedding breakfast, and then the happy couple left for the Continent, seemingly carrying with them the good wishes of all Oxford.

The list of wedding gifts was impressive. The Members of the House presented a magnificently mounted writing cabinet and book, containing the names of all the subscribers. Prince Leopold gave a beautiful wall mirror with oxidised silver enamel and four matching candlesticks. The Dean gave a despatch box, and the Archbishop of Canterbury a family Bible. The Students of the College gave a picture of the marriage of the Virgin, and Gathorne Hardy gave antique vases. Lady Rothschild gave a gold antique bracelet of considerable value, and Lady Anstruther a card tray set with onyx stones. The bridegroom, who had given Lorina an engagement ring of emeralds and diamonds, now added a splendid gold and pearl bracelet. And there were many more gifts besides.

Tears are never far away on occasions such as this, and while Alice was happy for her sister, it would have been impossible to ignore the fact that this marked the parting of the ways for a trio who had formerly been inseparable. Rhoda and Violet would be less affected by their sister's departure, for the age gap meant that they had not spent so much time in Lorina's company. But now Alice and Edith drew together in an ever-increasing bond of love. Though William Baillie Skene, or 'the laird' as he came to be known in family circles, lived at 39 Broad Street in term time, Lorina would naturally spend much of her time in Scotland from now on.

The other major family event of the year was the raising of the Barony of Ravensworth to an Earldom on 2 April 1874—a date which delicately avoided All Fools' Day. The Dean had always been close to his cousin, Henry Thomas Liddell. Though the latter was some fourteen years his senior, they had much in common, notably a keen interest in the Classics. Though *The Times* described him as a minor poet, it was to be said that he was very minor indeed. Apart from his translations of Horace, his little volume *The Wizard of the North, The Vampire Bride and Other Poems*, published in 1833, represents virtually his entire poetic output. Nevertheless, he was a good parliamentarian, who frequently spoke on the Tory side in the House of Commons until his father died of gout in 1855 and he inherited the title. Now he became Earl of Ravensworth and

Baron Eslington, but it was a title he did not live long to enjoy, for he died suddenly at Ravensworth Castle on 19 March 1878, leaving five sons and eight daughters.

Though Dodgson had been largely out of touch with Alice and other members of the Liddell family in recent years, he had continually opposed the Dean in College affairs, and had published his controversial views in a series of clever squibs. In the main these had been generalised, but he had now moved into an area of more personal conflict. In 1872 he published a monograph *The New Belfry at Christ Church, Oxford*, under the thinly disguised transposed initials D.C.L. The governing body had decided to create a direct approach to the Cathedral from Tom Quad by cutting an archway, called by its critics 'the tunnel', and to relocate the bells from the Cathedral tower over the staircase of the Hall. The bells were cut free from the stonework by a 'trench' and housed in a plain wooden case. In his squib Dodgson derided this wooden belfry, calling it a *Lexicon*, likening it to a tea chest and claiming that it had given a new impetus to Art in England. 'Already an enterprising maker of bonnet-boxes is advertising "the belfry pattern": two builders of bathing machines at Ramsgate have followed his example: one of the great London houses is supplying "bar-soap" cut in the same striking and symmetrical form: and we are credibly informed that Borwick's Baking Powder and Thorley's Food for Cattle are now sold in no other shape.'

Liddell had accepted all Dodgson's taunts in dignified silence: but in 1873 Dodgson published *The Vision of the Three T's*, a parody of *The Compleat Angler*. This squib took the form of a dialogue between an angler and a hunter who converge on the pond in the centre of Tom Quad and in the intervals of angling sing the 'Ballad of the Wandering Burgess', the burgess being Gladstone, who since his defeat in the Woodstock election had variously represented South Lancashire and Greenwich. Many of the Dean's cultural and architectural projects were satirised, even the performance of Bach's *St Matthew Passion* that he had arranged for a paying audience of twelve hundred in the Cathedral. Dodgson's 'Bachanalian Ode' beginning, 'Here's to the Freshman of bashful eighteen', was a direct reference to this occasion.

But most offensive to the family at the Deanery were the hints that Mrs Liddell was seeking noble, even royal husbands for her daughters. Describing the fish in the Christ Church pond, Dodgson wrote:

The Common kinds we may let pass: for though some of them be easily Plucked forth from the water, yet are they so slow, and withal have so little in them, that they are good for nothing, unless they be crammed up to the very eyes with such stuffing as comes readiest to hand. . . . I will say somewhat of the Nobler Kinds, and chiefly of the Gold-fish, which is a species highly thought of, and much sought after in these parts, not only by men, but by divers birds, as for example the King-fishers.

Alice may even have felt some implied criticism of herself in this squib, for she and her sisters had entered into the scheme of playing Bach in the Cathedral with enthusiasm, helping out with the secretarial tasks and in particular with the ticket allocation. Ruskin had written to her, 'I'm delighted with my ticket—please express my gratitude properly to the secretaries—what darlings they must be to think of me.' On 20 March 1873, the very day when the music was played, Ruskin wrote again to Alice:

I am sure I shall like to hear you telling me about the music—or about anything else you like to tell me—much better than any music (unless you would sing it without all the organs and trumpets and showmen and things). But even in that bright historical light I'm afraid I shall never come to feel Bach more than wonder of Wonderland. But I'll come of course—on any pretence—being ever your Faithfullest servant.

Dodgson wrote of the occasion, 'I did not go. I think it a pity churches should be so used.' He objected not only to the principle, but also to the notion of paying to go into church. In 1874 he took the offensive again, with *The Blank Cheque: A Fable*. This time he was attacking, with justification, the decision of Convocation to leave the matter of building a new Examination School on the site of the Angel Inn entirely to a nine-man committee, who would put the work in hand without further consultation. What was not justified was a serious attack on Mrs Liddell herself. She was thinly disguised as Mrs Nivers, representing, with her husband the Vice-Chancellor, in a very real sense the U *Nivers* ity. 'Her broad, good-humoured face wreathed itself into a sunny smile as I entered and we were soon embarked on that wayward smooth-flowing current of chat about nothing in particular.' She goes on to complain of her husband's habit of taking in boarders—a sly reference to Gladstone and Gathorne Hardy, both of whom stayed at the Deanery:

'He says it looks respectable, and that they talk so well, they make the House quite lively. As if *I* couldn't talk enough for him!'

'It isn't that!' muttered John. 'It's—'

'They're well enough sometimes,' the lady went on (she never seemed to hear her husband's remarks).

Liddon, Pusey, Stanley and many other leading favourites of the Liddells were held up to ridicule, but Mrs Nivers remarks, 'They're a set of dear good boys on the whole: they've only one real Vice among them.' Small wonder that Alice's family took offence.

During that same year another Oxford squib was published. This time it came from a different hand, and Dodgson as well as the Liddell family was lampooned. The squib was called *Cakeless*,[11] and was written by an undergraduate called John Howe Jenkins. It took the form of a drama, and, hinting that William Baillie Skene, Lorina's husband, was not wealthy enough to please the Dean and his wife, centred round the triple marriage of Ecilia, Rosa and Psyche (Alice, Edith and Rhoda).

Ecilia comes to her parents, Apollo and Diana, and announces that she wishes to marry:

> *You always wished that I should marry one*
> *Or Prince, or Peer, or else a Member's son.*
> *The last have I at length securely trapped,*
> *And in the toils of courtship firmly wrapped.*

Her bridegroom is revealed as Yerbua, Aubrey Harcourt, grandson of the Earl of Sheffield, and son of the Member for Oxford. Diana is delighted with this news:

> *My blessings on you daughter! would that she*
> *Who's gone before had made a match like thee.*

Rosa's bridegroom is Rivulus, alias Lord Brooke, an undergraduate who ultimately became Earl of Warwick. Psyche's match is even more splendid:

> *I've trapped a Prince, the youngest of his race,*
> *Of tender flesh, but yet of handsome face.*

11 See Appendix II

The reference to Leopold is all too obvious. At the wedding breakfast Apollo proposes a toast:

> *Another bride before them went;*
> *Her money must be well nigh spent.*
> *May these for ever moneyed be.*

Just as the wedding is about to begin, Kraftson (Dodgson) intervenes. The British Library copy has a contemporary note that Dodgson had been rejected.

> *Kraftson:* 'I do protest against this match, so let me speak.'
> *Apollo* (irate): 'Strip, strip him, scouts! This is the knave we seek.'. . . .
> *Rosa:* 'Take him through trench and tunnel to the chest,
> Nor ever leave the cursed fiend at rest.
> Leave him in Wonderland with some hard-hitting foe,
> And through the looking-glass let him survey the blow.
> Confine him in the belfry, not in Peck
> And make him sign at pleasure your blank cheque.'

Dodgson as a Student had been relatively immune from disciplinary action. Not so John Howe Jenkins, who was merely an undergraduate. He was sent down for his part in the affair.

DREAMING AS THE SUMMERS DIE

In a Wonderland they lie,
Dreaming as the days go by,
Dreaming as the summers die.

Through the Looking-Glass

ON 7 APRIL 1874 Prince Leopold came of age. In honour of the occasion Parliament voted him an income of £15,000 a year, and at the same time he was made a Member of the Privy Council. Usually there were sharp criticisms of expenditure among the Royal Family, for Parliament had not forgotten the irregular habits of the sons of George III. But such was Leopold's reputation that the resolution was received most favourably in the House, and went through to win approval without a division.

In the summer term he had a serious illness and was confined to Wykeham House for several weeks. Afterwards Sir Robert Collins, the Prince's tutor, wrote to Dr Acland: 'I don't know what we should have done without you at Oxford the whole time the Prince has been there, but especially have I reason to be grateful to you for all you have done during the last two months.'[1]

Worse was to follow. Eighteen months later, when the Prince travelled to Osborne for Christmas, he developed typhoid, and it was later discovered that the cause lay in the drainage at Wykeham House. During the Prince's absence that summer, the drains had been connected without authority to the main drainage of the town, with results that could so easily have proved fatal to the frail young Prince.

Alice and her family waited in desperate anxiety for news of the young man. A letter from the physician to King Leopold to Sir Robert Collins, written on 21 January 1876, underlined the seriousness of his condition: 'Your kind note this evening has done away with what little hope I was beginning to feel from the fact of his having lasted so long . . .

1 J. B. Atlay, p. 367

155

Prince Leopold at Oxford

one has felt it almost impossible to hope. It is indeed a most harassing time.'[2] Leopold's friend F. W. Meyers remarked that the 'sight of the Prince's look of brave patience and Ruskin's look of yearning melancholy made me feel as if they two typified to me all that the world contains of dignity, delicacy and sadness.'[3] As for Alice's father, he wrote to the Prince, 'Your friends here, than whom I am sure you have none warmer, have watched from day to day with trembling anxiety the accounts of your health.'[4]

It would appear from a letter from Collins to King Leopold's Equerry, Yorke, that symptoms of haemophilia were also causing anxiety. 'Thank God that the bleeding has ceased and that the weakness does not

2 HRH Princess Alice, *For My Grandchildren*, 1966, p. 16
3 ibid, p. 17
4 ibid, p. 17

increase,' he wrote.[5] Mercifully the Prince recovered gradually and was able to return to Oxford to complete his studies.

That unlucky satirist, John Howe Jenkins, was not wrong when he suggested that Prince Leopold was romantically attached to a daughter of the Dean. But the object of Leopold's attentions was not Rhoda, the Psyche of his drama: it was Alice.

Just when the feelings of liking and regard between them developed into something stronger cannot be said with any certainty. They were frequently thrown into each other's company, but then so too were all the family. Their love of music, art, literature and languages was a natural bond, but these interests were also shared by Edith, Lorina, Rhoda and Violet. All the girls were beautiful, though Violet was still too young for romantic notions. But a romance blossomed between Alice and the Prince, though it was carefully kept a secret by the Liddell family. As feelings deepened between the two young people, the subject of matrimony constantly recurred.

And now, so far from proving herself the 'King-fisher' that some people imagined, Mrs Liddell demolished the proposal from the outset. The Queen was known to expect all her sons to marry princesses, so that Alice was ineligible from the start. The Dean was now a man of considerable substance, but he had a lot of children to provide for. He and his wife had settled £8000 on Lorina when she married, from which she would reap an annual income. They would do the same for Alice. It was a comfortable sum, but hardly princely. In a sense, moreover, the Dean and his wife were acting *in loco parentis* to the Prince while he was in Oxford, and it was unthinkable that they should betray the Queen's trust by giving encouragement to notions of matrimony between their daughter and her son.

There were certain circumstances which may have inclined the young people to imagine that the Queen might relent. Leopold was most unlikely to succeed to the throne. He was only fourth son, and the Prince of Wales had in any event produced children of his own. Leopold's steady conduct, hard work, sympathetic public image and academic ability had all endeared him to the Queen. He had exhibited certain qualities possessed by none of his brothers, and in his patronage of the arts he resembled his father closely. He had earned the title 'scholar prince'. Above all there was the delicate state of his health to consider. Perhaps this might make the Queen more willing to indulge his wishes.

5 ibid, p. 16

Matters were still unresolved when the Prince finished his studies in the summer of 1876. This looked like being an auspicious year for the Liddells as another marriage was now in the offing. Harry, perhaps surprisingly, had not inherited the Dean's academic ability. He did not go to university, nor was he cut out for the army: he had little interest in horses and did not seek the excitement that a military career seemed to offer. He was pious and charitable, but his dislike of academic pursuits ruled out a career in the Church. The lifestyle of a country squire seemed much more suitable. In short, there was only one thing to be done, and Harry did it. On 13 June 1876 he married an heiress. His bride was Minnie Cory, second daughter of the late William Cory of Devonshire Place House, who had died in 1867, and whose substantial fortune derived largely from mining interests.

And now Alice and her sisters had another very special secret. Edith had decided to become engaged and planned to announce that fact at the beginning of Commemoration week. The girls' time was now almost exclusively taken up with chatter about what they would all wear for the wedding, who should be invited, where the couple would go for their honeymoon, and other such matters. Perhaps Alice felt a twinge of regret that she had as yet no wedding to plan; but she was deeply attached to her sister, and was very happy for her.

Edith's prospective bridegroom was in fact the 'Yerbua' of John Howe Jenkin's satire, *Cakeless*. He was the only son of Edward William Harcourt of Nuneham Courtney and Stanton Harcourt, who was High Sheriff in 1874 and Member of Parliament for Oxford from 1878–85, and for Henley Division from 1885–6. In June 1849 Edward Harcourt had married Lady Susan Holroyd, daughter of the second Earl of Sheffield. Besides Aubrey, who had been born on 16 August 1852, they had only one other child, Edith, who on 27 October 1875 had married the twelfth Earl of Winchelsea and Nottingham.

The *Oxford Times* described Nuneham Courtney, to which Aubrey Harcourt was heir, as 'One of the finest and most beautiful country seats in England,'[6] as undoubtedly it was. Its two creators were men of very differing tastes and temperaments. The first Earl Harcourt had been born into the world of Dryden and Pope, and had sought orderly nature. A founder of the Dilettanti Society, he had been Lord of the Bedchamber to George II. He had spent many years abroad as an Ambassador, and had a reputation for fine apparel. His plan for an ordered landscape involved

6 23 April 1904

Nuneham Courtney

moving a whole village, an episode which Goldsmith recorded in *The Deserted Village*.

The Second Earl was influenced by Rousseau. He called in Capability Brown who remodelled both house and gardens. His romanticised landscapes contrasted with the formal vistas of the first Earl. With lush meadows and hanging woods, he created a setting which looks like nature unadorned. Later Earls added to the house and gardens, and without a doubt it was in Aubrey Harcourt's day a splendid heritage.

Prince Leopold arrived in Oxford for Commemoration week on Friday 16 June. That evening he attended a meeting at the Provincial Grand Lodge of Oxfordshire Freemasons, of which he was Master, before proceeding to a banquet at the Clarendon Hotel. Saturday was spent fairly quietly, the only formal engagement being a concert given by the Musical Society of Wadham College. On Sunday morning the Prince went to hear the Bishop of Oxford preach, and in the evening he went to the Cathedral to hear Jowett preach in the Cathedral. Everywhere he went, Alice was with him, always accompanied by her mother or sisters.

After the evening service a large crowd collected in the Broadwalk to watch the Prince promenading with Mrs Liddell and her daughters. It was a fine evening, and the *Oxford Times* reported: 'Owing to the presence of His Royal Highness and the mildness and brilliancy of the weather, this time-honoured promenade was more largely patronised than has been usual of late years, and many striking and handsome toilettes were worn by the ladies.' Only one thing marred the afternoon. While the family had been sitting in Church, Edith had suddenly felt unwell and had had to go home and retire to her room.

On Monday there was a procession of boats on the Isis, which drew large crowds. Leopold watched from the Loder Club Barge with Alice and her sisters; but Edith was still indisposed. That evening the University Ball was held in City Buildings: it was attended by three hundred and forty people. In charge of the arrangements was Charles Foster, husband of Alice's former governess, 'Pricks'. The ballroom was the Corn Exchange, now splendidly transformed, with maroon drapes eight feet high on the walls, finished with blue and gold cord. There were gilt girondelles with brackets for wax lights and bouquets, and drapes of tarleton, lace, cord and tassels. In the centre was a regal crown, Bible, sword and sceptre. The banqueting room looked elegant, with white and gold panels and huge baskets of flowers. 'A charming effect was added to the presence of the room by a pyramid of ice-blocks, which further greatly cooled the atmosphere,' wrote the *Oxford Times* reporter.

Violet, drawn by W. E. Miller, 1876*

Mrs Liddell and Alice were in the Prince's private party, for whom a charming small room had been prepared, but Aubrey Harcourt appeared without his bride-to-be, for she was still indisposed. Nor was Edith present on the following day when the Prince joined the party on an excursion by water to Nuneham. The Queen sent a telegram asking why the engagement had not been announced, for she knew nothing of it. But by now it was realised that Edith was suffering from measles.

That year's Encaenia at the Sheldonian Theatre was a splendid pageant. All the University was in academic dress. Once again the *Oxford Times* reporter was quite carried away: 'The entrance of Mrs Liddell, wearing an elegant robe of dark green and cream colour, accompanied by two young ladies, was the signal for a hearty cheer for "The ladies in pink", as typified by the Misses Liddell, who were wearing charming toilettes of the most delicate rose. . . . A storm of applause greeted one of the younger daughters of the Dean of Christ Church, who was most elegantly attired in pale pink, and wore a broad-brimmed hat lined with black velvet, the tasteful effect of which may be imagined.'

As the clock struck twelve, the great gates opened and the procession advanced. Prince Leopold, bronzed and handsome, was wearing the gown of DCL over the naval officer's uniform, crossed by the blue ribbon of the Garter and adorned with numerous decorations. When the Vice-Chancellor presented the Prince with his diploma, the crowds cheered and sang 'For he's a jolly good fellow'. It was a proud and emotional moment, especially for Alice as she watched the young man who had come to mean so much to her.

That evening the Prince attended the ball at Christ Church with Alice and Mrs Liddell. It was a fitting climax to a wonderful week. Next day he left Oxford.

Since the preceding Sunday, Edith had had to keep to her room. Everybody felt sorry for her, including Alice, despite her preoccupation with the Prince. She had missed all the fun, all the excitement.

Suddenly, on Sunday 25 June, Edith began to complain of severe pain. Dr Acland was sent for at once. He in turn immediately sent for Sir James Paget from London, but Acland already knew the terrible truth, without that eminent man's confirmation. Edith was going to die. She had peritonitis, and at that time there was no remedy. Nothing could now be done except try to alleviate the terrible pain and wait for the end. She died on Monday afternoon.

The family was stunned. Their fortunes had never been higher and Edith's illness had seemed trivial. They could not believe that she had been taken from them, young, beautiful, happy and with everything to live for. The autumn wedding she had planned so happily would never happen. The wedding peal would be replaced by the death knell. In her closet hung the beautiful dresses, identical to her sisters', that she should have worn during commemoration week: the ball gowns, the rose pink dress for the Encaenia. They would never now be worn.

They sought relief by making plans for the funeral. The details to Messrs. Elliston and Cavell, the undertakers, were absolutely specific. There were to be none of the ordinary gloomy symbols of mourning. No scarves or hatbands were to be worn. The funeral, a strictly private affair, took place on Friday 23 June, and Prince Leopold arrived from London in time for the service.

The canons and choir waited at the door to the Cathedral for the procession to arrive. The Prince, that frail young haemophiliac who all his

life had had to avoid strenuous activity, was one of the foremost
pallbearers, with Dr Acland leading on the other side. The coffin was
draped with a white pall, on which there were two wreaths, including one
from the Queen. Immediately behind came the chief mourner, Aubrey
Harcourt. Only a few days before his future prospects had seemed so full
of promise. Now, instead of waiting for his Titian-haired bride at the altar
rail, he walked beside her cold, sad corpse.

Behind him came Alice, Rhoda and Violet, dressed in virgin white, like
bridesmaids at a wedding. Following on behind were the parents and
young Lionel. Next, Lorina, her husband, and Harry, followed by the
Fellowes, aunt and cousin of the Dean; and finally came Aubrey
Harcourt's father, his uncle, Sir William Vernon Harcourt, and an
assortment of family members, plus the devoted Robert Collins.

After the service came the interment in the family vault—Edith was
the first to be buried there. It was in a somewhat secluded spot called the
Verger's garden, to the south-east of the Cathedral, and approached
through an ornamental door. At the conclusion of the ceremony, so many

163

lovely chaplets of white roses, camellias and lilies were placed upon the coffin by the mourners that it was completely submerged in flowers. Prince Leopold, who appeared profoundly affected throughout the ceremony, laid a magnificent wreath of white roses on the coffin.

It was impossible to remain unmoved by the pathos of Edith's death. Sir James Paget, who had been called in for a second opinion in her last hours, wrote to Acland: 'This is surely the saddest thing that we have known among all the sadnesses that our calling has brought us to the sight of—a very tragedy. Nothin seems wanting for the perfection of sadness, and one cannot discern, in any of this world's hopes, a gleam of consolation.'[7]

The grief of the family was terrible. Sir Thomas Acland let them have the use of his house at Holnicote, where they all stayed for about three weeks. To his co-lexicographer, Robert Scott, the Dean wrote, 'We are all better, though what some of us had gone through, both in actual watching, and still more in terrible anxiety, cannot soon be overcome.'[8] As for Alice, she never really got over the terrible shock of Edith's death. They had been so very close, and the end had been so sudden and tortured. Though she lived to be a very old woman, Alice could never speak of Edith's death without being overcome with emotion. The lips still trembled, tears still stung the eyes; and those who were closest to her, knowing how sad it still made her, carefully avoided the subject.

Later a stained glass memorial window by Burne-Jones was placed in the east end of the south choir aisle of the Cathedral; but Alice wanted a personal memento. From Holnicote she wrote to their old friend William Richmond asking him if he would paint a portrait of Edith. He had been travelling about Cornwall, but the letter eventually caught up with him and he replied, 'I shall be delighted to try and do something of your poor sister, if you will send me any photographs, etc., that you care for, I will at once set to work and do what I can, I have felt very much indeed for you.' He was indeed much affected by the tragedy, recalling the child whom he had painted in 'The Sisters'. In later years he described how Edith 'in the gravity of whose demeanor an imaginative onlooker might fancy some premonition of the tragedy which awaited her—died in the dawn of her womanhood, under peculiarly pathetic circumstances. One Sunday "the happiest of the happy", she was receiving the joyous congratulations of her friends on her engagement to Mr Aubrey Harcourt, on the next she lay dying of appendicitis.'

7 H. L. Thompson, p. 257
8 ibid, p. 258

The St Catherine window in St Michael's
Chapel in Christ Church Cathedral, dedicated to
Edith by Burne-Jones

The photographs were forwarded to Richmond, and on 9 May 1877 he wrote to Alice, 'I have finished the little picture and send it off to you the day after tomorrow. . . . It has been a great pleasure to try and do you a little 'poem' of your poor sister and in doing it I recollect one of the happiest periods of my life. . . . I have made her looking towards "The Light".'

Alice responded immediately, telling him how much she liked the picture. 'I sincerely hope it may continue to give you pleasure,' he wrote back. 'As I know that the question of payment in such cases is often difficult, to prevent your asking I tell you that if you pay £70 to The Union Bank, Argyle Place, it will repay me.'

The life of the Liddell family now began to return to some sort of normality. There was new life in the family, but fresh bereavement also.

Harry's wife Minnie had borne him a son, born on 29 March 1877, and baptised Henry Lyon Liddell. Only two months earlier that grand old woman, Lady Pleasance Smith, Alice's great aunt, had died at the remarkable age of a hundred and three, having remained in possession of her faculties to the end. In December 1872, as she neared her hundredth year, she wrote Alice a five-page letter in an excellent hand, which shows how active an interest she had in current affairs: 'There was also in Monday's *Times* an excellent speech of the Lord Chancellor's (Sherborne) on the value of a good education not merely as a means of acquiring wealth that we place at a Banker's, but the wealth of a rich well-cultivated *mind*. . . .' Despite the clarity of her letters she ends on a note of apology: 'I am ashamed of my letter dear Alice—yet can write no better and am thankful I can see large objects and prospects—I now say farewell and am always your affectionate auntie.'

The following year saw the death of two cousins of the Dean, the Earl of Ravensworth and Lady Williamson. And on 11 October 1879 Alice's grandmother, Lorina Reeve, died also. She had endured more than half a century of widowhood, and her chief delight had been her children and grandchildren. Her visits had been pleasurable, and she had gone out of her way to avoid giving trouble to anyone. Of the arrangements for her own funeral she wrote: 'It is my wish that my funeral may be of a very private nature and that no hatbands be worn and that it may be attended by such of my children as may find it convenient to do so but I desire that they should not come from any distance for the purpose being assured of their affection towards me without any such mark of the same.' Mrs Liddell received a bequest of a thousand pounds, plus a portrait by Oakeley and all the ornaments, furniture and china from her mother's drawing-room. She was also given various items of jewelry, and Alice, along with all the other grandchildren, received ten pounds with which to buy a memento.

Prince Leopold had gone to Italy immediately after Edith's funeral. He was in need of some form of regular occupation and Disraeli wrote to him on 25 August 1876 suggesting that he might consider assisting the Queen with her despatches. In particular he felt that the Prince might help in foreign affairs. He wrote:

Your Royal father's criticisms on the draft despatches submitted to the Queen, I know, were of much moment, and frequently adopted by the Ministers. You could keep an unbroken précis of important despatches, and you would occasionally draw up memoranda of your own views as to the questions at issue. In this manner, you would, in due course, obtain such a knowledge and command of affairs, as to find great interest and excitement in life, and critical occasions might even occur, when your talents and acquirements might be appealed to for the public service of the nation.'[9]

The Queen had hitherto been unwilling to allow any of her sons to participate in this way in affairs of state; but Disraeli had considerable influence with her, and she saw the good sense of his arguments. As Leopold tackled these often tedious tasks, he exhibited a mature judgment and conscientious approach which encouraged the Queen to lean more and more on this, the youngest of her sons.

In 1877 the Prince took up residence in Boyton Manor in Wiltshire, where he often entertained his Oxford friends. Soon Disraeli attempted to intervene again on Leopold's behalf. The Queen had so far failed to deviate from her insistence that all her sons should marry princesses. Now Disraeli suggested to her that Frances Maynard, a seventeen-year-old auburn beauty, though not a princess, might make a suitable bride for him. The Queen accordingly invited her to Windsor.

Frances did in fact have royal blood in her veins, for her mother was directly descended from Charles II and Nell Gwynne. At the age of five years she had inherited substantial estates and an income of thirty thousands pounds a year. But Leopold declined to consider her at all. Perhaps he was still too much preoccupied with another young woman with no royal blood who had a special place in his heart. Instead, Frances married Lord Brooke, the Rivulus of *Cakeless*, and a great friend of Leopold's. The Prince of Wales signed the register at their wedding, and Leopold was best man.

Since Lorina's marriage Alice had taken a greater share of responsibility in organising the family's social life. It was she who in February 1874 had written to G. F. Watts about the family plans for meeting him in the Isle of Wight. He replied: 'The plan you propose could be very agreeable and I will do my very best to ensure its being carried out. I shall be much engaged in Town all the Spring and Summer but must run down here occasionally and I think the matter might be managed, agreeably to your wishes.'[10] On 27 March he wrote to Alice again: 'Not being at Freshwater I have only just received your letter so could not reply

9 HRH Princess Alice, p. 23
10 and 11 Autograph letters in the private collection of the Marquess of Bath

left, A letter from
Alice to Sir Robert
Hadfield which she
wrote in 1932, giving
him her painting of
Christ Church
Cathedral*; *right*, The
Dean, painted by G. F.
Watts, 1876

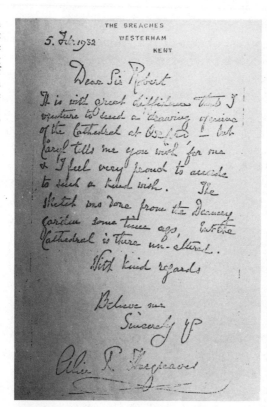

sooner. I will go to Freshwater unless prevented by accident. I meet with
the Dean on the 8th or 9th.'[11]

It was Watts who was chosen to paint a portrait of the Dean in 1875
in celebration of his twenty years of office, and the members of Christ
Church presented it to him at the Gaudy in the summer of 1876, shortly
before Edith's death.

The controversial Benjamin Jowett, whose salary had caused an
uproar in Christ Church, was another notable who received letters from
Alice. Immediately before the performance of Bach's *St Matthew Passion* in
the Cathedral he wrote to Alice:

My dear 'Alice'

You see what liberties I take with young ladies who write
notes to me. But have I not a vision of you and your sisters
singing little songs to Mrs Stanley more than twelve years ago?

I shall always remember (though I hardly remember

Christ Church Cathedral Oxford
1898

Alice's drawing of Christ Church Oxford

anything, being very old and stupid) that Bach was born in 1684 and Handel in 1685.

Fare you well, but not for ever, for on Thursday I hope to see you and other princesses.

Yours sincerely,

B. Jowett[12]

There were other letters, invitations to dinner and the like, between Alice and Jowett. On one occasion he invited her to dinner to meet the novelist George Eliot:

My dear Alice

Can I persuade you to give me the pleasure of your company at dinner either on Sat at 7.45 or Sunday at 7.30 and do you think that the Dean and Mrs Liddell can be persuaded to come with you?

I want you to meet Mrs Lewis: She is a very remarkable and interesting person even more so in Conversation, I think than in her books. It is a pleasant recollection to have known her.

Excuse the levity with which I address you. I must remind you that you began the correspondence, and remain Yours very sincerely,

B. Jowett[13]

By this time Alice had apparently buried all hopes of marrying Leopold. Now she sought to forget the sorrows of her blighted romance and Edith's death in a whirl of gaiety. The summer of 1878 was typical. The Liddells had taken a rented property called Waltham House in Queen's Road, Cowes, on the Isle of Wight. The King and Queen of Denmark and their daughter Princess Thyra with whom the Liddells mixed socially were staying next door at Lisburne House, home of the Countess of Lisburne. They enjoyed a summer of socialising and sport, and on 2 September they said goodbye to the Danish Royal Family across the tamarisk hedge and travelled by steamer and train to London.

Lord Colville had ordered a saloon for their exclusive use, and after dining at King's Cross they set out on the Scottish Express for Inverness. There they embarked for Skye, having written ahead to reserve rooms at the Portree Hotel, the only one on the island. They were accompanied by

---

12 and 13 Autograph letters in the private collection of the Marquess of Bath

only two maids and, since there were no porters, they had extreme difficulty in managing their luggage. Unfortunately it soon became apparent that all the rooms had been taken already, for their visit coincided with the judging of the Highland Games, and all Scotland seemed to have turned out for the occasion, 'creating a somewhat alarming crowd, and a still more alarming ring round the front door of the Hotel'.[14] There was nothing to be done but press on to Dunvegan Castle, where they were staying with friends. The weather was indifferent, but they managed to go on a number of excursions and patronised a typical Highland crofter with a visit. In the evenings, or when the weather was inclement, they played whist, billiards and Dumb Crambo, entertaining the company by singing and playing Gilbert and Sullivan on the piano in the smoking-room of the castle. One evening Alice and Rhoda astonished the company with conjuring tricks, a relic no doubt of the days when Charles Dodgson had taught Alice to practice sleight of hand. The highlight of the holiday was an excursion to Quirang, and the return by steam launch in torrential rain, with the wind and tide against them. In her diary, which she illustrated with amusing little sketches, Alice wrote: 'After some agony of fright suffered by Mama, and Lord Fortesque, who could see nothing, hear very little, and repeated the steering orders mostly wrong that he did hear, we were safely landed on the rocks at Grishinish, very wet, very cold, but very glad to be there once again.'

Before they returned to Oxford, Alice and the family paid a visit to Lorina's house at Pitlour, which was to be a home from home for them all for many years to come. The views from the house were superb, and Lorina and William Baillie Skene raised four daughters and a son there, in isolated but idyllic surroundings.

14 Alice's personal diary

THE STAR OF PERFECT WOMANHOOD

His heart stood still in sudden trance:
He trembled with a sweet suspense—
All in the waning light she stood,
The star of perfect womanhood.

'Three Sunsets'

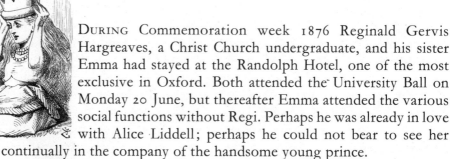

DURING Commemoration week 1876 Reginald Gervis Hargreaves, a Christ Church undergraduate, and his sister Emma had stayed at the Randolph Hotel, one of the most exclusive in Oxford. Both attended the University Ball on Monday 20 June, but thereafter Emma attended the various social functions without Regi. Perhaps he was already in love with Alice Liddell; perhaps he could not bear to see her continually in the company of the handsome young prince.

On Wednesday 7 July 1880, Regi wrote to his best friend, Arthur William Ridley:

My dear Ribsy,

You will be glad to hear that you have succeeded in saying a clever thing at last and that I am engaged to Alice Liddell. I don't think I need say any more, as from what you know I think you will be able to form some idea of my happiness, it is worth all I have suffered a good many times over. Ah how I wish you could be happy in the same way. It was settled yesterday and the next letter I am going to write is the one we talked about to my cousin to throw him over for the 12th, I hope at that time to be at Cowes 'sailing on the summer seas' with her. I am afraid I shall not see you now before I leave town which will be about the 22nd, but I shall expect a letter, which I know will be full of good wishes for me, before then.

By the bye you need not repeat what I told you abroad. I don't think Lewie's example in that matter is a desirable one to follow.

Yours ever
Reginald Hargreaves[1]

1 Autograph letter belonging to Dr Jeffrey Stern

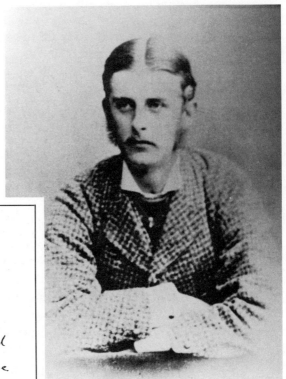

right, Reginald Hargreaves

Wed'y

JUNIOR CARLTON CLUB,
PALL MALL, S.W.

My dear Ribsy,
You will be glad
to hear that you have
succeeded in saying a
clever thing at last & that
I am engaged to Alice
Liddell, I don't think I
need say any more, but (as)
from what you know I
think you will be able
to form some idea of
my happiness, it is worth

The letter sent by Regi
to 'Ribsy', informing him
of his engagement to Alice*

Regi's family was wealthy and their history full of interest. His grandfather, born on 21 December 1871 and called Thomas because he was born on St Thomas's day, was the second son of John and Alice Hargreaves, who had a farm at Wheatley. Though their circumstances were relatively comfortable, Thomas received no education except that which he obtained at night school, being put out to work at an early age as a hand-spinner earning a penny a day.

When Thomas was old enough he was sent to Sabden, to learn calico printing. He proved hard-working and intelligent and was soon transferred to Broad Oak, and in 1801 he became a partner in the firm which was now called Fort, Hargreaves and Co. He married Margaret, daughter of Benjamin Wilson of Baxenden, by whom he had two daughters, Alice and Helen, and a son called John, all born at Oak Hill, the house which he himself had built. When Margaret died he married Nancy, daughter of John Hoyle of Haslingden. For her he built a new house called Oakenshaw, where they had five sons: Thomas, Lawrence, Benjamin, Robert and Jonathan. All these six sons of the family were at one time engaged at Broad Oak.

In 1811 the firm fell into serious financial difficulties, having accumulated debts of a hundred thousand pounds. The company was bailed out by friends who loaned some thirty thousand pounds, allowing all liabilities to be cleared within two years; but the shock of what had happened led Thomas Hargreaves to dissolve the partnership. He appointed a new partner, the designer Adam Dugdale, a man of talent who had married his elder sister, Mary.

The firm now moved into a period of unprecedented prosperity, due partly to the sophistication of its chemical and mechanical processes, and partly to the beauty of its designs, which enjoyed a remarkable vogue. Two of the sons, Lawrence and Thomas, decided to go to Glasgow University before joining the firm, but in 1822 Lawrence died of typhoid. The bereaved father wrote: 'I have lost Lawrence, the pride of my house, and might have been the staff of my old age.'[2] Within two months he too was dead, and of the same disease. His son Benjamin wrote of him: 'His leading mottoe seemed to be honour and integrity, which he carried out in every transaction of life. His discreet sound judgment was at the command of all who sought his advice, and his kindliness of nature made him ever ready to shelter and protect the oppressed.'[3]

The firm was well able to continue, even without the leadership of

2 Benjamin Hargreaves, *Recollections of Broad Oak*, 1882, p. 52
3 ibid, p. 53

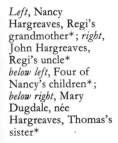

Left, Nancy Hargreaves, Regi's grandmother*; *right*, John Hargreaves, Regi's uncle*
below left, Four of Nancy's children*; *below right*, Mary Dugdale, née Hargreaves, Thomas's sister*

Thomas Hargreaves. Besides his partner, Adam Dugdale, there were enough sons to carry on. In recent years two other sons had been born, William in 1815, and James in 1820. Fortunately the finances of the family were now ample, so that William was able to proceed in due course to King's College, Cambridge, and James to King's College, London. Neither of these sons showed any interest in the family business, William turning his attention to politics, and James to botany, astronomy and music.

Jonathan, who had been born in 1810, was of a less academic turn of mind. He was educated by the Reverend Allen of Clitheroe, afterwards joining the firm and working his way up through the drawing department and laboratory, until he became a junior partner in 1832. By this time Benjamin Hargreaves had left the firm to engage in philanthropic pursuits, and Thomas had died of consumption in October 1825.

The death of Adam Dugdale in 1838 left only Robert and Jonathan to run the business. In 1846 Jonathan became engaged to be married to Anna Maria Harland, second daughter of Christopher Harland of Ashbourne, Derbyshire. They married in 1849 at Oak Hill.

Matters proceeded smoothly in the firm until 1854, when Robert Hargreaves died from injuries sustained in a riding accident. After his death Broad Oak could never be the same. Jonathan felt his isolation particularly keenly. His brother Benjamin wrote of him:

Jonathan was of a quiet turn of mind, very much liked by the employees because of his mildness of disposition and non-assumption of severity. He was most punctual in his rounds of supervision, and everyone seemed to know the time of his appearance amongst them, so much so, as to have been not inaptly compared to the regularity of clockwork. It could scarcely be expected that his was the spirit to contend with business in all its

A nineteenth-century
view of Lyndhurst

phases, and the anxieties of a large concern that had engaged the assistance of several active, zealous partners, but had never one too many for the work to do.'[4]

Jonathan managed to dispose of the business without detriment to the employees who relied on it for their livelihood. He then bought a magnificent country house called Cuffnells, in Hampshire, and moved there with his family in 1856, though always retaining the fixed intention of returning to Oak Hill. But circumstances were against it. He was in somewhat uncertain health, and the damp climate which had proved so favourable to the family business had been unsuitable for his condition.

By now Joni and Anna had three children: Fanny Helena, Emma Caroline, and Reginald Gervis, Alice's future husband. Reginald was a few months younger than Alice, having been born on 13 October 1852. His mother was a romantic figure, fond of writing, an avid reader of romantic novels, and an amateur artist of taste and talent. Her drawing master was Copley Fielding, and later his brother, Newton Fielding. Anna continued with her lessons for a year after her marriage, and she collected his paintings.

Regi was still only seven years old when Anna and Jonathan invited the Bishop of Lichfield to stay with them at Cuffnells. The Bishop held the key to admission to Eton, where they were both determined that Regi should go. But shortly after the visit the Bishop sent them a letter in which he said: 'I doubt not that you have judged rightly, in determining not to place your boy at Eton so soon as you had intended.'

In 1862 the family went abroad for the sake of Jonathan's health. For a while this afforded him temporary relief, but he was suffering from the same dreaded illness that had carried off his elder brother Thomas: consumption. On 27 January 1863 he died in Rome. Sadly the family returned to this country with his remains. In February he was interred in what was to become the family grave in the churchyard of Lyndhurst Parish Church. Inside the church Anna erected a very lovely monument in his honour.

Regi went to Eton in the autumn of 1862, and on 10 September 1864 John Lonsdale, Bishop of Lichfield, wrote again to Regi's mother: 'I should like Reggy to be placed under Mr Cornish's care, if you could be satisfied in respect to his house.' Regi was a well-behaved boy, but he was no scholar. He hated Latin and Greek and did not even care for French,

4 ibid, p. 141

though in later life he developed quite a taste for it. Inevitably he preferred the cricket pitch to the classroom, and it was there that he excelled. Most important of his friends at Eton were his cousin George Meyrick, son of his mother's sister Fanny, and Arthur Ridley. When George's father died in 1896, he became a baronet. Arthur was a month older than Regi, and was a great-grandson of Sir Matthew White Ridley, second baronet. His father was Nicholas James Ridley, a clergyman, and he had two elder brothers. His skill at cricket and athletics was even greater than Regi's, and he was in the Eton First Eleven in 1870 and 1871. He also represented Eton at rackets.

Regi seems to have entertained wild hopes of getting to Oxford at the end of 1869, but he was not up to it. Ridley matriculated at Christ Church on 25 November 1871, and Regi followed suit on 23 May 1872. He was the most delightful young man imaginable, but he was simply not a great academic, and took a long time plodding through his undergraduate work. Though Ridley got his B.A. degree in 1876, Regi did not manage it until two years later.

Anna Hargreaves lived just long enough to see Regi safely embarked upon his career at Christ Church. She died at Cuffnells on 15 November 1872, and her remains were interred in the family grave at Lyndhurst. Later her children raised a memorial plaque to her beside that of her husband, in the sanctuary of Lyndhurst Parish Church. They added two inscriptions: 'God is the strength of my heart and my portion for ever', and 'Her children arise up and call her blessed'.

Anna had never really recovered from the loss of her husband, and to her children she wrote: 'I leave my blessing to my dear children and may God bless and keep them. I ask them to hold in loving remembrance the memory of their excellent father who was the purest and most unselfish man I ever knew and to remember his beautiful life and character as their best inheritance.'[5] Her sister Lady Gervis was appointed Reginald's guardian.

Regi was now head of the family; but his mother's death did not make him master of Cuffnells, for that was his already, under the terms of his father's will. Jonathan had left Anna £500, the use of Cuffnells free of rates and taxes for life, and an income of £1500 a year, provided that she remained a widow. On attaining the age of twenty-five years Reginald would inherit Cuffnells, and after his death the estate was to pass to Regi's eldest son. The two daughters, Fanny Isobella and Emma Caroline, were

5 Anna Hargreaves' will, Somerset House

to receive £12,000 each, held in trust until they reached the age of twenty-five.

In 1870, Fanny had married Willoughby Edward Bryan, eldest son of the Rector of Cliddesden, near Basingstoke. An Oxford man, Willoughby had taken his B.A. degree in 1867. On 24 September 1878 Emma married Robert Henderson, who later became a director of the Bank of England. He was of Scottish descent and could trace his ancestry back to Patrick Henderson of Borrowstones, born in the year 1600. Robert Henderson's home was Sedgwick Park and his estates extended to some 624 acres, including a ruined castle. When Robert Henderson acquired the estate he greatly extended the house, which had magnificent views of St Leonard's Forest on the north and east, and on the south side a wide prospect of the Sussex Downs extending from Beachy Head to Selsey Bill. All the Hargreaves had inherited from Jonathan and Anna a keen interest in horticulture, and when Emma Henderson married, she turned her attention to creating a superb garden. From the house one looked down on to a semicircular terrace, framed with yew hedges on the homeward side, lined with seating, and finished with a pair of bronze athletes. Beyond was a miniature lake, called by Emma's children 'the White Sea', beautifully landscaped with fine shrubs, exotic plants and superb trees. Still further

The memorial to the Hargreaves at Lyndhurst Parish Church*

179

below lay the great wooded park, ending in the distant prospect of the Downs. The skill that Emma showed in planning and creating such a garden was truly remarkable.

Alice and Regi were married on Wednesday 15 September in Westminster Abbey by special licence, that special prerogative of the upper classes, enabling them to marry without the banns being read. Dean Stanley, the old family friend, performed the ceremony, and Dr Stainer played the organ. At three o'clock Reginald was waiting with his friend Arthur Ridley, his best man, when Stainer began his voluntary and the door opened to reveal the bridal procession. Alice, leaning on the arm of her father, looked very lovely. Her dress was of rich silver brocade and white satin, and the front was covered with valuable old Spanish point lace, the gift of her mother. Sprays of natural orange blossom looped back her magnificent tulle veil, and on her head was a circulet of diamonds, the gift of Robert and Emma Henderson. About her throat was a superb diamond and pearl pendant, Regi's gift to her, and pinned to the front of her bodice was a horseshoe-shaped brooch sent as a wedding present by Prince Leopold.

Alice was followed by her four bridesmaids, Rhoda, Vio, her cousin Maud Fellowes, and George Meyrick's sister. All four were identically dressed in cream-coloured cut plush bodices over Madras muslin skirts with capotes of old gold plush. Each carried a bouquet of gardenias and yellow daisies, and each wore on her bodice an olive branch of pearls and diamonds, the traditional gift from the bridegroom to the bridesmaids. After the ceremony the couple retired to the sacristy and signed the register, leaving the Abbey to the strains of Mendelssohn's 'Wedding March'. Afterwards a reception was held in the Jerusalem Chamber, following which the couple left for Sedgwick Park, where they were to spend a few days with Emma Henderson, who was expecting the first of her four children, before going on to Scotland. Thereafter the couple went on to tour Spain: honeymoons in those days were more leisured affairs than they are today.

Alice's wedding caused a great deal of excitement in Oxford. The bells of the Cathedral rang for an hour to coincide with the ceremony, and many and costly were the gifts that were showered on Alice and Reginald. Lorina and William gave them some fine silver plate, and Harry and his wife Minnie gave a gold sugar bowl and spoon. From Vio, Eric and Lionel came a fine Japanned screen, and from Rhoda a pearl initial brooch. Alice's Uncle Charles, the engineer, gave diamond earrings, and Mrs Mary Foster, alias 'Pricks' the governess, gave a pair of candlesticks.

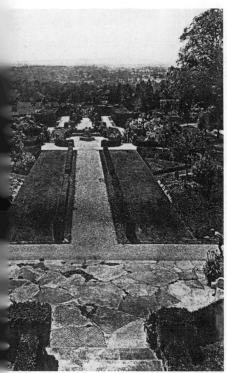

Emma Henderson, Alice's sister-in-law (*above right*)*, and the garden she created at Sedgwick Park where Regi and Alice began their honeymoon

Dean Stanley

Aubrey Harcourt, no doubt still thinking of the happiness he might have enjoyed with Edith, gave the couple a silver tea kettle and liqueur stand. He never did marry, but spent his life alternating between local social functions, and yachting and gambling in the casinos of the world. When he died in 1904 in Monte Carlo he left a fortune of £130,000, all of which passed, with his title and property, to his uncle.

The list of wedding gifts is enormous;[6] but there is one significant omission: the name of Charles Dodgson. Yet Dodgson did, in fact, give a wedding present to Alice, jointly with his old friend Thomas Vere Bayne, who was a frequent and welcome visitor at the Deanery. Their gift consisted of a gilt-framed original watercolour painting of the Great Quadrangle at Christ Church. It was painted by R. P. Spiero and was a well-executed piece of work measuring $19\frac{1}{2}''$ by $12\frac{1}{2}''$; Alice treasured it until her dying day.

And what of Prince Leopold? He had sent a fine gift, which Alice wore on her wedding gown, and it symbolised his good wishes for her future. But he who had walked in Lorina's wedding procession with the Dean's aunt on his arm, he who had hastened to Oxford to help carry Edith's body to its last resting place, did not come to Alice's wedding. He was not abroad, nor was he detained on some major royal function. While Alice was walking up the aisle of Westminster Abbey, he was at the Aboyne highland gathering in Scotland. The inference is obvious: he simply could not bear to see her being married to another man.

6 See Appendix I

THE HARGREAVES FAMILY

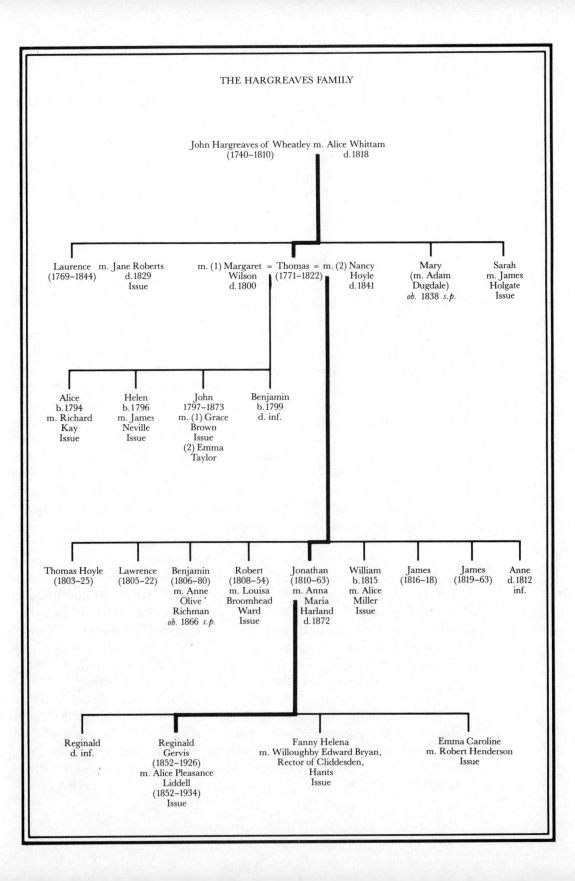

John Hargreaves of Wheatley m. Alice Whittam
(1740–1810)   d. 1818

Laurence   m. Jane Roberts   m. (1) Margaret = Thomas = m. (2) Nancy   Mary   Sarah
(1769–1844)   d. 1829   Wilson   (1771–1822)   Hoyle   (m. Adam   m. James
               Issue   d. 1800   d. 1841   Dugdale)   Holgate
                                                                            ob. 1838 s.p.   Issue

Alice   Helen   John   Benjamin
b. 1794   b. 1796   1797–1873   b. 1799
m. Richard   m. James   m. (1) Grace   d. inf.
Kay   Neville   Brown
Issue   Issue   Issue
                                (2) Emma
                                Taylor

Thomas Hoyle   Lawrence   Benjamin   Robert   Jonathan   William   James   James   Anne
(1803–25)   (1805–22)   (1806–80)   (1808–54)   (1810–63)   b. 1815   (1816–18)   (1819–63)   d. 1812
                           m. Anne   m. Louisa   m. Anna   m. Alice   inf.
                           Olive   Broomhead   Maria   Miller
                           Richman   Ward   Harland   Issue
                           ob. 1866 s.p. Issue   d. 1872

Reginald   Reginald   Fanny Helena   Emma Caroline
d. inf.   Gervis   m. Willoughby Edward Bryan,   m. Robert Henderson
                   (1852–1926)   Rector of Cliddesden,   Issue
                   m. Alice Pleasance   Hants
                   Liddell   Issue
                   (1852–1934)
                   Issue

CHILDREN THREE

Children three that nestle near,
Eager eye and willing ear,
Pleased a simple tale to hear.

Alice's Adventures in Wonderland

THE HOUSE and estate of which Alice now found herself mistress were of rare beauty. There were a hundred and sixty acres of rich Hampshire earth, some of the most fertile in the country. It had been referred to on a map of 1375 as 'Bocus De Cuffenore'. In 1784 it was bought by an important politician, George Rose, Privy Councillor, Chancellor of the Exchequer, a parliamentarian who had drifted into politics after being a midshipman in the Navy. At various times he was Member of Parliament for Lymington and for Christchurch, near Bournemouth. He was Secretary to the Treasury under Pitt, Vice-President of the Board of Trade, and Joint Paymaster General of the Forces. Besides being favoured by frequent visits by the Prime Minister, Sir George also entertained King George III and Queen Charlotte on several occasions when they were travelling between Weymouth and London.

It was Rose who made the principal additions to the house, comprising a drawing-room forty-two feet by twenty three, connected with a dining-room of similar proportions by an oval vestibule: these rooms formed the south front. A major feature was an orangery a hundred feet long and twenty-three feet wide. A balcony ran the length of the upper storey, and the rear of the house afforded magnificent views over the Solent to the Isle of Wight. The drawing-room, besides having the traditional wood panelling, had a frieze of peacocks, two feet deep, painted by an Italian artist. There was a large billiard room, and a grand staircase.

In 1831 the estate was bought by Sir Edward Poore, passing on his death to his widow. Regi's father acquired it in 1856. Even in Sir George Rose's day the gardens were particularly fine, with luxuriant American shrubs, and one enormous rhododendron bush, measuring fifty paces round, with all the branches proceeding from a single stem. Anna and Joni Hargreaves had thrown themselves with enthusiasm into the task of

above, Cuffnells, the
home of Regi and
Alice after their
marriage, and *left*, seen
before George Rose's
extensions

A view from the foot of Alice's driveway in Lyndhurst*

enriching the garden, stocking it with a wide variety of plants, trees and shrubs from many parts of the globe. One of the features had been a 'wilderness', ideal for Fanny, Emma and Regi to romp in as children. There was also a small lake suitable for fishing, stocked with fish and water plants of exceptional quality.

One remarkable feature of the house was the so-called 'gold room' on the upper floor. This was the room which the King had slept in when he used to visit George Rose. It had been kept in exactly the same condition as when he and Queen Charlotte had used it, and it was the finest bedroom in the house, affording wonderful views from its huge shuttered windows. The principal feature of this room was a giant four-poster bed with a golden coverlet. The bed itself was gilded, and bore above it an inscription to the effect that the King had slept there. Though there was no hot water, the room had its own little porcelain basin, with gold-plated taps, and there were gold doorknobs and gold-plated handles. This room was never slept in, but to the end of Alice's life it was kept as a curiosity to show to visitors.

Cuffnells had a beautiful library. Relatively few books had found their way on to its shelves from Thomas Hargreaves, but there was a substantial number from Jonathan and Anna's time. Over the years Alice and Regi built up a very fine collection of books which reflected the breadth of their tastes. Many of the books were given to Regi by Alice, suggesting that she was the arbiter of taste in matters of literature and art. But even more belonged to Alice herself or were given to her by Reginald. The range of subjects included poetry, literature, art and music. There was a wide selection of books on travel, and some on forestry and horticulture. Sporting pursuits such as shooting and fishing were well represented, as were archaeology, architecture, ornithology and philosophy. The many books on religion included some by men well known to Alice, such as Jowett and Liddon. There was a biography of Dean Stanley by Prothero and Bradley, and a selection of his letters and verses. Pride of place was, of course, given to Liddell and Scott's *Greek Lexicon*, and there were large quantities of books on languages and in other tongues. A copy of *The Romance of Princess Amelia*, daughter of George III, suggests that his royal visits to their home had given Alice and Reginald a special interest in him.

A large staff was required to run a house the size of Cuffnells and to maintain the social prestige of its young owners. There was a special kind of hierarchy among the servants: the butler, the cook and the head housekeeper were considered a cut above all the rest, and took their meals separately in the housekeeper's room, while the rest ate in the servants' dining-room. Included among these were the head housemaid and two under-housemaids; two kitchen maids and a scullery maid; a laundry maid and two footmen; a ladies' maid and a ladies' maid/housekeeper. Later a boot boy was taken on as well. The outside staff comprised the coachman—later chauffeur—the groom and gardeners, quite apart from all the staff employed in the running of the farm, which was principally given over to dairy farming.

The running of the kitchen would have been a revelation to the modern reader. The table on which the food was prepared was made of solid wood, three inches thick. It was fifteen feet long and six feet wide. The fireplace was used for charcoal spit-roasting. The basting tray was four feet square. Copper pots, jugs and moulds had to be burnished regularly, the knives ground and the silver polished. Discipline was very strict and all the servants knew their stations. Alice exercised tight overall control, and through the senior staff she saw that the running of the house continued smoothly. It was exactly the situation her mother had brought her up for, and she brought precisely the right skills to her new way of life.

The journal which Alice kept of her honeymoon in Spain and later letters and diaries indicate the warmth of feeling and the tender teasing affection she felt for her new husband. As for Regi, he absolutely idolised his wife, and regarded her as the epitome of good taste and breeding. His marriage brought him all he wished for.

In a way Regi had been a surprising choice of husband for Alice. Her own idol had always been her father, and few men could of course compare to his intellectual stature. All her life she had mingled with men of academic distinction. Her father enjoyed the outdoors, liked riding, even hunting and walking; yet he was never an athlete. Leopold had been a very serious-minded young man, but because of his haemophilia he had been totally unable to indulge in strenuous pursuits. Alice herself had been trained to take an interest in absolutely everything, but her preferences had tended towards the academic and artistic. Yet the husband she had chosen was no scholar. Academic studies had been hard and uncongenial work to him. He was the nicest, kindest young man imaginable, and not totally unintelligent by any means; but intellectually he was simply not in the same league as Alice.

Regi was, however, well-favoured, many might say handsome. His kindly nature seemed to show in the gentle, sympathetic eyes. He had wit and humour, and he liked to dress in style. In every sense a gregarious and sociable fellow, he wanted to cut a bit of a dash socially. Both he and Alice were united in their desire to bring to Cuffnells the cream of society. Anna and Jonathan had pointed the way to this: their friends had included Charles Kingsley and his wife, who not only visited often but wrote long letters on such subjects as religion, art and the upbringing of children; Copley Fielding, Anna's former art teacher, who became a personal friend of Alice and Regi's, received letters and gifts of game from them, and often came to stay; Hamilton Aidé, the artist and novelist, who had been equally friendly with Alice's parents; Sir John Leighton, and many others. With Alice by his side, trained by her mother as an impeccable hostess, Regi was now well able to carry on and extend that tradition.

The sudden acquisition of wealth had brought its problems to some branches of the Hargreaves family. All the sons of Thomas Hargreaves, who had initially set the family on the road to fortune, were serious-minded and hardworking, perhaps because they were not far removed from their artisan beginnings. But the next generation was brought up to the notion of great wealth, and in some instances with no understanding of how to manage financial affairs. One of Jonathan's brothers, for example, produced four sons and four daughters, all of whom relied on

Arthur Hargreaves, Regi's cousin*

him absolutely to supply their needs. The child of one of his daughters wrote: 'Of course there were fearful rows about their extravagance, as when mother ordered from Truslove and Hanson no less than £45 worth of engraved writing-paper, mauve, gilt-edged and tastefully embellished with ivy-leaves; but these rows never lasted long. . . . When grandpapa died, his widow actually had to be shown how to make out and sign a cheque.'[1]

Some of the Hargreaves cousins thought nothing of hiring a special train if they missed the last one back to Oxford, or putting their own carriages and horses aboard and returning to university in style. It was the custom of the four sons of Jonathan's brother to hire a special train to take them and their entourage to Scotland for the season to shoot and hunt. And so matters went on for some sixty years. But after the First World War they began to realise that their finances were dwindling somewhat, and to economise, they contented themselves by simply adding a couple of saloon carriages to the back of the Highland Express. But that, too,

1 Charles Chevenix Trench, *My Mother Told Me*, 1958, pp. 26–7

eventually had to be cut out. One of the family, Guy Hargreaves, who had twice been Master of the South Berkshire Hounds, was glad enough in his old age to become Berkshire Rat Catcher.

The family had its eccentrics, too, though very amiable ones. One formidable lady, without male escort, but often with a grand piano which none of them could play, and always with a mahogany commode, toured India, Ceylon, China, Japan and North America with her sister and daughter, for whom she sought eligible husbands.

Regi, though an indulgent husband who spent money reasonably freely, avoided the pitfalls of over-extravagance and eccentricity. While Alice looked to the smooth running of the house, he kept an eye on the running of the estate. He was a keen sportsman, making up with his physical energy and adroitness what he lacked academically. Cricket was still his major preoccupation, and in this he was joined by his brother-in-law, Mr Willoughby Bryan, who also lived in Lyndhurst. The latter had had the misfortune to lose an arm, but it was said of him: 'He was a one-armed player, a good bowler, and a quite wonderful bat, for with a wrist of steel he could hit as hard as any man.'[2] Even as early as 1869 he had knocked up a score of fifty-five for the Gentlemen of North Hants versus the Gentlemen of South Hants. In due course Regi became President of Lyndhurst Cricket Club, the New Forest Cricket Club and Hampshire Cricket Club. In 1874 he had had a cricket pitch laid at Cuffnells, and a number of important local matches were played there, as well as at Bolton's Bench, where cricket had been played from 1828 onwards. Usually Regi captained the New Forest Club team himself, and it was he who encouraged Lord Londesborough, who owned a neighbouring mansion called 'Northerwood', to bring the Yorkshire County second eleven to play against them. From time to time he also led the New Forest side against them on their home territory at Scarborough.

Regi was a fine lob-bowler and a strong batsman of county class. He did not play regularly for Hampshire, but appeared in twelve matches between 1875 and 1885, scoring a total of 307 runs with a personal best of thirty-eight not out. Fourteen wickets fell to him over the years, and in one match he took four wickets for fifty-five runs. On that inglorious occasion in May 1883 when Surrey scored 650 runs against Hampshire at the Oval, Regi was on the defeated side.

Arthur Ridley was an even better cricketer. In *Hampshire County Cricket*, H. S. Altham wrote: 'The most distinguished cricketer who

2 F. E. Stevens, *The New Forest Beautiful*, 1925, p. 193

Princess Leopold's wedding dress

played for our county in these years was A. W. Ridley. A first-rate batsman of the true old Eton type, a superb fielder, especially to his own bowling, he was the last of the line of amateur lob-bowlers.' Ridley went on to play for Middlesex, where he enhanced his reputation still further.

Alice, however, had other matters with which to occupy herself now. On 25 October 1881 she gave birth at Cuffnells to a fine healthy son. Her father baptised him, following the practice he had established with his own children. The names that Alice chose for him were Alan Knyveton. From the start it was obvious that he was a fine, sturdy boy.

Prince Leopold did not choose a wife until some months after Alice's marriage. In the year that saw the birth of Alice's first child, he was created Duke of Albany, Earl of Clarence and Baron Arklow. A short time afterwards he met and was captivated by Princess Helene Frederica Augusta, daughter of His Serene Highness George Victor, Prince of Waldeck-Pyrmont. Queen Victoria readily assented to the match and *Punch* promptly published a 'Song for the Royal Betrothal':

> *Helen of Waldeck! Thou has won*
> *England's cultured and student son;*
> *Earnest ever at desk and book;*
> *His to rule with an eager heart*
> *Over the wide domain of Art;*
> *Thine to aid like a loyal Wife,*
> *All that's best in a Husband's life.*
>
> *Helen of Waldeck! When our strand*
> *Welcomes thee from the fatherland:*
> *When all the best farewells have rung*
> *On thine ears in the Teuton tongue:*
> *Trust us thou never wilt repine*
> *Leaving the land of haunted Rhine.*
> *Here is a greeting, frank and free,*
> *Waiting thee, Princess, over the sea.*[3]

The Victorian era saw nothing absurd in this pathetic attempt at a loyal tribute, which was well meant.

The wedding took place at St George's Chapel, Windsor, and the Prince personally expressed the wish that Alice should be present to witness the ceremony. To her mother he said that the entire family would be welcome, 'particularly Alice and Ina to witness my wedding in the nave of St George's. It would give me such pleasure to see them there.' He went on to speak with nostalgia of 'the dear old days' at Christ Church.

News of the approaching royal marriage threw Alice's mother into a flurry of activity. Assisted by Mrs Max Müller, she personally chose the present which was given to the Prince collectively by his friends at Oxford. It consisted of a beautifully designed set of old silver-mounted ornaments for the Prince's writing table. Besides the inkstand and candlesticks there was a mirror, an album bound in silver which contained the autographs of all the subscribers, and a silver frame containing a portrait of the bride. The mounting of the blotting-case was in dark blue velvet, bound with bands of old silver, delicately chased with figures and foliage. In addition the Christ Church Society presented a pair of chased silver candelabra, weighing 445 ounces.

The *Illustrated London News* described the bride's dress as 'one of the most novel and exquisite creations imaginable, and it is difficult to

3 November 1881

understand how it can have been so elaborately made, and yet could look as though it had never been touched by hands.' It was made of rich white satin, with small openings near the bottom of the skirt through which masses of myrtle and orange blossom could be seen. It was trimmed with *point d'Alençon* lace flaked with silver, and on the train large bunches of fleurs-de-lys stood out in relief.

The bridesmaids' dresses, eight of them, were almost as splendid, being made of thick white satin ornamented with flounces of pearled net. The dresses were made in Paris, and a little model showing the dress was seized on by Princess Beatrice, the Queen's youngest daughter. The bride's going away dress was of ivory stamped velvet.

After the wedding the couple went to live at Claremont, the magnificent house and estate given by Queen Victoria. There the Prince settled down to the life of a country squire, adding a lodge and a fine avenue of chestnut trees, and effecting a number of improvements. But he felt the need for other occupation, and soon embarked on a highly successful royal tour of North America.

On 8 January 1883 Alice gave birth to her second child, another boy. Only a few weeks afterwards, on 25 February, Leopold's bride gave birth to their daughter. Alice wrote at once, congratulating him on the birth and inviting him to be godfather to her new son. He replied at once from Windsor:

> Dear Alice,
> Many thanks for your very kind letter of good wishes on the birth of our little girl. The event is, as you can imagine, a source of great pleasure to us. It is very good of you asking me to be godfather to your boy, and I shall have *great* pleasure in being so. Please let me know what his names are to be. . . . Our child will probably be christened on Easter Monday, we mean to call her Alice.
> Yours very sincerely,
> Leopold

Alice's son was called Leopold Reginald, but to the family he was always known as Rex. Leopold's daughter had been born with greater ceremony, with Sir William Harcourt the Home Secretary keeping watch in the next room, just to make sure that the child was genuine. To the Prince he wrote: 'I trust that the infant Princess may remain all her life as lively and

left, Prince Leopold;
centre, His home,
Claremont; *right*, The
soldiers guarding
Prince Leopold's body
at the Villa Nevada

cheerful as I can testify to her having been in the first few minutes of her experience of this troublesome world.'[4] His wishes were fulfilled. Princess Alice, later Countess of Athlone, outlived all Queen Victoria's other grandchildren, and spent a lifetime in happy and devoted service as a much respected member of the Royal Family, dying in January 1981 at the age of ninety-seven.

On 15 February 1884 Prince Leopold attended an amateur concert at Esher in aid of the funds of the village national schools, and sang 'The Sands of Dee' with such pathos that he had to give an encore. Soon afterwards bad weather made it advisable for him to go to Cannes, where he travelled incognito as the Baron Arklow, and took up residence in the Villa Nevada. His wife, who was seven months pregnant, could not go with him. He attended a number of functions, including a Bachelors' Ball at the Mediterranean Club, and various garden parties and dinners. He took daily drives and went yachting with his host, Captain Perceval. His health appeared to have benefited considerably, and he was looking forward to travelling with the Queen to Darmstadt for the wedding of his sister Victoria. On Thursday 27 March he went at two o'clock to the *Cercle*

4 HRH Princess Alice, p. 8

Nautique to watch the 'Battle of Flowers' from the balcony over the promenade. Wishing to take part in the festival himself, he had arranged for the Baron Hoffman to call for him shortly after four o'clock. But at the foot of the staircase leading to his private room his legs seemed to give way under him, and he fell. He was carried instantly into the salon, where his doctor found that he had injured his knee. Dr Royle bathed and dressed the knee, which did not give much pain. He was taken by carriage back to the Villa Nevada, where he retired immediately to bed as a precaution. He dined and chatted with his host, but though he seemed to suffer very little discomfort, he was in a melancholy frame of mind and began to talk of his own death, and of the royal tombs at Windsor Castle. At about eleven o'clock that night Dr Royle read him to sleep and then prepared for a night of vigil in the Prince's room. Until about half-past two in the morning the Prince slept soundly. Then he was suddenly seized with convulsions, and in a few minutes was dead: the cause, a brain haemorrhage.

News of his death reached the Queen at noon on 28 March, and shortly afterwards the news reached his young widow at Claremont. Her grief can be imagined. The Prince of Wales was at Aintree when his telegram arrived, and it was he who had the unenviable task of travelling to Cannes to bring the body home.

They dressed the young prince in the violet satin frock-coat which he was to have worn to the Battle of Flowers, and laid him in a glass-topped coffin. It was ornamented with violet and white satin bows, and white lace was draped on top. The insignia of the Order of the Garter was placed on his chest. On his finger was the betrothal ring given him by his wife, and around his wrist the heavy gold bracelet that he always wore. The coffin, heaped with flowers, was taken by train to Cherbourg, and returned to England aboard the royal yacht *Osborne*. After lying in state at St George's Chapel and a most affecting funeral service, the Prince joined his ancestors in the royal vault. His son was born on 19 July 1884.

Alice was stricken at the news of Leopold's death. Though they had gone their separate ways, though each had sought and found a different kind of fulfilment with someone else, she could not help but be moved by the news of this tragedy. All the nation mourned him. What then must Alice's feelings have been as she lamented his death.

On 19 November 1887 Alice's third son was born at Cuffnells. As with Alan and Rex, he was christened by the Dean at St Michael's and All Angels, the Parish Church at Lyndhurst. His names were Caryl Liddell. Asked if the first name had anything to do with Carroll, Alice replied that it was simply a name from a novel.

By the time Caryl was born, Alan and Rex were already riding Tinker, the pony who was used to pull a little cart to collect up the dead leaves from the estate. All her boys were fine and healthy, and Alice was immensely proud of them. Her family was now complete. With her husband and her boys, and her fine house and estate, Alice had every reason to be happy.

And so she was; and yet curiously everyone who knew her commented on an air of sadness which was somehow never very far from the surface. However much she laughed and sang, however much she indulged that insatiable curiosity, the sadness was somehow always there. The family believed that the death of Edith was the cause of it, and certainly that had powerfully affected her. But a young woman with a husband and sons to live for does not grieve for a sister for ever, however much loved. Surely the reason ran even deeper than that. What seems to have happened was that the death of Edith and the parting from Leopold became inextricably interwoven in Alice's mind. A young woman as discreetly brought up as she could not speak openly of her blighted romance, and Edith's death alone was the reason she gave for the continuing melancholy of her attitude. And in the end renunciation was not enough.

Separation had been followed by death. Small wonder that she appeared forever sad.

Of course her feelings for Regi were a wonderful comfort to her. Though he had not won her easily, his perseverance had borne fruit and he had won not merely her hand but also her heart. Yet his inability to match her intellectually left her with a feeling of isolation which nothing could ever take away.

Alice*

ECHOES FADE

Long has paled that sunny sky:
Echoes fade and memories die:
Autumn frosts have slain July.

Alice's Adventures in Wonderland

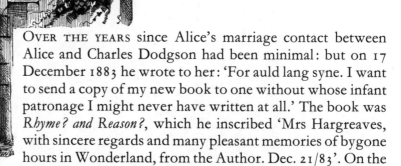

OVER THE YEARS since Alice's marriage contact between Alice and Charles Dodgson had been minimal: but on 17 December 1883 he wrote to her: 'For auld lang syne. I want to send a copy of my new book to one without whose infant patronage I might never have written at all.' The book was *Rhyme? and Reason?*, which he inscribed 'Mrs Hargreaves, with sincere regards and many pleasant memories of bygone hours in Wonderland, from the Author. Dec. 21/83'. On the day that he posted off her copy he wrote to her, 'Perhaps the shortest day in the year is not *quite* the most appropriate time for recalling the long dreamy summer afternoons of ancient times: but anyhow if this book gives you half as much pleasure to receive as it does me to send, it will be a success indeed.'[1]

Some fifteen months later Alice heard from him again:

Christ Church, Oxford
March 1, 1885

My Dear Mrs Hargreaves,

I fancy this will come to you almost like a voice from the dead, after so many years of silence—and yet those years have made no difference, that I can perceive, in *my* clearness of memory of the days when we *did* correspond. I am getting to feel what an old man's failing memory is, as to recent events and new friends (for instance, I made friends, only a few weeks ago, with a very nice little maid of about 12, and had a walk with her—and now I can't recall either of her names!) but my mental picture is as vivid

1 M. N. Cohen, pp. 560–1

198

as ever, of one who was, through so many years, my ideal child-friend. I have had scores of child-friends since your time: but they have been quite a different thing.

However, I did not begin this letter to say all *that*. What I want to ask is whether you have any objection to the original MS book of *Alice's Adventures* (which I suppose you still possess) being published in facsimile? The idea of doing so occurred to me only the other day. If, on consideration, you come to the conclusion that you would rather *not* have it done, there is an end of the matter. If, however, you give a favourable reply, I would be much obliged if you would lend it me (registered post I should think would be safest) that I may consider the possibilities. I have not seen it for about 20 years: so am by no means sure that the illustrations may not prove to be so awfully bad, that to reproduce them would be absurd.

There can be no doubt that I should incur the charge of gross egoism in publishing it. But I don't care for that in the least: knowing that I have no such motive: only I think, considering the extraordinary popularity the books have had (we have sold more than 120,000 of the two) there must be many who would like to see the original form.

Always your friend
C. L. Dodgson

An inscription from Lewis Carroll to Alice in *Rhyme? and Reason?*

Lewis Carroll's only drawing of the real Alice

Alice acceded to his request at once, though she apparently had some reservations about the publication of the little photograph of herself aged seven which Dodgson had pasted at the end of the original. On 7 March he wrote back: 'Many thanks for your permission. The greatest care shall be taken of the MS (I am gratified by your making *that* a condition!). My own wishes would be definitely *against* reproducing the photograph.'

Beneath the photograph referred to was the only surviving drawing Dodgson ever produced of the real Alice. Clearly he was not satisfied with his own draftsmanship and preferred the little photograph. But the drawing has a special poignant intensity and seems to give a rare insight into his feelings for the little child. In later years he drew many of his child friends, but not one of those drawings contains the emotion portrayed in his little vignette of Alice Liddell.

The book duly arrived on 21 March, but apart from the formal acknowledgement of its safe arrival, Alice did not hear from Dodgson again until 15 July when he wrote:

> After a good deal of casting about among various photographers and photozincographers, I seem at last to have found out *the* man who will reproduce *Alice's Adventures Underground* in really first-rate style. He has brought his things to Oxford, and I am having all the photographs taken in my own studio, so that no one touches the MS book except myself. By this method I hope to be able to return it to you in as good a condition as when you so kindly lent it me—or even better, if you will allow me to have it rebound before returning it. May I?

Whether the publication is a source of gain, or not, it is impossible to say: but if it is, I hardly like the idea of taking the whole profits, considering that the book is now *your* property, and I was thinking of proposing to send half of them to *you*. But a better idea has now occurred to me, which I now submit for your approval: it is to hand over the profits to Hospitals, and Homes, *for sick children.*

The following is the announcement which I propose to make (if you approve) at the beginning of the book, and also at the end of all advertisements of it:

'The profits, if any, of this book will be devoted to Hospitals, and Homes, *for sick children*: and the accounts, up to 30 June each year, will be published in the *St James's Gazette* on the second Tuesday in the following December.'

I hope to be able to return the book to you (or to send it to the binder, as you prefer) in about a week.

Alice approved in principle, but suggested a slight alteration to 'Children's Hospitals and Convalescent Homes for Sick Children'. Dodgson replied:

I adopt your emendation most gladly: it is very pleasant to think that you are thus connected with the facsimile edition. Of the existence of the original you were the chief, if not the only cause. You shall have the original back again in (I hope) exactly the state in which I received it, and (of course) one of the earliest copies of the facsimile. May I also have the pleasure of presenting one to your eldest daughter (even if she be *not* an Alice—which I think unlikely)?

By this time the pages had all been photographed, though Dodgson asked leave to keep the MS a little longer to compare the reproductions with the original. But all did not go as smoothly as he had hoped. On 11 November 1886 Dodgson wrote to Alice to explain the saga of events:

Messrs Macmillan recommended a certain Mr Noad, an excellent photographer, but in so small a way of business that I should have to *prepay* him, bit by bit, for the zinc blocks: and *he* was willing to come to Oxford, and do it here. . . . Mr Noad did a first-rate set of

> 7. Lushington Road,
> Eastbourne.
> Aug. 14 /85
>
> Dear Mrs Hargreaves,
> I adopt your emen-
> -dation most gladly: it is
> very pleasant to think that
> you are thus connected with
> the fac-simile edition. Of
> the existence of the original
> you were of course the chief,
> if not the only, cause. You
> shall have the original back
> again in (I hope) exactly the
> state in which I received
> it, and (of course) one of the
> earliest copies of the fac-simile.

A letter sent by Lewis Carroll to Alice

negatives, and took them away with him to get the zinc blocks made. These he delivered pretty regularly at first, and there seemed to be every prospect of getting the book out by Christmas 1885.

On October 18, 1885, I sent your book to Mrs Liddell, who told me your sisters were going to visit you and would take it with them. I trust it reached you safely?

Soon after this—I having prepaid for the whole of the zinc-blocks, the supply suddenly ceased, while 22 pages were still due, and Mr Noad had disappeared!

My belief is, that he was in hiding from his creditors. We sought him in vain. So things went on for months. At one time I thought of employing a detective to find him, but was assured that 'all detectives are scoundrels'. The alternative seemed to be to ask you to lend the book again, and get the missing pages re-photographed. But I was *most* unwilling to rob you of it again, and also afraid of the risk of loss of the book, if sent by post—for even 'registered post' does not seem *absolutely* safe.

In April he called at Macmillans and left 8 blocks, and again vanished into obscurity.

This left us with 14 pages (dotted up and down the book) still missing. I waited awhile longer, and then put the thing into the hands of a Solicitor, who soon found the man, but could get nothing but promises from him. 'You will never get the blocks,' said the Solicitor, 'unless you frighten him by a summons before a Magistrate.' To this last I unwillingly consented; the summons had to be taken out at Stratford-le-Bow (that is where this aggravating man is living), and this entailed 2 journeys from Eastbourne (my *personal* presence being necessary) and the other to attend in Court with the Solicitor on the day fixed for hearing the case. The defendant didn't appear; so the Magistrate said he would take the case in his absence. Then I had the new and exciting experience of being put into the witness-box, and sworn, and cross-examined by a rather savage Magistrate's clerk, who seemed to think that, if only he bullied me enough, he would soon catch me out in a falsehood! I had to give the Magistrate a little lecture on photo-zincography, and the poor man declared the case was so complicated he must adjourn it for another week. But this time, in order to secure the appearance of our slippery defendant, he issued a warrant for his apprehension and the constable had orders to take him into custody and lodge him in prison, the night before the day when the case was to come on. The news of *this* effectually frightened him, and he delivered the 14 negatives (he hadn't done the blocks) before the fatal day arrived. I was rejoiced to get them, even though it entailed paying a 2nd time for getting the blocks done, and withdrew the action.

The 14 blocks were quickly done and put into the printer's hands; and all is going smoothly at last: and I quite hope to have the book completed, and to be able to send *you* a very special copy (bound in white vellum, unless you would prefer some other style of binding) by the end of the month.

Dodgson finally received the first copy for his approval on 17 December

1886, and shortly afterwards Alice duly received her special copy. Apparently Alice invited Dodgson to be godfather to one of her sons, presumably Caryl, but he did not in fact accept, for reasons which are unknown. Nevertheless, they were clearly on very cordial terms once again. On 1 November 1888 Regi was taken to the College by Lorina's husband. In his diary Dodgson recorded: 'Skene brought, as his guest, Mr Hargreaves, the husband of "Alice", who was a stranger to me, though we had met, years ago, as pupil and lecturer. It was not easy to link in one's mind's eye the new face with the once-so-intimately-known and loved "Alice", whom I shall always remember best as an entirely fascinating little seven-year-old maiden.'

Alice's family commitments made her visits to Oxford infrequent, but she nevertheless maintained a keen interest in all that went on there. Her sisters, Rhoda and Vio, had largely taken over the role that she had previously adopted, helping Mrs Liddell with all the social engagements. Violet had studied art under Sir William Richmond, who had become Slade Professor of Art when Ruskin gave up the post in 1879. Under his tuition she became a very fine portrait artist, and produced fine oil paintings of both Alice and Lorina in the mid-1880s. The Dean had been made an Honorary DCL of Edinburgh University. Mrs Liddell was much

occupied with the Acland Memorial District Nursing Fund of which she was President and prime instigator, having been moved to start the fund by the death of her old friend Sarah Acland.

While Vio painted and sang to large public assemblies, Rhoda took up a remarkable hobby: woodcarving. She was not content with small items like ornaments and book-ends, but carved altar screens, tables and sideboards. She took rubbings of mirror frames and coffee tables which she admired, and used them in her own work. When Thomas Vere Bayne saw an item which Rhoda had carved as a wedding present for a friend, he remarked that it would almost be worth getting married to receive such a gift. He never married, but he got his woodcarving just the same.

Alice also enjoyed woodcarving, and she put her skill to excellent use for one charitable purpose. For years Christ Church had operated a mission to the East End of London, and early in 1889 Henry Parry Liddon delivered an impassioned appeal for funds for the building of a church to replace the rude hall which had hitherto been used. The Dean, too, added his own personal appeal when he preached in the Cathedral on St Frideswide's day. The Duchess of Albany, Leopold's widow, who had maintained the Prince's former friendship with the Liddells, laid the foundation stone. A considerable sum of money was raised, but it was insufficient to complete the building and the Bishop of London Fund agreed to contribute to the cost, provided that the freehold of the site was conveyed to the Ecclesiastical Commissioners. The Church, which was built by an architect named Willey, was opened on 15 July 1890, and a large number of members of the choir of Christ Church attended. Alice's contribution was a vestry door, which she carved herself, and which depicts St Frideswide, who reputedly preserved her honour from a royal lover by hiding in a pigsty, arriving in Oxford by boat. During the Second World War the church of St Frideswide, as it was called, was bombed, and was never rebuilt. But amid all the rubble Alice's door remained intact and was transported to Oxford, where it now stands in the Church of St Frideswide, Osney.

In 1889 Alice's father had enthroned the new Bishop of Oxford: this was only one of the many public duties he had had to perform over the years. The Dean was now a very old man, and although his health was still robust and his brain as active as ever, he began to feel that it was time to retire. As well as those duties arising from his position as Dean, he had been acting as Professor of Ancient History at the Royal Academy, and Trustee of the British Museum. Finally, on 8 August 1891, he wrote to Lord Salisbury, announcing his intention to retire. He wrote:

> You will believe that it is not without many searchings of heart that I have come to this conclusion. Christ Church has been my

A family group in the Deanery garden, *c.* 1885: *l to r, standing,* William Baillie Skene, Lionel Liddell; *seated,* Lorina, the Dean, Mrs Liddell; *front,* Violet, Alice, Eric, Rhoda

home (barring nine years at Westminster) for more than sixty years. But it is my affection for the place that induces me to take this step. I am now in my eighty-first year, and feel that my work ought to be committed to younger and more vigorous hands. I will not say that I am unable to perform the routine duties of my office. But I am conscious of various infirmities incident to advancing years, and I cannot now take such part in academical and other business as ought to be undertaken by a person in my position.'[2]

The date fixed for the Dean's retirement was Christmas 1891. The impending event brought many members of the family to Oxford, including Alice and Lorina. Dodgson had recently received a brace of grouse from Lorina, who still remained on cordial terms with him. In mid-November he was favoured with a visit from Princess Alice and her little brother Charlie, Prince Leopold's children. They were staying with the Duchess of Albany at the Deanery, and they went over to visit him in his rooms twice. Afterwards he wrote to Mrs Liddell:

> The honour I now covet is that a certain pair of young ladies should come over some day and take tea with me. I have a store of ancient memories of visits from your elder daughters, but I do not think that Miss Rhoda and Miss Violet Liddell have ever been inside my rooms. . . . If I were twenty years younger, I should not, I think, be bold enough to give such invitations: but, but, I am close on 60 years old now, and all romantic sentiment has quite died out of my life: so I have become quite hardened to having lady-visitors of *any* age!'[3]

They duly went; and a few days later, Lorina and Mrs Liddell also visited him in his rooms. And then word got around that Alice was coming to stay at the Deanery also. She received the following letter from him:

Christ Church, Oxford
December 8, 1891

My Dear Mrs Hargreaves,

    I should be so glad if you could, quite conveniently to yourself, look in for tea any day. You would probably prefer to

2 H. L. Thompson, pp. 266–7
3 M. N. Cohen, p. 873

Herkomer's portrait of the Dean

bring a companion: but I must leave the choice to you, only remarking that if your husband is here he would be ~~most~~ very welcome. (I crossed out most because it's ambiguous; most words are, I fear.) I met him in our Common Room not long ago. It was hard to realise that he was the husband of one I can scarcely picture to myself, even now, as more than 7 years old!

Always sincerely yours,
C. L. Dodgson

Your adventures have had a marvellous success. I have now sold well over 100,000 copies.[4]

Alice could not go to tea, but she went over with Rhoda for a short time. It was the last time she ever saw the man to whom she owed her immortality.

The Dean's leaving ceremonies were very moving. Although Herkomer had been working on a portrait of the Dean, it was not ready in

4 Caryl Hargreaves, 'The Lewis Carroll that Alice recalls', *New York Times Magazine*, 1 May 1932

time, and Mrs Liddell received it on her husband's behalf on a later occasion. There were many fine speeches and gifts, and a superb morocco-bound volume bearing the names of the Dean's well-wishers was also presented. Curiously, Dodgson's name was not there, but this must have been sheer accident. A letter he sent to Mrs Liddell expressed his sentiments:

> It is *very* hard to find words which seem to express, adequately, how strongly I feel the very *great* loss to the University, the College, the City, and to myself, involved in the going away of the Dean and yourself. We, as the Governing Body, have had a chief of such exceedingly rare qualities that it would be vain to hope that *any* successor can *quite* fill his place. I am sure that the whole of Oxford, and all the good and charitable work carried on in it, will suffer great and permanent loss by the absence of yourself. And, to *me*, life in Christ Church will be a totally different thing when the faces, familiar to me for 36 years, are seen no more among us. It seems but yesterday when the Dean, and you, first arrived: yet I was hardly more than a boy, then; and many of the pleasantest memories of those early years—that foolish time that seemed as if it would last for ever—are bound up with the names of yourself and your children: and now I am an old man, already beginning to feel a little weary of life—at any rate weary of the *pleasures*, and only caring to go on, on the chance of doing a little more work.[5]

Alice's parents and her two unmarried sisters now moved to Ascot Wood House, a leasehold property of enormous proportions and large grounds, not far from the home of Alice's brother. There they were to live out their days in tranquillity, still maintaining their social contacts, still keeping up with Oxford affairs. Some of their friends were now gone. The greatest loss outside the family had been Dean Stanley, who died in 1881, only a few months after he had married Alice and Regi. The Dean had been staying with Lorina when he heard the news. 'It is a sad privilege to survive,' he commented.[6] In 1894 the Dean's brother Charles died. During his distinguished career as an engineer he had built many railways, including the Taff Vale Line and the extension of the Metropolitan Line to Aylesbury, and in the Crimean war he had laid a cable from Varna to the Crimean Peninsula. He had been active to the last.

5 H. L. Thompson, p. 259
6 ibid, p. 259

During recent years Regi had been occupied with business matters relating to Oak Hill, the family house and estate in Accrington which he had inherited from his father. For some years it had been let, but had now become something of a white elephant, having stood empty and decaying for a decade. The town council, wishing to convert the estate to a public park, approached Regi, but regarded his asking-price of £10,500 as too high. Regi refused to budge, even though the grounds alone needed a minimum expenditure of £2000, but offered to donate £1000 if the purchase went through at his price. The park was duly opened by Regi on 22 May 1893, and with the Mayor and Corporation, and the town bands, he paraded through the streets, being hailed as a public benefactor. Yet not everybody applauded Regi's 'generosity'. One local paper pointed out that he had converted a rapidly deteriorating estate which had been a financial liability for ten years into gold, securing the best bargain he could for himself.

Alice's boys, meanwhile, were growing rapidly. All three of them went to Eton, like their father before them. In character, Alan resembled his father most closely. His daredevil streak emerged at an early age. Possessing boundless physical energy, he threw himself into every sporting activity and every adventure with tireless enthusiasm. He was a complete extrovert and possessed a flamboyant streak into the bargain. Everybody adored him, not least his mother. He was also the friendliest fellow imaginable, polished in his manner, and an absolute charmer.

Rex had an adventurous spirit, too; and there was a strongly competitive streak in him that led him into friendly rivalry with his brother. But though he was a fine, athletic boy, he rarely came out on top in these sporting activities. Academically, he had more of his mother in him than his father, and although he was a sound scholar rather than a brilliant one, he outpaced Alan. Caryl tended to compete less with his brothers in sport and physical combat, on account of the age gap between them. He was a much more introverted character, intellectually gifted, and with a keen interest in most forms of cultural pursuits.

Alice was absolutely devoted to her children, yet it must not be imagined that her management of them in their early days was significantly different from her mother's care of Alice and her brothers and sisters, except, of course, that Alice had fewer children. But a lady of Alice's social position did not involve herself in the hourly needs of her children, which were the concern of a nanny or governess, supported by nursery maids. Alice was content with three children, and had no wish to emulate her mother's state of almost permanent pregnancy. It is curious that Alice's sisters Rhoda and Vio never married, for both were beautiful, talented, and socially distinguished. But it was known in the family that one of them had been decidedly put off the idea of marriage by the sight of sisters and friends spending seemingly half their lives lying around on couches, waiting for the next offspring to arrive.

None of Alice's boys was unaware of their mother's affection for them, which manifested itself in the keen interest she took in all their activities—in their academic and sporting successes, and in the general development of their characters. They were never allowed to forget their social class. There was no hob-nobbing with the people in the village. Regi was daring enough to introduce a professional cricketer into the New Forest cricket team, but this man was not permitted to socialise with the rest of the team because of his inferior status. Artisans were not allowed to use the gentlemen's changing-rooms, much less join them for refreshments and conversation after the game. Good works and charitable acts were one thing, but Alice was acutely class-conscious. It was part of the life to which she had been brought up.

Cuffnells was a focal point for high society. There were parties, balls, and shooting parties. Regi was a crack shot and he received as many invitations as he gave. Lord Grafton regularly invited him over to Norfolk in the season, and Alice with him. 'I am so anxious you should come *home* to Euston,' Lord Grafton wrote to her once. They went to Scotland every year, too, for the sport, usually spending at least some of the time with Lorina and her family.

Leighton's famous mural in Lyndhurst Parish Church

A unique posthumous portrait of Lewis Carroll, by his
illustrator and friend, Miss E. Gertrude Thomson

Alice kept a Houseparty book, listing all the functions that went on
at Cuffnells, and the guests who came to stay there. Many were the
distinguished visitors who enjoyed the Hargreaves' hospitality. They
included the Duchess of Albany and Princess Alice—who might just
conceivably have qualified to sleep in the royal four-poster in the Gold
Room; Mr and Mrs Gladstone, who never forgot their affection for the
Dean and his family; Lord Londesborough; Sir William Harcourt;
Millais; and of course Lord Leighton, who had painted a remarkable
fresco in Lyndhurst Parish Church shortly before Alice and Regi were
married. Though Alice had exchanged life in the cultural centre of Oxford
for that of a country gentlewoman, it should not be imagined that hers was
a life of quiet retirement. All the family loved travel, and though Alice did
not always accompany Reginald, she enjoyed many tours to Switzerland,
Germany, and other European countries.

On 14 January 1898 Charles Dodgson died. A few days before he had

developed a cold, but bronchial symptoms soon made his breathing
laborious. He suffered relatively little. Some time previously he had
written: 'I sometimes think what a grand thing it will be to be able to say
to oneself, "Death is *over* now; there is not that experience to be faced
again."'[7] By his own wish he had a simple walking funeral and was buried
at Guildford, where the family home was situated. Many were the floral
tributes that were laid upon his grave, including one from Alice.

But Alice did not attend the funeral. She felt deeply the loss of her old
friend, who had never ceased to shower her with copies of his books and
Alice memorabilia. Gifts of the later years had included an ivory-handled
parasol, carved in the shape of Tweedledee and Tweedledum, which was a
unique and personalised item; the postage-stamp case which he had
invented; and the 'Alice' biscuit tin, manufactured in an 'edition' of
50,000 by Messrs Jacobs with Dodgson's permission, and now a most rare
and valuable item.

Saddened though she was by the news, an even greater sorrow had
recently overtaken Alice, for on 18 January her father died peacefully at
his home. Only eighteen months before, he and his wife had celebrated
their golden wedding anniversary, surrounded by their children, of every
one of whom they had cause to be proud, and by many old friends. Many
were the gifts that were showered on the couple on that occasion, but
none had been more appropriate than that of Mr Hamilton Aidé, once a
friend of Anna and Joni Hargreaves, and still a friend of Liddells and
Hargreaves alike. It was a picture called 'A Golden Sunset'. In accepting it
the Dean had said: 'So long as I live—it cannot be long—I shall look on it
with delight, though I feel that the golden glow will gradually fade into
darkness. I only hope that the twilight may be short, and that I may "cross
the bar" before the glow has quite vanished.'[8]

His wish was fulfilled, for he suffered no pain and was in full
possession of his faculties until the end. Only a few days before, Thomas
Vere Bayne of Christ Church had visited him, and had found him vaguely
unwell, Violet decidedly ill and Mrs Liddell with a swollen face, leaving
Rhoda the only member of the family in ordinary health.

On Friday 21 January the Dean's body was taken from Ascot Wood
House to Christ Church, where it was met by the Dean Paget and all the
canons in their robes. The procession preceded it to the Latin Chapel,
where it remained until the following day, when it was placed on a
catafalque draped in purple in the choir. Many distinguished men and

7 S. D. Collingwood, *The Life and Letters of Lewis Carroll*, p. 330
8 H. L. Thompson, p. 277

An illustration taken from the Charles Robinson
edition of *Alice*

women attended the funeral, and it was a comfort to Alice and the rest of
the family to see so many tokens of the universal esteem in which her
father had been held. Both the Queen and the Prince of Wales, as well as
the Duchess of Albany, were represented at the funeral, and all of them
sent wreaths. The Prince's wreath was of arum lilies, camellias, lilies of the
valley, white roses and lilac, flaked with myrtle, and bore a card on which
he had written in his own hand: 'For Auld Lang Syne. From an old Christ
Church friend, Albert Edward.' After the choral service the oak coffin was
lowered into the grave beside Edith's. Mrs Paget, wife of Dean Paget, had
personally decorated the grave by lining it with moss and evergreen,
stranded with white flowers.

Neither Violet nor Lionel was present at the funeral, the former
being too ill. Lionel was serving as HM Vice-Consul at Galatz in
Rumania. For the children of Henry George Liddell, the funeral marked
the end of an era. It was extraordinary that he and Dodgson should have
died within a few days of each other.

LIVING SEAS OF MEN

Anon a distant thunder shook the ground,
The tramp of horses, and a troop shot by—
Plunged headlong in that living sea of men—
Plunged to their death.

'The Path of Roses'

AFTER ETON both Rex and Caryl went on to Christ Church. Not so Alan. He had never been in any doubt about the career he wanted to follow and went instead to the Royal Military College at Sandhurst, from where he was gazetted to the Rifle Brigade as a second lieutenant. His arrival coincided with the centenary celebrations of the regiment, which was based in Dublin.

This new life of excitement and adventure suited Alan perfectly, and when he embarked on the SS *Orient* for South Africa in December 1901 he was frankly glad at the chance of getting in some active service. They reached Cape Town on 5 January 1902, and ten days later he was promoted lieutenant, fighting at Kronstadt. Peace was declared in June of that year.

Alan was immensely popular in the Battalion, partly on account of his physical prowess. Back in this country he played polo regularly. He was an excellent horseman and his horse called Spider, from the stables at Cuffnells, was reputed to be the biggest horse in the whole of Hampshire. Point-to-point riding was his speciality, and on this horse Alan won the annual regimental point-to-point four years in succession.

His service in South Africa, though brief, had won Alan the Queen's Medal and three clasps. In 1908 he sailed with the 4th Battalion to Malta. One of his major concerns was how to procure decent ponies for the polo club, and eventually he and his companions shipped their own mounts at a cost of £5 10s. each. Alexandria, Suez, Khartoum: such were the destinations he visited with the regiment. In 1913 he bagged a leopard on the Blue Nile. His only regret was that there was no time to go on into elephant country. When the Battalion moved on from Egypt to Karachi, they arrived in pouring rain to find barracks that had stood empty for six

Alan Hargreaves, wearing the Queen's clasp

months. For three days their baggage stood in the rain. The lesson in church on their first Sunday began, 'Why hast Thou brought us out of Egypt to this place where no water is?'

In the summer of 1913 Alan was on leave, and he spent it in Muttra for the pig-sticking. He was one of the fortunate few who had his own motor car, and his reckless driving was described by his fellow officers as 'like that of Jehu, and one day's bag, of one dog, two "byles", and an old lady in a pair of green velvet trousers may be taken as typical'.

Neither Rex nor Caryl chose a military career. Rex developed business interests in Canada, a country which held a powerful fascination for Caryl and Regi also. Perhaps the magnificent trees had something to do with it; for all the boys were keen on forestry, and all brought home specimens from their travels for the grounds at Cuffnells. Caryl toyed with the notion of becoming a writer, but frankly he lacked real talent, though he could turn out a reasonable short prose passage from time to time if the need arose. He was artistic, too, and very musical, having won prizes even as early as his Eton days for his fine performances as a solo pianist. There were some who saw this as a somewhat unmanly pursuit and criticised him for it, which was a pity, for he was not an effeminate man, and indeed had a good deal of business acumen.

On 25 June 1910 Alice's mother died at Ascot Wood House, aged eighty-four. Alice and Regi, Alan and Caryl attended her funeral, but Rex was abroad and could not get back in time. There was a preliminary service at St Andrew's Church, South Ascot, after which the mourners travelled with the coffin to Christ Church. Almost twenty years had passed since the Liddells had left Oxford, but the large congregation in the Cathedral and the impressive service gave a clear indication that the work of the Liddells could not be forgotten. The Bishop of Oxford personally conducted the choral service, and when it was over Alice's mother was interred beside her husband and Edith. The grave had been lined with ivy, white carnations and white sweet peas. The wreath from the immediate family was a cross of pink malmaisons, and the quantity of floral tributes was almost beyond belief.

The *Oxford Times* wrote an appreciation of Mrs Liddell's work as a committee member of the Girls' Old Bluecoat School, and as President for twenty-five years of the Oxford Prize for Needlework, to which she had always managed to bring a person of distinction to preside over the annual judging. But her main interest had been the establishment of the Sarah Acland District Nurses to help the poor, and the establishment six years later of the Acland Home. 'Those who were with her from the beginning can best testify to her indomitable perseverance and untiring energy, and also to her generosity in becoming a guarantor to the then treasurer for a loan of a considerable sum, when the funds of the Home were at a low ebb, and an immediate demand on them seemed probable.' Once in Ascot, she had founded the Royal Victoria Nursing Home. Under her influence the tradition of hospital work had become strong in the family, and in 1920 both Rhoda and Violet received the MBE for their services to nursing. Though Alice did not apparently take up the same cause on any appreciable scale, Reginald was closely associated with the work of two hospitals.

Mrs Liddell left more than £80,000, which was divided in the main between her children. For them she also left a rather touching farewell letter:

My dear Children,
    I wish to avoid a formal disposition of certain gifts to each of you. You are quite at liberty to make any exchange you please,

and I am quite sure you will carry out my wishes without dissatisfaction or any feeling of favouritism. I have loved all of you equally and have tried to do my best for each and all. God forgive me my shortcomings and I pray that the love I bore you will dwell in your memories.

The old lady left many splendid treasures, but the item she appears to have valued the most was Richmond's splendid painting of Lorina, Alice and Edith, 'The Sisters', which was to pass from one to the next in succession until the last of her children was dead, when it was to go to the person judged to be the Dean's legal heir. The insurance value which she set on it was £500. Alice was to receive her Burne-Jones screen and the clock which Sir William Harcourt had given to Dean Stanley on his marriage.

Sadly, Harry only survived his mother by about a year. His elder son had died unmarried in 1901, and his son Geoffrey now succeeded him. Born in 1884, Geoffrey was a young man of great personal charm; educated at Eton and Sandhurst, like Alan he was in the Rifle Brigade. A man of courage, he was awarded the DSO in 1915 and became a Lieutenant-Colonel. His wife, whom he married in 1915, was doubly a Liddell, her father being the son of the Dean's brother Charles. Mary Sophia Liddell still retains the clearest recollections of Alice and her family, and of the numerous family gatherings which they jointly attended.

Though the children were now grown up and rarely at home, Alice and Regi were happy enough. Regi was much preoccupied with his work as Chairman of the local magistrates' bench and with his sporting activities. A staunch Conservative, he became Chairman of the local Conservative Club. He was President of the Golf Club, too, and every year he allowed the New Forest Pony Club show and the Lyndhurst flower show to be held at Cuffnells. Both Alice and Regi were devout Christians, and they had had their own pew both in Lyndhurst Parish Church and in the church at Emery Down. In due course Regi became a church warden.

There was at times ominous talk of war but on the whole people tended to imagine that it would never come to anything, and that even if it did, it would soon be put down. Lyndhurst went on with its annual flower shows, when bands played and there was dancing on the lawn at Cuffnells; it still held its annual carnivals, still exhibited its ponies, and put all such thoughts firmly out of mind.

When the order to mobilise was received on 4 August 1914, Alan was with the 3rd Battalion in Ireland. He had been promoted Captain in 1910,

above left and centre, Alice's nephew, Geoffrey Liddell, and his wife Mary Sophia, portraits by Dick Peddie*; *above right*, The Hargreaves pew at Lyndhurst Parish Church*; *left*, Lyndhurst Carnival, just before the war

and had been Adjutant to the 4th Battalion for three years. Now he was officer in charge of 'D' Company of the 3rd Battalion. Mobilisation was completed on 9 September and the Battalion was shipped to England, where they headed for Cambridge and spent time in a number of route marches for the sake of the new recruits. Shortly afterwards they set sail for France.

Things did not begin to get really tough until they crossed the Aisne and relieved the Royal Berkshire Regiment in the trenches two miles north of Soupir. The existing trenches were nothing more than a series of isolated holes, and they had to set to work to dig new ones. By late September they were beginning to suffer heavy casualties, and they were grateful when the South Staffordshire Regiment arrived to relieve them. In three days about fifty men had been killed or wounded or reported missing. As they had tried to rush the German trenches, Alan had been conspicuous for his courage and tenacity.

By the second week of October they were in the thick of things again, this time at Hazebrouck and along the 'Bailleul 30' ridge. A headquarters had been established in a farmhouse on 13 October. The Colonel had been wounded and there was what seemed to be a screen of cavalry with machine-guns and a light battery. Gunfire continued until dusk, advance having proved impossible. During the course of the afternoon Alan was severely wounded by gunshot in the right lung and had to be brought back to England. Alice, of course, was filled with anxiety; but he was a tough young man, and gradually he recovered. At least for a short time he was safe.

Rex, meanwhile, had joined the Irish Guards immediately war broke out. He joined his regiment on 10 November 1914. Its condition when he arrived was deplorable. In a week, during the long battle of Ypres, they had had 613 casualties, including 16 officers. Immediately after Rex arrived, the Battalion occupied dug-outs, being heavily shelled and sniped most of the day. And so it continued. On 30 December 1914 Captain Gough was killed by a stray bullet and thereafter Rex was in command of No. 1 Company. He had been promoted Lieutenant on 23 December.

The regimental diary gives a clear picture of what things were like at that time:

The country round this part is very low-lying, intersected with ditches with pollarded willows growing on their banks. No sooner is a trench dug than it fills with water. . . . The soil is clay, and so keeps the water from draining away even if that were possible. In order to keep the men at all dry, they have to stand on planks rested on logs in the trenches, and in the less wet places bundles of straw and short fascines are put down. Pumping has been tried, but not with much success. The weather continues wet, and there does not seem to be any likelihood of a change. Consequently, we may expect some fresh discomforts daily.

Alan had meanwhile been mentioned in despatches by Sir John French and he was awarded the DSO for his gallantry on 25 September and 13 October 1914. Despite the severity of his wound, he was back in France on 26 March 1915 when he took over command of 'C' Company. For the next month the Battalion alternated with the Royal Irish Rifles, holding trenches some two or three miles south west of Armentières. On 9 May he was killed in action leading an attack near Fromelles. He was buried in Le Tron Aid Post Cemetery, Fleurbaix, in the Department of the Pas-de-Calais.

The rest can be readily imagined: the telegram, the trembling fingers that tear open the envelope, the desperate hope that all is not lost; and then the cold blank words that leave the bereaved mother and father crying out in their hearts at the utter waste of a brave young life; the flood of memories: the infant clinging on to the pony, the fun, the laughter; the bright hopes for the future, all dashed in a few official words of regret.

Alan Hargreaves (*2nd from l*), a month before his death

And Rex and Caryl were both still out there, for Caryl, too, had enlisted in the Scots Guards. It was a time fraught with bitter regrets and deep anxieties for Alice.

The year 1915 brought incredible hardship to the Irish Guards. For much of the time the trenches were filled with two feet of water, and the order was given that men were not to stand in the water for more than twelve hours at a time. It took the men most of their rest in the billets to scrape themselves moderately clean before going back to face the enemy again. To save portage through the mud, the men were each given two days' rations at a time, plus some dry tea and a couple of tins of Maconochie to heat over the braziers. The naked braziers flared up to the sky as the Irish 'drummed up', or brewed their tea and stewed their rations. 'Trench feet', severe swellings caused by long exposure to the water which filled the trenches, was a serious problem, only partially curbed by rubbing on a gruesome mix of lard and mustard.

And so the year continued, with heavy casualties in the most appalling conditions. In September 1915 Rex was 'permitted to wear the badge of Captain pending his temporary promotion to that rank being gazetted'.[1] But on September 10 he was badly wounded and had to be invalided home.

The respite did not last very long. On 20 August 1916 he was back again with the regiment, taking over No. 2 Company. Soon they reached Méault, where the billets were damp, dirty and flea-ridden. There was no let-up from the torrential rain and the clinging mud of the Somme. In those indescribable conditions they trained at bombing and signalling visually to aircraft. Kipling described the situation:

> Yonder but a very little way, stretched horizons, downs and tablelands as far as imagination could range. All the firmament groaned to the artillery hidden and striving within them; and statelily, regularly and unceasingly, the vast open spaces were plumed with vertical columns of shell-smoke. Men perceived that everything they had known, till then, had been a field-day. Here was The War![2]

On 10 September 1916 Rex, now a fully-fledged Captain, and his men bivouacked in some old trenches at the north of Bernafoy, where they

---

1 Rudyard Kipling, *The Irish Guards in the Great War*, 1923, p. 221
2 ibid, p. 179
3 ibid, p. 179

were used to carry fatigues for the 3rd Guards Brigade in the front line. Two days later they were stationed in a small copse near Trones Wood, which was choked up with corpses and wreckage. There three of their Lewis-gunners were killed and five more wounded by shells.

Rex and his men were left in reserve in the wood on 15 September, but later they were ordered up and Rex was wounded before he reached the front line. But he continued in spite of that, leading out a mixed party of Coldstream and Irish Guards to a chain of disconnected shell-holes a few hundred yards in advance of the trenches. There they endured field battery fire at less than half a mile, and the regular machine-gunfire which devastated them from their right. The Battalion was cut to pieces. As dusk fell the Scots Guards attacked without success.

On the morning of 16 September enemy aircraft spotted them at first light, and soon the artillery began again. The total brigade casualties were 1776, and only seven officers were left alive, including Rex who was injured. When they returned to the Citadel the sun was shining and breakfast was laid out for them by the trees. 'It struck their very very tired apprehensions that there was an enormous amount of equipage for a very few men, and they noted dully a sudden hustling off of unneeded plates and cups. They felt as though they had returned to a world which had suddenly outgrown them on a very terrifying scale during all the ages that they had been away from it.'[3]

left, Rex, wounded on 25 September 1916, was carried back to the base hospital on a stretcher, but he died during the night; *right*, Rex's grave

The musical setting of a song by Lewis Carroll

By 25 September all four companies were together. But there was tragedy and disaster to follow. Just as they had sent off a carrier pigeon to report their capture of their objective, British guns, misranging, inflicted further casualties and a second pigeon was sent off begging them to stop. While these guns were pitting the open terrain behind Lesboefs with shell-holes, the men dug themselves into a potato field, setting aside the potatoes as they did so for supper.

Then the British barrage wavered and stopped almost on the line where the men were digging in. Not many survived to tell the tale, but some say that this lasted for a quarter of an hour, others for as much as two hours. But the outcome was fearful. Among the carnage, Rex fell, wounded once more, and this time most severely. The men managed to carry him back, but he died during the night. This was an ironic tragedy: that after having fought so gallantly, he fell a victim to British guns.

Rex was posthumously awarded the Military Cross, and this was gazetted on 14 November 1916. But what good are medals, and a little pile of letters, written as and when the state of battle permitted, to a sorrowing father and mother, robbed of two fine sons in the prime of their lives? And worst of all, Caryl, the only child left to them, was still out there.

Wilfred Ewart, a brother officer in the Scots Guards, described what it was like in a way that Caryl thought captured the way it seemed at the time:

> It seemed as though the Almighty had passed judgment upon mankind and were levying execution of it inexorably. It was always a crooked and a twisted and a broken memory in after-years, yet starred with strange intervals of lucid, unexpected peace, during which men saw visions of a wondrous ultimate purity and splendour.... For if the eves were terrible, the dawns were beautiful. And if there was naked horror in the bright noonday when the sun scorched down upon the livid, festering corpses, and every grinning feature of the land was laid bare and the buzz of the clustering blue-bottles mingled with a nameless stench—there was sleep sometimes, too, and dreams scented with the thyme of Paradise.[4]

Even the strongest of men reach the limit of their physical endurance in conditions like those the Scots Guards endured. When men stood knee-

4 Wilfrid Ewart, *Way of Revelation*, 1921, p. 288

high in the mud, when their rest was broken by sudden emergency, when they were exposed alternately to the sweat of physical exertion and long waits in icy blasts, it was inevitable that the senses were dulled and that alertness which preserves a man from danger lost its focus. But the greatest pressure is that of responsibility, the fear that had one acted differently, one might have saved this or that man from destruction. Side by side with that feeling of responsibility came that terrible fatigue which brought many to death's door and beyond.

> It is the deadly journey, back and forth to the front line with material, the known and foreseen war in darkness and mud against the natural perversity of things, that shifts the foundations of the soul, so that a man, who scarcely regards Death hunting him at large by the hour, will fall into a child's paroxysms of rage and despair when the wire-strand rasps him across the knuckles or the duckboard for the hundredth time tilts sideways underfoot.[5]

Finally, towards the close of 1916, Caryl was recalled to England. He did not have to suffer that experience again.

Alice and Regi were relieved beyond words when their only remaining child was removed from danger; but it was not until Armistice was actually declared that they could sleep easy in their beds, for fear that Caryl might even yet be torn from them. Theirs was not a unique experience, for mothers and fathers, wives and sweethearts up and down the country were shedding the same tears, feeling the same heartache. Something died in them with their two eldest boys, and that bright prospect of the future could never be the same again.

It comforted them a little to place a memorial plaque to Alan and Rex's memory in Lyndhurst Parish Church, and a stained glass window in the church at Emery Down. And in due course, when the residents of Lyndhurst got round to raising a war memorial to the dead of the village near Bolton's Bench, where so many of their young men had played cricket on warm summer afternoons, the names of Alan and Rex were naturally included.

When the war was over, Caryl went to live in London; but he always regarded Cuffnells as his home, returning there at weekends. Alice and Regi now lived for his visits. All the affection that had been divided three ways in former years was now focused on him alone. He was the hope of their old age, the light of their declining years.

5 Rudyard Kipling, pp. 198–9

Arthur Ridley, a famous Hampshire and Middlesex
cricketer, who was best man at Alice and Regi's
wedding*

Regi remained active in local affairs. He still haunted Lord's Cricket Ground, though he missed his old friend Ridley, who had died suddenly in 1916 of a heart attack at Thistleworth, his home in Tadworth, Surrey.

Caryl and his father had a great deal in common. Both were excellent shots, and keen fishermen, who went to Scotland every year for the salmon; both were lovers of nature, with a special interest in arboriculture. They enjoyed a good round of golf. Each of them had a certain gentleness of disposition inherited from Jonathan Hargreaves.

Like his father a Justice of the Peace, Regi had sat on the local magistrates' bench, in time becoming senior magistrate of the New Forest Division. For a while he was chairman of the magistrates and carried out his duties conscientiously; but as he advanced in years he was increasingly troubled by deafness, so that eventually he was reluctantly forced to retire. He was a member of the parish council, and was district commissioner of the local boy scouts. Although he gradually began to suffer from those minor afflictions that come with age, he had much to occupy his time. And his devotion to Alice never faltered. His marriage to her was the best thing that ever happened to him.

The flower shows and pony club shows, usually a combined event every August, had come to be major events at Cuffnells. Marquees were erected to exibit the entries, and there were stalls for the local charities, including that of the Emery Down Women's Institute, of which Alice was the first president. There was always a band for the afternoon and evening, and usually bowling for a pig, a steam roundabout, and numerous sideshows. Outside caterers were brought in for the event. The gymkhana was a great attraction, and everyone loved the pony races. The fur and feather competition somehow never really caught on, but there were many sporting events. For the artisan classes there were horticultural competitions: as the judge in 1925 remarked, 'It was an excellent thing for the working man to grow his own vegetables, and he ought to be encouraged in every way.'[6] In the evening there was always dancing on the lawn, an event much looked forward to locally.

The beginning of 1926 was exceptionally cold, and falls of snow in the New Forest were the heaviest for several years. Here and there, wild ponies patiently scraped and nosed away the snow to get at the grass underneath. Fortunately the snow was soft and they managed to get food without too much difficulty. Traffic had come to a virtual standstill, for the roads were dangerous. Little local lads took their toboggans out on Bolton's Bench and enjoyed hours of exhilarating sport there.

From the windows at Cuffnells, the views were enchanting. The grand old trees were heavily laden with snow, which glistened in the early sunshine. From the summit of the little hillock in the garden one could see the sea at the end of a long white vista of untrodden snow. It was the kind of sight to bring back nostalgic memories of childhood, when tramping the untrodden snow and skating and sledging were a wonder and a delight; to think, too, of those three little lads whom Regi and Alice had brought into the world there.

On 14 February 1926, Regi died at Cuffnells. He was seventy-three years old. *The Times* obituary said of him:

None who had the privilege of knowing 'Regi' Hargreaves could fail to realise in him a quite uncommon fineness of spirit. With the more obvious accomplishments of his class he was well endowed, being more than a commonly good shot, fisherman, and cricketer. But he was far from being a mere sportsman and player of games. Widely read, a good French scholar, and a lover of nature, he found,

6 *Southern Evening Echo*, 5 August 1925
7 17 February 1926

as was natural for one born in the New Forest, one of his principal interests in forestry, and his grounds at Cuffnells contained some of the finest specimens of Douglas Pines and Red Woods in this country. . . . Until the last year or two he was a very faithful spectator at Lord's of the principal cricket matches and a well-known figure in the pavilion.[7]

The obituary also mentioned his having married 'Alice in Wonderland'. He was buried in the Hargreaves family grave with his father and mother in the cemetery of Lyndhurst Parish Church.

Alice was devastated by Regi's death. Though initially hers had been the driving force behind their social life, in recent years she had looked increasingly to Regi to take the lead. In a volume, *Miscellaneous Essays*, by Richard William Church, which Alice had given to Regi eight years after their marriage, Alice had written:

> *So we through this world's waning night*
> *May, hand in hand pursue our way;*
> *Shed round us order, love and light,*
> *And shine unto the perfect day.*

A watercolour by Alice*

left, Antony Brazier,
the butler*, and *right*,
Vera White, the head
housemaid at Cuffnells*

They had indeed lived their lives hand in hand. The romanticism of their early life together had given place in their final years together to a companionable relationship which made it almost impossible for either of them to think of life without the other. The terrible bereavements of the war years had brought them even closer than ever before. Now he was gone, and Alice felt his loss deeply.

Furthermore, she now had to think rather carefully about her personal finances. In the days when her mother was alive, she had never imagined that the time would come when she would not have ample means, but under the terms of Jonathan Hargreaves' will she could not inherit Cuffnells, which inevitably passed to Caryl. In a sense this did not matter, for Caryl was deeply, almost passionately attached to his mother and could be relied upon to look after her in an appropriate way in her old age. On Regi's death he was very much worse off than his father, who had been left £40,000. Regi left only about £26,000: a very considerable sum, yet very much less than might have been expected. In other words, even though he had inherited Alan's entire estate of £4201:13*s*:8*d* and Rex's of £6440:14*s*:8*d* he had done no more than preserve the financial status quo. Alice had become legally entitled to her marriage settlement of £8000 from her parents when her mother died, but Mrs Liddell clearly had not imagined that Alice would ever need it, and had specified that it could be disposed of as Alice herself directed. It had never been her custom to call upon her annual allowance in the past.

To Alice, Regi had bequeathed 'all the wines, liquors, fuel and consumable provisions of which I shall die possessed also my carriage horses with the harness and other appendages thereto respectively belonging also my motor cars and motor accessories and all the implements and utensils stock of hay corn straw petrol oil and tyres and other moveable effects in or about my coach house stables and motor house and all my jewelry and the sum of £200 and all furniture, plate etc. and domestic effects she wants to set up home for her life'. Alice was to insure this property and to pass it on to Caryl at her death.

Mrs Benger, the cook at Cuffnells*

Caryl was now perfectly entitled to ask his mother to move out, but he did not do this, leaving matters exactly as they were, retaining his own home in London and returning to Cuffnells at weekends. Alice continued to keep a close eye on the running of the house, though with a somewhat depleted staff by her earlier standards. But there were still plenty of them looking upon her as mistress and addressing her as 'Lady Hargreaves', while Caryl was simply the mistress's son. There was Miss Wasley, the housekeeper, who had been with the family for many years, and Antony Brazier, the butler, who for a time went out with Vera White, the head housemaid. Everyone knew how keen he was on her, but they never got married. The cook, Mrs Benger, was a stout, motherly sort of woman who had been there a long time, and was first-rate at her job, as was only to be expected, considering the style in which the family liked to entertain. There was a footman, a hallboy and a daily maid, and outside, Mr Richards, the gardener, a man of great experience who really loved his work. In the lodge which Regi had built was Charles O'Dell who had also been with the family for very many years and was fiercely loyal to them. The other servants were of the opinion that he had rather an easy job, for 'Lady Hargreaves' rarely went out in her later years.

Unfortunately Alice's health at this time was not good. When her sister Violet died on 9 December 1927 Alice was too infirm to attend the choral funeral service at Westerham Parish Church, near Hoseyrigge, the house in which Rhoda and Violet had set up home after their mother's death. So many of the people who had been close to Alice were now dead and gone. Some years earlier that grand old lady Mary Foster, who had been Alice's governess, had died at the age of eighty-three. After her husband's sad death on Christmas Day 1888 she had continued as proprietress of the Mitre Hotel in Oxford until a few years before her death, when she formed a public company. When she died her effects stood at £9264:12s.

Alice was now frankly lonely. Most of her days were spent in her library, where she read continually. There was no heating at all on the top

231

Mrs Foster, née Prickett, the Liddell
children's former governess

floor of the house for most of the time. Those stately and impressive
rooms were difficult to heat and the house was draughty. She had her own
little suite of rooms consisting of a small drawing-room, study, bedroom,
bathroom and w.c. But though most of her days were now spent alone, she
always dined in the main dining-hall and used the big drawing-room. Few
people came to visit her now. The piano was silent, and her piano
accordian, too, which she had once loved to play. The voice that had once
sung so charmingly had lost its range. Her social superiority isolated her
from the rest of the village, who might expect cordial treatment, but knew
their place.

Now Caryl was all she had; but he was a young man with lots of
friends and many interests. He had a habit of arriving late on Saturday
night or early on Sunday morning, long after Alice was asleep. She did not
like that, and it was a cause of contention between them: there were often
raised voices and banged doors. But they showered affection on each
other for all that. He was her life now.

STILL SHE HAUNTS ME

'Still she haunts me, phantomwise,
Alice moving under skies
Never seen by waking eyes.'

Alice's Adventures in Wonderland

OVER THE YEARS Alice had continued to cherish the books and mementos that Charles Dodgson had given her and they were now kept locked up in her private study. They included many fine items: first editions of almost everything he had ever written. After his death she had demonstrated her continuing interest in her adventures by collecting new editions as they appeared. She loved fine illustrations, though she never saw any she liked so well as those of Tenniel. But the new additions to her collection that she prized most were the foreign editions, translations into more languages than they could ever have imagined on that golden afternoon when the story was first told. The most treasured possession of all was the presentation manuscript of *Alice's Adventures Underground*.

It was not easy to maintain Alice in suitable style at Cuffnells. The old house needed constant attention to keep in good repair, and that, plus the cost of maintaining the estate and the bevy of servants, was now a continual drain on Caryl's financial resources. They talked the matter over, and finally Alice came to a major decision: she would sell the precious manuscript.

Sotheby's stage-managed the whole affair with impeccable style. It was one of the truly great book sales, the kind of occasion that few people are ever privileged to witness. There were Carroll items from other sources: an 1865 copy of *Alice's Adventures in Wonderland* and a facsimile edition of *Alice's Adventures Underground*, both autographed by the author. The Wilcox family, Dodgson's cousins, were offering autographed letters, including the original manuscript of 'Verses to Matilda Jane', a

The famous auction of
the *Alice* manuscript at
Sotheby's

poem addressed to a doll, and sent to Dodgson's cousin, Menella Wilcox.
Fine items from other authors were also up for sale. A large selection of
Johnsoniana included the last letter Dr Johnson had ever written. A
contemporary theatre manuscript copy of Thomas Middleton's *A Game at
Chess* and Lord Byron's duelling pistols were also catalogued.

The auction was held in a great gallery at Sotheby's auction rooms in
New Bond Street. Old Master paintings looked down from the walls,
which were of oak, like the auctioneer's rostrum. Before the rostrum was
the horseshoe-shaped table covered with green baize where the dealers
always sat; and in front of that, rows of chairs to seat three hundred
spectators, some there to bid, but most just for the excitement of it all: for
word had got around that Alice was to be there in person, and many were in
their seats a full three hours before the auction was due to start.

As the auction began, attention was focused on an American, Dr
A. S. W. Rosenbach, a distinguished book dealer seated on the right of the
table, nearest to the auctioneer. Opposite him was E. H. Dring, President
of Quaritch's, the well-known London dealer, who was bidding for the
British Museum. Nearby sat Mr Maggs, another London dealer, whose
client remained anonymous. Alice was seated on the rostrum, a frail
figure, retiring, yet stylishly dressed in a tall, wide-brimmed hat with a
contrasting hatband and a coat with a fashionable astrakhan collar. Next

A. S. W. Rosenbach

to her was Sir Frederick Kenyon, Librarian of the British Museum.

Promptly at one o'clock the auctioneer, Mr Des Graz, began. Many items came on before Alice's, including the manuscript of Hardy's 'An Ancient Earthwork', which fetched £600. Maggs and Rosenbach fought fiercely over the 1865 copy of *Alice's Adventures in Wonderland*, but the former dropped out when Rosenbach bid £5000. Finally it was time for item 319, and a rustle of excitement went round the assembled people.

The bidding started at £5000, and bidding rose at £100 per second. Alice looked thrilled and fascinated. The excitement was so intense that few people present could actually hear the bidding. At £12,500 Quaritch, on behalf of the British Museum, had reached his limit. At this stage Dr Rosenbach—smooth-shaven, thickset, dark-haired and wearing a pince-nez—and Mr Maggs were the only people still bidding. When Rosenbach bid £15,400 Maggs dropped out. Rosenbach had won, and the manuscript was now his. Alice, visibly affected by events and by past memories of days in Wonderland, was escorted from the room by friends to the car which awaited her. 'I am very pleased at the price,' she said before she drove away. 'It is a large sum of money and I do not yet know what I shall do with it.'[1]

1 *Daily Sketch*, 4 May 1928

It seemed that the sale, which also included other major items from her Carroll collection, had solved her financial problems. Next day the *New York Times* ran a large article on the auction and included a comment on the state of her finances:

Before the lodge-keeper's gate of her old country place is a sign reading: 'To rent, furnished, this historic mansion.'

'She won't see visitors, sir,' the butler tells you. 'You see sir, she's pretty old and not very well. She rather feels things are slipping away from her.'

After the auction the sign could be taken down. But the sale of the manuscript to America caused an uproar. The magazine *The Passing Show*, carried a caricature of Dr Rosenbach with *Alice* under his arm and crates of other treasures bound for the USA, and below it a verse:

> *What are the wild waves saying? Alice where art thou?*
> *Though dear to us you've always been, You're dearer to us now!*
> *The Rosenbachs have been and gone (just hear the dollars roar!)*
> *And left some muddy footprints on the British nursery floor.*

This was the highest sum ever paid for a book in Britain at that time. Immediately after the sale, Dr Rosenbach said that he felt the book properly belonged to the British nation and offered to sell it back to the British Library for the sum he had paid for it. He even offered £1000 to start a fund to buy back the book. The offer was not accepted.

It was in 1928 that a new housemaid was taken on in the house at Cuffnells. Mary Gailor was fifteen years old, and her father ran a local off-licence. She had been born in a little thatched cottage about three miles from Lyndhurst, which had been rented by her family since 1822, and where she still lives today. Like all the other indoor staff she had to live in, and received a weekly wage of three shillings and sixpence, plus her board and lodging. It was not a particularly high wage for the job, but she was at least within cycling distance of her family.

Every morning, like all the other servants, she had to be ready to start work at 5.50am. Her first job was to go to the top floor of the house and open all the shutters, then clean all the grates, in that order. Mary always had trouble opening the shutters, which were absolutely enormous, and secured by a heavy iron bar. She suffered from chilblains on her hands, which broke as a result of the cold weather outside and the chill conditions in the vast empty rooms. One morning her hands were so painful that she simply couldn't open the shutters, so thinking that she would get one of the other servants to help her a little later, Mary began cleaning the grate. She had hardly begun when she was startled by an icy voice from the doorway.

'I thought I told you to open the shutters before you begin the grate. You know I want it done first thing. Why have you disobeyed me?'

'I'm sorry, Lady Hargreaves, but you see it's my hands. I've got dreadful chilblains and they've broken, and I just can't move the shutters.'

She lifted her hands for Alice to see. Clearly the excuse was genuine; but Alice was a strict disciplinarian, and she had no intention of allowing any of the servants to imagine that she could be disobeyed. The housekeeper was summoned, and another servant detailed to open the shutters on that occasion. Then O'Dell was sent into Lyndhurst to get some ointment from the chemist. The cost was the equivalent of one week's wages for Mary Gailor and it was deducted from her earnings.

Mary Gailor had been surprised to see her mistress up and about at six o'clock in the morning, but she soon learned that Alice always rose early, following the pattern established in her childhood days at Christ Church. Mary's next job when she had finished the windows and grates was to put in an hour's needlework each day on the household linen. Like all girls of her generation she had been trained from early childhood to darn and mend with skill, and to turn out items like curtains and other home furnishings as and when the need arose. But when things got a bit quiet, she sneaked off with Antony Brazier, Vera White and Mrs Benger for a quiet game of cards—and heaven help them if Miss Wasley the head housekeeper caught them, or, worse still, Lady Hargreaves herself, for hers was a continual presence: she had been brought up to deal with servants, and knew well the value of letting know that she was continually on the watch and might turn up at any time to see what was going on, even in the servants' quarters.

Mary Gailor, the housemaid at Cuffnells*

Neither Alan nor Rex had married, though each had been thirty-three at the time of his death. Caryl was now forty-one, and still a bachelor. Perhaps it was difficult for a man with a mother possessed of such exceptional qualities as Alice to find a woman who matched up to her standards. Despite their occasional ups and downs, they still clearly adored each other.

It was about this time that Caryl began courting seriously. Madeleine Hanbury-Tracy was the widow of the Hon. Felix Charles Hubert

Hanbury-Tracy, and the only daughter of Brigadier General George Llewellen Palmer, CB, of Lackham, Lacock, Wiltshire. Madeleine, who was always called 'Missy' by her family, had married Felix on 11 June 1908, and had two sons, Michael David Charles, born on 29 March 1909, and Ninian John Frederick, born on 7 December 1910.

On 19 December 1915 Felix, a Lieutenant in the Scots Guards, was killed in action at Destages La Ventre near Armentières. His total effects amounted only to £394:3s:4d. Luckily Madeleine's family was independently wealthy, but her early days of widowhood were nevertheless a great struggle. When the early days of grief were over she began going into society again in an effort to quell her grief in the kind of life she had once known, but many a time she had to refuse social invitations because she felt she had nothing suitable to wear.

Madeleine was a very affectionate mother, but as was the custom with women of her class, she placed her boys in the care of a governess. 'Frizzie Freeman' was absolutely devoted to David and John—both boys were known by their second Christian names—and they to her. It was she who attended not only to their education but also to their daily needs, and Madeleine was content that it should be so. Even till the day she died 'Frizzie' never tired of talking about 'her boys' and the little incidents of their daily lives. In the early years they all lived together in a house in Brompton Square, which in those days was a very modest area. When her mother died, Madeleine went to live with her father at his home, Berryfield, Bradford-on-Avon, and ran his home for him. Their grandfather was the nearest thing to a father that the two boys ever really knew.

Madeleine was not young when she and Caryl became serious about each other, but she was a supremely beautiful woman and she had had numerous suitors, all of whom she had rejected firmly. Hers was a restless and nervous personality. In her own attitudes she was very conventional; yet she could accept unconventionality in others. She was always impeccably dressed, and she could be perfectly at ease in any setting. She had known a great deal of sorrow in her life, and it is hardly to be wondered at that she took refuge in society gossip and platitudes. But she was a cultivated and gifted person, fond of music and art. She was what used to be referred to as a 'soul', but Caryl teased her about that, and afterwards she rarely talked about it.

One might think that Alice would have welcomed the idea of having a daughter-in-law, but as the attachment between Caryl and Madeleine became apparent, she began to show her disapproval. Caryl had known

Madeleine's late husband socially, and the tragic circumstances of his death were well-known. Having lost two sons herself, Alice ought to have had more sympathy for Madeleine's situation as a war widow with children to bring up. But Alice was rooted conventionally in the mid-Victorian era. The powerful influence of her mother still persisted, and even though Mrs Liddell had been dead for many years, that influence still lived on in Alice's thoughts and feelings. According to her way of looking at things, a widow should emulate Queen Victoria and go on sorrowing alone until she joined her husband in the next world. Even the thought of the two orphaned boys did nothing to soften Alice's attitude, for it simply served as a remainder that Madeleine's fertile years were nearing their close.

Social occasions were few and far between now. The old days when there had been hunting and shooting at Cuffnells were over. Alice was living there alone, possibly fearful that Madeleine and Caryl would settle in at Cuffnells and dispossess her of her home altogether; but that, of course, was a thing that Caryl did not mean to allow. Alice was becoming increasingly edgy with him, but although he was sympathetic, he remained firm. He understood that his mother's feelings in the matter of his relationship with Madeleine were the result of the strength of her attachment for him. It was not easy for an old lady of seventy-seven to accept the idea of having a daughter-in-law for the first time. He rode the see-saw between these two most important women in his life with a skill born of wisdom and love.

Initially Madeleine's two sons were not too happy at the idea of acquiring Caryl as a stepfather—somehow he was not exactly a father figure—but by this time they were virtually off hand: even John, the younger, was about to leave Eton for Trinity College, Cambridge. Madeleine idolised her sons but, like Caryl, she could not allow anything to stand in the way of her romance.

The wedding took place on 6 June 1929 not at Lyndhurst, nor near the Llewellen Palmer or Hanbury-Tracy homes, but at Westerham in Kent. Alice's sister Rhoda, who was much attached to her nephew, organised everything from her home at Hoseyrigge. By the social standards of the day it was a relatively quiet affair, but there was still a substantial family turnout for the occasion. Madeleine, of course, looked wonderful. Caryl arrived at the last moment by car and presented his bride with her wedding bouquet—an enormous but pathetically wilted offering, but he had had a long drive.

After the wedding Caryl and Madeleine set up home in a charming

house in Montagu Square, London, moving on shortly afterwards to a much larger one in Portland Square. On 10 June 1931 Alice's only grandchild was born. It was a girl, and they called her Mary-Jean Rosalie Alice. This event, more than any other, reconciled Alice to the idea of Caryl's marriage.

Even so, she was now a very lonely old lady. Lorina, who had moved to a flat in the Brompton Road after her husband had died, leaving the house at Pitlour to their son Moncrieff, had died in October 1930. The funeral was at Strathmiglo on Saturday 1 November 1930, and afterwards she was interred in the family grave with her husband who had died in 1911. A memorial service was held for her in St Saviour's Church, Brompton, and Alice attended with Caryl and Rhoda. According to the *Oxford Times*, although she was frail, she had kept remarkably well right up until the time of her death and taken a keen interest in everything. Only three months beforehand she had visited her son Moncrieff in Scotland. 'She was the eldest of the three sisters in the well-known picture by Richmond. . . . She had endeared herself to a large circle of friends by whom she will be greatly missed.'[2]

As an antidote to her sense of social isolation and to escape from the cold of winter at Cuffnells, Alice decided to rent a house called 'The Breaches' at Westerham. It was a large house of Elizabethan origin, situated next to the parish church and overlooking the village green. Most

2 *Oxford Times*, 7 November 1930

left, William Baillie Skene, Lorina's husband*, and *right*, Moncrieff Skene, her only son*

important, it was sited only about a mile from Rhoda's home at Hoseyrigge. She began to spend the winter months there, with Caryl, Madeleine and Mary Jean joining her for Christmas. When the warmer weather came, she always returned to Cuffnells, drawn by its unique atmosphere, redolent of the days when she and Regi had set out on their married life together and raised their fine young family.

Even so, life was undeniably dull for Alice. Of the ten Liddell children only four now remained. Rhoda at Westerham was much preoccupied with the Women's Institute, as Violet had been before her. Lionel had retired to live at Dinard and Frederick, who had been knighted, had become legal adviser to the Speaker of the House of Commons. Few people now made their way up the long winding drive to the front door of Alice's large, rambling house with its cream walls, which still had the sconces on either side of the door. Alice mostly spent her days alone, gazing at Richmond's portrait, 'The Sisters', above the fireplace in the drawing-room, or at Burne-Jones' original drawings for Edith's memorial window. There was little use now for that private seal with her initials 'APH' on it. Sometimes she looked at her numerous items of jewelry; she had a special sentimental affection for the gold curb initialled bangle bequeathed her by Lorina, and the gold filigree ball necklace that had been a gift from Ruskin.

It was in 1932 that the world sought her out again, and in a way that nobody could have anticipated. On 27 January 1932 there were plans to celebrate the centenary of Lewis Carroll's birth and Alice was invited by

Columbia University to go to the United States to participate. In view of her frailty, it was agreed that she should not make the journey until April. Services of thanksgiving were held in Liverpool and in Guildford, where the Mayor laid a wreath on Lewis Carroll's grave. Neither ceremony was attended by Alice, who was saving her strength for her visit to America. In the centenary week the Detroit Symphony Orchestra played the Stillman-Kelley suite 'Alice in Wonderland', and the Boston, Chicago and Cincinnati symphony orchestras played the Deems-Taylor suite 'Through the Looking-Glass'.

In April Alice returned to Cuffnells from Westerham, and Caryl spent a few days with her. Shortly before she was due to set sail, she autographed a copy of *Alice's Adventures in Wonderland* for Princess Elizabeth, 'From the Original Alice'. The book was put on exhibition in St Mary's Hospital, Paddington, where a children's ward was being established as a memorial to Lewis Carroll.

The Lewis Carroll memorial cot at St Mary's Hospital, Paddington

Alice was accompanied on the liner *Berengaria* by Caryl and Rhoda, and when the liner reached quarantine on 29 April, Professor J. Enrique Zanetti, Chairman of the Columbia Carroll Centenary Committee and Roger Howson, the University Librarian, went aboard with a crowd of newspapermen to meet Alice. It was an ordeal that Caryl said she was dreading, but in the event she was very gently treated, and judging by the Paramount newsreel she seemed to enjoy the experience. Zanetti found her taking tea on the sun-deck. He described her as being 'of medium height and build, grain-haired [*sic*] and had charming old-fashioned manners in receiving those who were introduced by her son. She spoke in low tones and had a quaint sense of humour. She wore a blue flowered dress, a black camel's hair coat with a squirrel collar, and black hat with feather. A large bunch of orchids was attached to her coat. She used two canes in walking. . . . In order to save his mother as much as possible, Captain Hargreaves read the questions put by the reporters, and then gave the answers, with interpolations from time to time by her.'[3] She said that her favourite rhyme was 'Soup of the Evening' and her favourite character was the Cheshire Cat. Somehow it is difficult to avoid the impression that Caryl was being a little too protective, and that Alice was much more capable of coping than he cared to give her credit for.

After a whole day spent resting in their private suite at the Waldorf Astoria, Alice was taken on a special tour of New York which really did rather tire her. Afterwards she stood in front of a microphone in her suite

3 *New York Times*, 30 April 1932

Alice on the occasion
of the presentation of
an honorary doctorate
at Columbia
University in the USA

and broadcast to the people of America. The *New York Times* said: 'The
pace of New York seemed to have tired her and her voice trembled
somewhat with the fatigue and the excitement of it as she faced the little
quivering disc. . . . "America and New York City are such exciting places
that they take me back to Wonderland."[4] Her voice quavered as it sped
out over WABC Columbia network to thousands of eager ears.' Alice
went on to describe the memorial funds being raised in aid of children's
hospitals on both sides of the Atlantic. She then read letters she had
received from Lewis Carroll about the facsimile edition of *Alice's
Adventures Underground* and his request that the profits should benefit
children's homes and hospitals. Finally she read the acrostic that Lewis
Carroll had given to the Liddell children in the copy of *Holiday House* for
Christmas 1861.

The Columbia University Exhibition marking the centenary had
been opened on 31 March at the Avery Hall. Over three hundred guests
were present at the opening by Gerald Campbell, the British Consul
General. The original manuscript was displayed on a massive mahogany
table on which it was said to have been written. Nine copies of the fifteen
1865 editions of *Alice* then known to exist (a small number of additional
copies have since come to light) were on display, and eleven copies of the

4 *New York Times*, 1 May 1932

1866 edition. A fine collection of Carroll photographs was also exhibited, and a posthumous portrait of Lewis Carroll by E. Gertrude Thomson.

On the afternoon of 2 May Dr Nicholas Murray Butler, President of Columbia University, presented Alice in a private ceremony with the honorary degree of Doctor of Letters. Proudly she put on her academic cap and gown and posed for photographers on the steps of the university. She looked relaxed and happy: this was the kind of academic atmosphere to which she had been raised. Beneath her academic robes she wore a brown ensemble with a corsage of roses and lilies of the valley, and in her hand she carried No. 1 copy of the special edition of the catalogue of the Carroll exhibition.

Florence Becker Lennon described what happened after that:

Alice, aged 80, at Cuffnells

The wide aisle from the door to the carved wooden throne on the inner circle was tied off with white ribbons. The rotunda was a garden of live flowers. To welcome Queen Alice with ninety times nine, all the characters were present, not in costume, but not too heavily incognito. Oxford is not the only university from whose rostra Tweedledee and Tweedledum, the Walrus, the Carpenter, the Mad Hatter, the March Hare, and especially the Professor and the Other Professor, hold forth.

The hush deepened. The procession was assembling outside the door. At last Alice would be led to her flower-banked throne. The orchestra struck up, and more professors entered escorting Mrs Hargreaves in her cap and gown. She was carrying a cane, but not leaning on it. The president of the university entered too, and through some mischance sat on the throne. It must have been Rule Forty-two, for nobody said anything, and only one or two seemed astonished.

The escort tried to persuade the lovely old lady to sit down. She would not sit and would not lean on her cane. She swayed a little, but she stood throughout the ceremony. The quality that looks out of her child photographs endured past her eightieth birthday.

The old gentleman of the throne said: 'Alice Pleasance Hargreaves, descendant of John of Gaunt, time-honoured Lancaster, daughter of that distinguished Oxford scholar whose fame will last until the English-speaking men cease to study the Greek language and its immortal literature; awakening with her girlhood's charm the ingenious fancy of a mathematician familiar with imaginary quantities, stirring him to reveal his complete understand-

left, Alice, aged 80, in a
photograph which appeared in
Cornhill magazine in 1932

right, Alice in A. S. W. Rosenbach's
study

ing of the heart of a child as well as the mind of a man, to create imaginary figures and happenings in a language all his own, making odd phrases and facts, to live on pages which will adorn the literature of the English tongue, time without end, . . . you as the moving cause, Aristotle's "final cause" of that truly noteworthy contribution to English Literature, I gladly admit you to the degree of Doctor of Letters in this university.'

In her formal acceptance, Alice said 'I thank you, Mr President, for the signal honour bestowed upon me. I shall remember it and prize it for the rest of my days, which may not be very long. I love to think, however, unworthy I am, that Mr Dodgson-Lewis Carroll knows and rejoices with me.'[5]

An interpretation of the 'Alice in Wonderland' suite of Edgar Stillman-Kelley by a special chorus of 120 voices from the Barnard and Hunter College glee clubs, accompanied by the seventy-strong Columbia University Orchestra, completed the occasion. That evening, Oscar of the Waldorf presented Alice with a three-tier birthday cake decorated with Wonderland characters.

Alice stayed on in America for another ten days. During that time she met the great collector Arthur Houghton Jr. and told him the story of how for many years the original manuscript of *Alice's Adventures Underground* was casually kept on a table in the family home. Then one day some Americans came to the door and asked to see it. This gave Alice the notion that the book might have some intrinsic value and so she transferred it to a nearby bookcase! In her own view she was catapulted into fame 'by simply doing absolutely nothing'!

In the book *Rosenbach* by Wolf and Fleming is described the story of Alice's visit to Dr Rosenbach, who bought the manuscript, in Philadelphia. He had by this time sold the manuscript with two copies of the 1865 *Alice* for $150,000 to Eldridge Johnson, president of the Victor Talking Machine Company. Alice and Caryl stayed at Dr Rosenbach's home and Eldridge Johnson came to lunch, bringing the manuscript with him. 'Eldridge Johnson, towering over her, had the time of his life showing off the gadget-trimmed, watertight, fireproof, portable steel safe-deposit box which he had made to house the precious manuscript so that it would suffer no harm as it travelled on his yacht in tropical seas.'[6] But in

5 Florence Becker Lennon, *The Life of Lewis Carroll*, 1972, pp. 16–17
6 Edwin Wolf and John Fleming, *Rosenbach*, 1960

Alice, aged 80, opening the Lewis Carroll Exhibition

the excitement, Dr Rosenbach forgot to get Alice to autograph his own copy of the first edition.

On 14 May Alice and Rhoda sailed for home aboard the *Aquitania*, leaving Caryl behind in New York. One further centenary adventure was still to come. On 26 June 1932 Alice opened the Lewis Carroll exhibition at Bumpus, the London bookshop. Beside her was Peter Davies, the original Peter Pan. The Dean of Christ Church presided, and Sir Gerald du Maurier recalled meetings with Lewis Carroll. An old lady who had played with her as a child in the Deanery presented her with a bouquet of roses. Alice described herself as 'a very old person who got tired very easily, but she recalled the days when she was one of a number of small girls running about in cotton frocks, she knew Mr Dodgson before the name "Lewis Carroll" had been invented.'[7] The distinguished company included her son Caryl; Sir Harold Hartley, the greatest British Carroll collector of that era; Falconer Madan and S. H. Williams, authors of the first Lewis Carroll handbook; Sir Frederick and Lady Liddell, Alice's brother and sister-in-law; J. B. Priestley, Irene Vanburgh and Mr and Mrs Leonard Woolf. It was a splendid occasion.

7 *The Times*, 29 June 1932

EPILOGUE

ALICE SPENT Christmas 1933 at The Breaches and was joined, as usual, by her family. But this Christmas was to hold a novel experience in store for her: Paramount had made a film version of *Alice* with Charlotte Henry in the starring role and, with her grandchild, Mary Jean, on her lap, Alice watched a private preview in her own home. She wrote a long and not very original account of her opinion of the film for *Picturegoer*:

After seeing this film I was filled with delight, and am now convinced that the talking picture is the only possible medium for the interpretation of this best-loved of books. . . . The film meant a great deal to me, for although the book has been adapted frequently for the stage and beautifully illustrated by many artists, I always think of Wonderland as inhabited by people who speak Lewis Carroll's words and look like Tenniel's drawings. And here the costumes are wonderfully done and the words are not maltreated or changed. I myself am glad to hear that an edition of the book is shortly to be published with illustrations from the film. . . . You will understand that I cherish the hope that this picture will have a wonderful success.

Charlotte Henry's story is a sad one. A talent scout saw her in Pasadena Playhouse and arranged a screen test. She won the role that 6800 other young actresses had applied for. It seemed like the opportunity of a lifetime, but turned out to be a professional curse. 'I no longer existed as Charlotte Henry,' she said. 'With that costume I was transformed . . . to the creature people had read about as children. My identity was gone.'

One day early in November 1934, Alice was out in her car when she was taken ill and had to be taken home. The servants got her to bed and sent

248

'n huis teëgekom wat so al in mens se pad kom nie! Nooit!"
Tog staan die heuweltjie nog lewensgroot daar, dus moet sy maar weer van voor af begin. Dié slag kom sy by 'n groot blombedding uit, met 'n randjie gousblomme en 'n wilger-boom mooi in die middel.
„Ag, Tierlelie!" spreek Alice die lelie aan wat sierlik in die wind dans, „ek *wens* tog jy kon praat!"
„Natuurlik kan ons praat," sê die Tierlelie, „mits daar iemand is met wie dit die moeite werd is om te praat."
Alice is so verstom dat sy 'n minuut lank geen woord kan uitkry nie: dis asof dit haar asem skoon wegslaan. Uiteinde-

Foreign editions of *Alice* and other Carrolliana absorbed Alice until her death

for the doctor, but there was nothing that could be done. She was in a coma. Caryl and Rhoda were with her constantly, but from that time on she knew no one. *The Times* carried bulletins of her condition, but it was clear that there was no hope. She died peacefully at The Breaches on 15 November 1934.

A requiem mass was said by the vicar to the Parish Church of St Mary the Virgin in the room where the body lay, and all the servants were present. Alice was cremated at Golders Green and her ashes placed in the Hargreaves grave at St Michael and All Angels, Lyndhurst. While the service was being conducted at Lyndhurst, another memorial service was held in Westerham.

Alice left no will. Her effects amounted to £1371:10*s*:1*d*. She had been content to leave money matters to Caryl, who now inherited her entire estate.

For a short time after Alice's death Cuffnells operated as a hotel. A typical advertisement said: 'Come and see for yourself this historical English house, set in 160 acres of loveliness. The home of the original Alice of *Alice in Wonderland*, the home where King George IV, Queen Charlotte and Pitt stayed. Residential terms from 4½ gns. Lunch 3/6 (Sunday 4/6)

Dinner 4/6 Tea 1/6.' During the Second World War the house was requisitioned for use by a searchlight battalion, and afterwards its condition was so dilapidated that it had to be demolished.

Caryl served as a Wing Commander in charge of barrage balloons, and Alice's granddaughter, Mary Jean, was sent to America for the duration of the war. Her step-brother David was wounded at Dunkirk, and though he was brought back to England, he died on 22 August 1940. He left a widow and one son, Merlin Charles Sainthill Hanbury-Tracy, born on 17 June 1939. When he was only two years old, he succeeded his cousin, becoming the seventh Baron Sudeley.

Madeleine was deeply shocked at David's death. Her second son, John, was an explorer who went on a two year geographical expedition to Tibet, where he was trying to find the source of the Salween River. He and his wife had to abandon an expedition to the Andes when the Second World War broke out. Though he joined the Scots Guards, he luckily survived the war.

Caryl died on 26 November 1955 at his home at Longwood in Scotland, and his widow died on 5 August 1958. Caryl had asked to be cremated, and requested that his ashes be scattered from an aircraft over the English countryside. Alice's granddaughter, Mary Jean, grew up and married, and produced a fine family of children. So the line continues.

As for Carroll and his Alice, they remain immortal:

> *Ever drifting down the stream—*
> *Lingering in the golden gleam—*
> *Life, what is it but a dream?*

Alice's Grave*

APPENDIX I:
LIST OF ALICE'S WEDDING PRESENTS

Mr Arkwright, water jug and glasses with jewelled leaves
Miss Grace Ashhurst, silver scent-bottle
Miss Ashhurst, handsome lace handkerchief
Mrs Astley, old silver hand glass
A. Baldwin (Deanery coachman), riding whip
Miss Barnes, watercolour drawing of Chvist Church
Dowager Viscountess Barrington, gold bracelet, with pearls
Mrs I. Beech, ivory paper-knife
Mrs Beech, china butterfly inkhouses
Madame Belchman, white and gold fan
Mrs Bell, jewellery
Right Hon Montague Bernard, china vases
Lord Boston, silver necklace and locket
Mater of University and Mrs Bradley, Menton china
Mr and Mrs Bryan, oak and silver cup
Mrs Buckle, finely worked gold bracelet
Madame de Bunsen, Berlin china
Lady Burton, Tennyson's works and china
Hon H. Chateris, old gold tray
Mrs Clerke, Worcester jewelled china bowl
Miss Cleverly, green moss china bowl
Professor and Mrs Clifton, old gold spoons
Mrs and Miss Colson, white china flower vase (lilacs)
Mrs Coltman, handsome pair ormolu inkstands with horses
Mrs Combe, books
Mr and Mrs Conbeare, lotus-leaf silver toast-rack and a walnut tea-table
Miss Conybeare, Normandy cross
Mr and Mrs E. J. Cooper, crystal and pearl ornament
Mr and Mrs Courthorpe, silver letter-weigher
Dr Craddock, saddle and bridle
Viscount and Viscountess Cranbrook, silver looking-glass
Cuffnells servants, pair of candlesticks
Mr and Mrs Darby Griffiths, china cupids
Deanery servants, two brass inkstands
Deanery servants, two china figures and card-case
Countess de la Warr, Dresden vases
Earl de la Warr, hunting whip
Mrs Dundas, coffee spoons
Mr and Mrs A. Entwisle, fine old oak cabinet for hall
Mr B. Entwisle, letter-weigher
Mr C. Entwisle, gold compass
Captain and Mrs Entwisle, inkstand and tray
Miss Entwisle, silver salt-bottle

Mr Nevile Hamlyn Fane, picture with view of Clovelly
The misses Hamlyn Fane, gold sleeve-links
Lieut and Mrs C. Fellowes, calendar
Rev and Mrs E. Fellowes, white china cornucopias mounted in velvet
Mrs Foster, pair of candlesticks
Signora Galimierti, china dish
Mrs Garbutt, china figures
Colonel and Mrs Garrett, photograph-frame
Hon Emily and Evelyn Gathorne Hardy, silver stork sugar-tongs
Hon Katherine Gathorne Hardy, silver necklace
Mr Grenfell, strawberry dish
Lord and Lady Haldan, coffee set
Mr Aubrey Harcourt, silver tea kettle and liqueur stand
Mr and the Hon Mrs A. Vernon Harcourt, silver sugar basin and tongs
Mr and Lady Susan Harcourt, travelling clock
Mrs Hargreaves, clock
Mr C. Harland, silver plate
Rev E. Harland, hymn book
Mr and Mrs J. Harland, muffineers
Messrs J. and G. Henderson, silver tray, jug and cup
Mr and Mrs Henderson, diamond for the hair
Mr C. Hoare, silver and ivory owl inkstand
Miss Lucy Hope, Victorian blue glass flower vase
Canon and Mrs Huertley, brass sconces
The Misses Huertley, writing-case
Canon and Mrs Ince, girandoles
Miss Johnson (Christ Church laundress), a silver salver
Canon and Mrs King, Derby lily tea set (Louis Philippe service)
Mr and Mrs Kitchin, Scandinavian bosses
Prince Leopold, pearl horseshoe brooch
Hon Sir A. Liddell, yacht clock
Mr and Mrs Charles Liddell, fine diamond earrings
Mr and Mrs E. H. Liddell, Indian gold sugar bowl and spoon
Miss R. Liddell, pearl initial brooch
Miss V., Master E., and Master Lionel Liddell, Japanese fire-screen
Rev W. W. Liddell, old silver inkstand
Dean and Mrs Liddell, a set of sable and point lace and other gifts
Miss Liddell, Byron's works
Miss Lightfoot, pair of china jars
Rector of Exeter and Mrs Lightfoot, old silver
Miss Lloyd, silver bracelet
Mrs Lloyd, tea-cosy
Col and the Hon Mrs Lloyd-Lindsay, pair of Kaga, Japanese flower vases
Earl of Londesborough, black pearl and diamond pin
Walter Long Esq, cribbage board
Miss Loyds, photograph book and lace handkerchief
Miss Macleod du Maurier, sketches of society

Miss and Miss Effie Meyrick, liqueur set and silver-mounted tray
Sir G. and Lady Meyrick, fine hall chiming clock
Mr Meyrick, cigar cabinet
Mr F. Montifiore, hunting whip with coral horseshoe (brooch)
Mr and Mrs Montifiore, diamond and pearl spray of marguerites
Mr and Mrs H. Morrell, ormolu glove-case
Sir F. and Lady Mowbray, gold muffineer
Professor and Mrs Max Muller, last of the Olympic
Sir Stafford and Lady Northcote, a silver looking-glass
Rev E. Paget, amethyst and pearl brooch
Hon E. Palk, decanters
Hon Evelyn Palk, blue glasses
Mr T. L. Pearson, flask
Mr Alfred Penn, engraved travelling clock
Mr and Mrs J. Penn, blotter and envelope-case, silver-mounted
Mrs Penn, old finely carved fan
Mr F. H. Phipps, photograph stand
Miss Phipps, brass bell
Mr Pigeon (late coachman at Cuffnells), silver napkin-ring
Professor and Mrs Prestwich, antique silver bowl
Lieut-Col Reeve, old silver-framed photograph
Mr H. Reeve, gold-mounted travelling bag
Countess of Rothesay and Hon Mr Leslie, ivory card-case
Mrs A. Sandeman, Dresden china basket
Mrs Leo Schuster, silver Dornee pepper boxes
Lord Victor Seymour, strawberry and cream dish, blue china, silver-mounted
Mr J. A. Shaw-Stewart, Dresden china cupids
Mrs Simmonds, Indian gold tray
Mr and Mrs Skene of Pitlour, gift of plate
Mr and Mrs Spencer, post pillar box
Hon Fitz Roy Stewart, pair of Dresden china figures
Col and Mrs Stucley, oak table and chair
Hon Mrs Sturt, silver scent-bottle — Hon Mrs E. Talbot, antique silver spoons
Mr and Hon Mrs J. Talbot, brass candlestick
Rev and Mrs Thompson, silver cream jug
Viscount Trafalgar, tusk paper-cutter, silver-mounted
Rev R. St John Tyrwhitt, book
Mr C. Upperton, old oriental plate and stand
Hon Mrs Vivian, photograph frame
Lady C. Weyland, Venetian scent-bottle
Mr Wilkinson, a massive gold bracelet
Mr and Mrs Wilson, opera-glasses
President of the C.C.C. and the Misses Wilson, china clock
Mr and Mrs Wollaston, photograph album
Rev and Mrs Woods, china mirror
Hon A. G. Yorke, antique pins
Hon Mrs E. Yorke, silver tea-caddy

APPENDIX II:
CAKELESS,
By John Howe Jenkins 1874

ACT I

SCENE I

Apollo seated in boudoir asleep. Wakes suddenly, throws handkerchief off his face, and starts up.

APOLLO (*loquitur*) Methinks the air seems o'er oppressed this night.
What ho! some scout, here, hither bring a light,
That with its garish beams will flout the gloom
And show me what is happening in the room.

Enter Diana; advances with jaunty steps

DIANA   Great partner, are thou sad?   I bring good cheer,
To glad thine heart and drive away thy fear.
With fortune smiling thou must smooth thy brow,
And listen to the tale I bring thee now.

APOLLO   No time have I for trifles or for fun;
Let's cut the story short and so be done.
You always seem to have so much to say,
As walking Lexicon you would be *au fait*.

(Rapping heard without)

Who knocks without, and splits my head with noise?
It must be one of those accursed boys.

Enter their daughter Ecilia

ECILIA   Mother, it always has been your behest
That truth and confidence are ever best.
You always wished that I should marry one
Or Prince, or peer, or else a member's son.
The last have I at length securely trapped,
And in the toils of courtship firmly wrapped.
I trust my father will his favour show,
And let me with this handsome stranger go.

DIANA   Surely Yerbua's not the happy man?

ECILIA   He is, he is! he loves me all he can.

DIANA   My blessings on you, daughter! would that she
Who's gone before had made a match like thee!
Apollo! one would deem you whelmed with grief.

APOLLO   I've lost my daughter!
                    (Aside) What a blest relief!

(Diana and Ecilia embrace.   More knocking heard)

APOLLO   By Peck and Pusey, what an awful din!
        The door itself will next be coming in.

Enter their daughter Rosa

ROSA   Papa! your pet, you know, I e'er have been;
        And though I scarce have reached to seventeen,
        I've trapped a noble lord of high degree,
        And I his ladye gay am going to be.

APOLLO   True daughter mine, well done, I laud your pain,
        And every one shall have a share of gain.

DIANA   Rosa was ever yours, but I rejoice
        To hear that she has made so good a choice.

(Embraces her)

Enter their daughter Psyche

DIANA   Why, here's our youngest girl,—a perfect child!
        Surely no lover true she has beguiled!

PSYCHE   I've trapped a Pr*nce, the youngest of his race;
        Of tender flesh, but yet of handsome face.

APOLLO   Blest of my heart,—three daughters at a go!
        Whene'er it rains, it pours, some wits say so.

SCENE II

Chorus of drunken satyrs in a large quadrangle.   A fountain in the middle.

CHORUS   The scout and don to roost are gone,
          The *Owl* sits in his tree.
        List to the sough of the summer's wind,
          And the plash of Mercury.

(Apollo's head appears in nightcap at a window)

APOLLO   Who calls so loud, and wakes my slumbers sweet
        That chase away the hours with flying feet?

SATYR *(below)*. What ho! Brabantio, reverend signor, rise!
        Awake! and banish slumber from your eyes,
        Look where your daughters turn the night to day,
        And worship Venus in a quiet way.

DIANA *(above)*. Hence, satyrs, hence! and learn the true particulars,

(Flings out parchment)

        Then look no more for any "perpendiculars."
        My girls are matched and bend at Hymen's shrine:
        A fitting act; for it were wellnigh time,

SATYRS *(singing)* Apollo was a worthy peer,
> His daughters cost him many a frown;
> Diana held them all too dear,
> But Fife he brought the market down.

CUISINE *(a pious Satyr, addicted to the distribution of tracts)*
> Children of hell, and born in Stygian night,
> How can such deeds your sinful hearts delight?
> Here, take these tracts: they suit your case full well:
> "Where go'st thou, sinner, but the way to hell?"
> Your offerings give to heathens far away,
> Unlearned as you in light of Gospel day.

ACT II

SCENE I

Same place by day.   The doors of the Temple thronged by Scouts, Satyrs, and Vestal Virgins.

(Enter the three bridegrooms, Yerbua, Rivulus, and Regius)

CHORUS *of festive Scouts*
> Happy, happy scouts are we!
> For this day from labour free,
> Masters have we none to-day,
> They must their own luncheons lay.
> Double, double, toil and trouble,
> Kettles boil and cauldrons bubble.
> Then let us our perquisites take, take,
> Then let us our perquisites take.
>> A scout's but a man,
>> A term's but a span,
> Why, then, let a scout partake.

(Enter Clericus mounted on the lectern-eagle, with Thurifer I and II)

THURIFER I *(loquitur.)*   Here be we three met anew
> To celebrate a marriage true.

CLER   My trusty Pegasus I now bestride,
> What fears may touch, what evils may betide.

(Eagle canters gaily up the aisle, followed by Thurifers a bad second and third)

Enter Apollo, leading in his daughters as a sacrifice to Hymen

APOLLO   A pretty go I've had my way to find;—
> One on each side and one attached behind.
> Why where's your mother, Psyche? has she come?

(Leader of Teuton band, hired for the occasion, chimes in)

> Sound the trumpets, beat the drum.

(Wedding company settled in church.   Among them may be seen, Agonistes, Dutch Skipper, and at some little distance, Kraftsohn, biting his nails.   Service begins.)

KRAFTSOHN *(interrupting)* I do protest against this match, so let me speak.

APOLLO *(irate)* Strip, strip him, scouts! this is the knave we seek.

KRAFT   By circles, segments, and by radii,
        Than yield to these I'd liefer far to die.

ROMANUS *(waving his hood)* Arm, arm, ye brave! and rush upon the foe,
        Who never did to early temple go,
        Nor taste in lordly hall the luscious steak,
        Nor would his frugal luncheon e'er forsake.

(Scouts advance, throwing their "perquisites" at the head of Kraftsohn, who takes refuge in the cloisters)

ROM   Take him through trench and tunnel to the chest,
        Nor ever leave the cursed fiend at rest.
        Leave him in Wonderland with some hard-hitting foe,
        And through the looking-glass let him survey the blow;
        Confine him in the belfry, not in Peck,
        And make him sign at pleasure your blank cheque.

(Scouts obey, and lock Kraftsohn in the Belfry)

(Wedding procession issues from temple.   Satyrs cheer; Vestal Virgins wave their typical bonnets.)

DIANA   I hope the breakfast will be a success!
        I almost fear the cake will be a mess.
        They promised they would send it yesterday;
        No signs of it as yet, the servants say.

APOLLO   Bother the cake! yonder within the chest
        My foeman Kraftsohn bites his nails at rest.

(Procession enters Apollo's domicile.   Lapse of a few moments, when exit Apollo from the Ostium.)

APOLLO   'Twixt Scylla and Charybdis I am pressed.
        Is there for man quiet, all unrest?
        Ye scouts! to H—t—n's, all, for Heaven's sake!
        Diana's mad; she has forgot the cake.

(Rex advances from among scouts)

REX *(loquitur)* The cake is sent, and waits us in the street,
        A glorious spectacle, a splendid treat!
        But it can never come the gate within,
        It is forbidden, and 'twould be a sin.

SIRRAH *(another scout)* No more the path to H—t—n's can we tread,
        So Thurifer commands, that awful head.
        Farewell to cutlets hot and sparkling wine!
        On viands cold we must in future dine;
        The keen-eyed Cerberus nought must pass unseen,
        Save hot potatoes and the cabbage green.

SCENE II—*A room within the house*

(Absence of cake universally lamented; the unfortunate Thurifer II is hooted from society.)

Apollo rises to his feet, and proposes health of the newly married pairs

APOLLO   A health to brides and bridegrooms three!
This duty does devolve on me.
Needless their merits to unfold,
In this are all their virtues told:
Another bride before them went;
Her money must be well-nigh spent.
May these for ever moneyed be,
And may they ne'er the Union see.

YERBUA *(responds)* My cordial thanks to thee I give!
May we for ever happy live;
A pearl that is of such a price,
Unhappiness can ne'er entice.
My sire his absence doth repent,
His duty lies in Parliament;
He must retrieve a victory won
By Opposition's warlike son.

RIVULUS *(responds)* Thanks to friends all for cordial toast.
A fairer bride can no man boast;
Money's acquired, while beauty's only given,
A gift from Jupiter the King of Heaven.
My father, too, great sorrow does he feel
That he before our altar could not kneel;
Our noble hall, where fire has made its raid,
He must rebuild, when all our debts are paid.

REGIUS *(responds)* Last, but not least, my thanks I say
On this our happy bridal day.
When hearts are full then words are few,
So a long speech I will eschew.
To-day doth Buckingham *ma mère* contain,
So we her noble presence could not gain.

Clericus from his chair proposes bride's father and mother

CLERICUS   Excuse my rising, friends; my legs are bent
Since reared on Pegasus to church I went;
Gaily I cantered up the long-drawn aisle,
'Mid many a hustling laugh and sickly smile,
The Satyrs all declare that when I speak
In chapel, 'tis the eagle moves his beak;
Because with deep-drawn sign "Amen" I drone,
To rival him that holds the other throne.
Justice in stewards is my favourite theme,
When Sabbath sun darts forth his glorious beam.
Pardon digression; 'tis a fault of mine

Whene'er by stealth I've quaffed the luscious wine.
Apollo's health, coupled with virtuous spouse,
To day I drink amid this gay carouse.
Something there lies beneath the groaning board—
It is the pretty don, by all adored.
Come, Loose Cloak, help to raise your friend,
And to his verdant chamber him attend.

DUTCH SKIPPER *(rises)*   I'm nearly dumb, my arms are very stiff;
Down the long river I have rowed a skiff;
I yestern eve aquatic powers did try,
Fully resolved to conquer or to die.
I rise to drink the health of one saint more,
A saint whom all the Romans do adore;
May be *absolve* me if I poorly speak,
I must *confess* my voice is weak.
His eyes are dim, his head is getting bald,
"Rits" are his ranks irreverently called.
No *Rock* he stands on, of all power bereft,
No *Record* of his name will e'er be left.

(All drink long life to Romanus)

Enter Sirrah

SIRRAH   The cabs have come, the double three to take,
Who now this house for ever must forsake.

APOLLO   Ho! Sirrah! get some slippers—old, not new:
To waste new slippers it would never do.
Keep not the cabs, my children, at the door;
We'll have to pay another sixpence more.

DIANA   Come fetch my *mouchoir*, I require it now.
'*A fondre en larmes,*' 'tis the right thing I trow.

(Daughters appear in travelling attire)

APOLLO   Come, come, be quick! we'll have to pay a mite,
For keeping cabmen waiting all the night.
Goodbye, goodbye! let's get it quickly done.
Bless you! my children, bless you every one.

CHORUS *of cabmen*   Let us wait, let us wait,
Never hurry from the gate.
For every minute lost to-day
Apollo must a sixpence pay.
Plenty of luggage, that's the style;
Shilling extra every mile.

(Couples enter cabs)

(Slippers thrown in showers)

ACT III

SCENE I

SCENE—*The Belfry*

Kraftsohn biting his nails with rage

KRAFTSOHN (loquitur)   Ah, tea-chest! thou thy slanderer dost repay
    For all the calumnies that he did ever say;
    List to the captive's stifled moan,
    Take the unhappy pilgrim home.
    Ah, scouts! a pamphlet I will surely write
    Which with a serpent's tooth will keenly bite.
    Your perquisites, your pilferings I'll betray,
    And turn to hellish night your garish day.
    List! there's a step! who haunts this ghostly pile?
    Who comes my wretched sufferings to revile?
    Hark! by the sound it is a Roman's toe:
    It is Romanus, purgatorial foe.

(Romanus whispers without to his attendant satellites Rex and Sirrah)

ROMANUS   Pinch him and pull him and turn him about,
    Through bricks and through mortar the foe of the scout;
    Whelm him deep in the plashing sea
    Where the crocodile lives and the Kedgeree.

KRAFTSOHN   My fate is sealed; my race is run,
    My pilgrimage is wellnigh done.
    Farewell to pamphlets and to angles round!
    I seek a shore where Euclid is not found.

(Enter by Mercury's brink Romanus with his two attendants bearing Kraftsohn between them. They plunge him in,)

ROMANUS   Full fathoms five e'en now he lies,
    Of his bones are segments made.
    Those circles are that were his eyes.
    Nothing of him that doth fade
    But doth suffer a sea-change
    Into something queer and strange.
    Goldfish hourly ring his knell.
            Ding-dong.
    Hark! now I hear them, ding, dong, bell.

FINIS

APPENDIX III:

Hotel Hermer Salvio
Biarritz

12. March. 98

Dear Mr. Mercer

When you took the photographs of Euston Church last summer I think one of them showed the beautiful monument to the sixth Duke — I mean the one near the park with a white marble cross raised

in a sloping manner, at the head, & the grave surrounded by a white marble coping — the flowers inside they are always lovely. If you have a copy of the photograph might I have it for my Mother

see? I would return it carefully.

We shall be here with her till the 22nd inst. then home again to Cuffnells

Lyndhurst

I have not written to Lord Charles about this, but should do so of course, before

going any further. We have a fancy that some such ~~tombstone~~ might be what we should like at Christ Church. Please forgive my troubling you

Believe me

Sincerely yrs,

Alice Pleasance Hargreaves

This letter from Alice was written from Biarritz, where she repaired after the death of her father in January 1898. It would appear that her mother accompanied her. Clearly the matter of a suitable tombstone for the Dean's grave at Christ Church was much on their minds at this time, and that is the subject of this letter. The monument to which she refers is the tomb of the sixth Duke of Grafton, who was buried at Euston Church. Alice and Regi were close friends of Lord Grafton, and frequently stayed at Euston Hall, his seat at Thetford, Norfolk.

BIBLIOGRAPHY

Anon, *The Life of The Duke of Albany, The Scholar Prince*, 1884

Athlone, HRH Princess Alice, Countess of, *For My Grandchildren*, Evans Brothers, 1966

Atlay, J. B., *Sir Henry Wentworth Acland, Bart, KCB, FRS, A Memoir*, Smith, Elder & Co., 1903

Batey, Mavis, *Nuneham Courtenay, Oxfordshire*, 1979; *Alice in Oxford*, Pitkin Pictorials, 1979

Berkeley, Reginald, *The History of the Rifle Brigade in the War of 1914–18*, The Rifle Brigade, 1927

Bill, E. G. W. and Mason, J. F. A., *Christ Church and Reform 1850–69*, The Clarendon Press, 1970

Bowman, Isa, *Lewis Carroll as I Knew Him*, Constable, 1972

Carleton, John, *Westminster School*, Hart Davis Educational, 1965

Carroll, Lewis, *Alice's Adventures in Wonderland*, Macmillan, 1965; *Through the Looking-Glass*, Macmillan, 1872; *Notes by an Oxford Chiel*, Macmillan, 1874; *Alice's Adventures Under Ground*, Macmillan, 1886; 'Alice on the Stage, the *Theatre*, 1887

Cecil, Lord David, *The Cecils of Hatfield House*, Constable, 1973

Clarke, Anne, *Lewis Carroll: A Biography*, J. M. Dent, 1979

Cohen, Morton N., *The Letters of Lewis Carroll*, Macmillan, 1979

Consett, Matthew, *A Tour Through Sweden, Swedish-Lapland, Finland and Denmark*, 1789

Collingwood, Stuart Dodgson, *The Life and Letters of Lewis Carroll*, Macmillan, 1898; *The Lewis Carroll Picture Book*, Macmillan, 1899

Crutch, D. (Ed.), *The Lewis Carroll Handbook*, Dawson, 1979

Ewart, Wilfrid, *Way of Revelation*, 1921; *The Scots Guards in the Great War*, 1925

Gardner, Martin (Ed.), *The Annotated Alice*, Penguin, 1970

Green, Roger Lancelyn (Ed.), *The Diaries of Lewis Carroll*, Greenwood Press, 1970

Hardy, A. E. Gathorne, *Gathorne Hardy, First Earl of Cranbrook: A Memoir*, 1910

Hargreaves, Alice and Caryl, 'Alice's Recollections of Carrollian Days' *Cornhill, LXXIII*, 1932

Hargreaves, Benjamin, *Recollections of Broad Oak*, 1882; *Messrs' Hargreaves' Calico Print Works At Accrington*, 1882

Hargreaves, Caryl, 'The Lewis Carroll that Alice Recalls', *New York Times Magazine*, 1 May 1932

Jenkins, Rev John Howe, *Cakeless*, 1874

Kipling, Rudyard, *The Irish Guards in the Great War*, 1923

Lavie, Germain, *The Westminster Play: Its Actors and its Visitors*, by an old Westminster, 1855

Lennon, Florence Becker, *The Life of Lewis Carroll*, Constable, 1972

Lewis Carroll Society, The, *Mr Dodgson: Nine Lewis Carroll Studies*, 1973

Lewis Carroll Society of North America, The, *Lewis Carroll Observed*, New York 1976; *The Wasp in a Wig*, New York 1977

Liddell, Charles, *Plan for the Metropolitan Water Supply*, 1849

Liddell, A. G. C., *Notes from the Life of an Ordinary Mortal*, John Murray, 1911

Liddell, Henry George, *A History of Rome*, 1855; *Funeral Oration*, 1876; *St Frideswide's: Two Sermons*, 1889

Liddell, Henry Thomas, *A Poetical Effusion*, 1826; *The Wizard of the North, The Vampire Bride, and Other Poems*, 1833

MacDonald, Greville, *Reminiscences of a Specialist*, 1932

Magnus, Philip, *King Edward the Seventh*, John Murray, 1964

Markham, Capt F., *Recollections of a Town Boy at Westminster*, 1903

Ruskin, John, *The Art of England—Lectures given in Oxford*, 1883; *Praeterita*, 1885

Stirling, A. M. W., *The Richmond Papers*, 1926.

Taylor, Alexander L., *The White Knight*, 1952

Thompson, H. L., *Memoir of Henry George Liddell, DD*, 1899; *Christ Church*, 1900

Trench, Charles Chevenix, *My Mother Told Me*, 1958

Verner, Col Willoughby, *The Rifle Brigade Chronicle*, 1900–1917

Warner, Marina, *Queen Victoria's Sketchbook*, Macmillan, 1979

Watts, M. S., *George Frederick Watts: The Annals of an Artist's Life*, 1912

Wolf, Edwin and Fleming, John, *Rosenbach*, 1960

INDEX

THE REEVE FAMILY

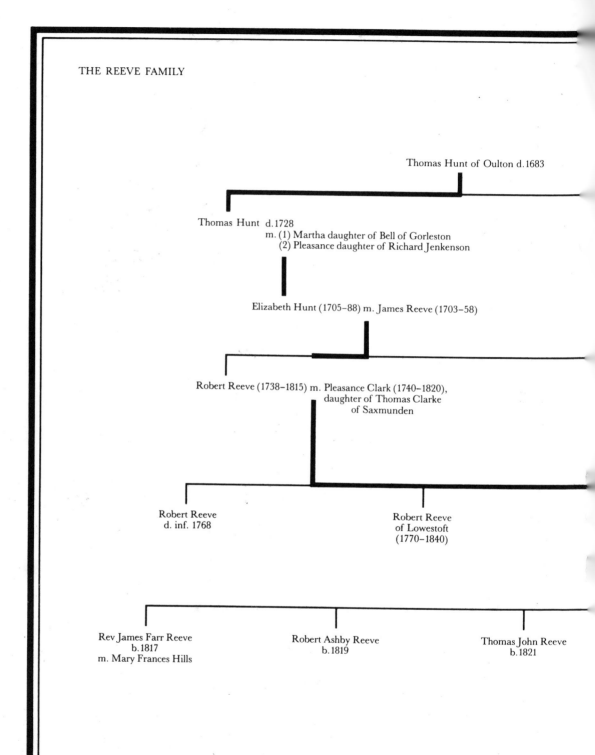

Thomas Hunt of Oulton d.1683

Thomas Hunt d.1728
m. (1) Martha daughter of Bell of Gorleston
    (2) Pleasance daughter of Richard Jenkenson

Elizabeth Hunt (1705–88) m. James Reeve (1703–58)

Robert Reeve (1738–1815) m. Pleasance Clark (1740–1820),
daughter of Thomas Clarke
of Saxmunden

Robert Reeve
d. inf. 1768

Robert Reeve
of Lowestoft
(1770–1840)

Rev James Farr Reeve
b.1817
m. Mary Frances Hills

Robert Ashby Reeve
b.1819

Thomas John Reeve
b.1821